IT in Marketing

Edited by Janet Chapman and Clive Holtham

ALFRED WALLER LIMITED
Henley on Thames

in association with UNICOM

Published by
Alfred Waller Limited, Publishers
Orchards, Fawley, Henley on Thames, Oxon RG9 6JF

First published 1994

British Library Cataloguing in Publication Data
A Catalogue record for this book is available from the British Library

ISBN 1 872474 36 5

Printed and bound in Great Britain by the Lavenham Press, Suffolk

Contents

3 Database Marketing

4 Geographic Information Systems in Marketing

5 Some Proprietary GIS Sources

6 Case Studies

Preface

Over the last ten to twenty years, organisations have become increasingly aware of the need for information in order that they may function efficiently and effectively in today's markets. A company's marketing strategy is closely bound up with its business strategy and is increasingly concerned with competition, especially in the expanding, diverse world marketplace. Information Technology (IT) is no longer seen as a background activity, a kind of enabler for the more routine functions, such as payroll or administration, whose costs have to be justified solely on grounds of increased clerical efficiency and reduced overheads. Rather, information, and the technology to collect, process and disseminate it are more and more becoming regarded as a corporate strategic resource which must be managed like any other.

Capturing or defending market share depends upon gaining or maintaining competitive advantage. Surveys show that the proportion of applications in UK companies which are regarded as contributing to or defending market share is expected to be nearly 50% by 1995. Indeed, many early IT innovations, such as point of sale terminals or smart cards, are now no longer a source of competitive differentiation, but are regarded as essential to keep a position in the market. IT is a rapidly developing field, and its effective exploitation, particularly in marketing, will continue to be vital to the successful business.

Focusing on business needs and benefits means a greater attention to the customer: who he is, where he is, what his needs are – both in terms of product and services. Customer profiling and targeting are essential, as is information about the competition. Reams of such data can be gathered, but the so-called 'Information Explosion' must be a contained one: raw data must be selected and refined into useful information – and this information must be continually updated to maintain its strategic value.

Each organisation has differing needs, and each marketing system will reflect these. The starting point will be different and the ultimate goals will be different, but there is advantage in learning from the experiences of others about what they are doing and what is becoming feasible.

This book contains a selection of outlooks – from academics, marketers, consultants and users. Techniques and case studies range widely, from improved direct operational costs to customer databases and the exploitation of spatial information via Geographic Information Systems (GIS). The topics included are both practical and forward looking, showing how the evolving nature of marketing can be supported by IT.

The first three chapters provide an overview of the IT issues facing today's marketers. Marketing IT strategy must form part of the overall organisation's IT strategy – the traditional '4 Ps' of marketing span several parts of the organisation's functions. For example,

- 'Product' impacts on R&D and subsequent product or service design and production, which are fed by market research, both in initiating a new product or service and in evaluating its performance after its introduction to the market. Hence there are links to production/manufacturing, finance and quality control.
- 'Price' is determined using production cost data, acceptable mark up, discount arrangements, etc. together with competitive factors – there are links here with the finance function and competitive market research.
- 'Promotion' requires campaign planning and ongoing top-up publicity. It requires product information, customer information (market research again), volume objectives, financial and budgetary objectives, and the means to measure response/conversion to the product or service – the customer services function.
- 'Place' concerns the sales channel, with obvious links to the sales function and sales monitoring and also to the corporate legal department.

Ideally, it should be possible to obtain inputs to the marketing function from all relevant sources of information throughout the organisation; many of the departments involved have IT systems already – the challenge to the marketing function is to deploy IT in such a way that this internal information, together with external information (e.g. demography, competitors) may be made available in a current, accurate and consistent manner.

Section 2 discusses various factors to be taken into account in choosing a marketing IT solution, from the analysis of system requirements to discussion on the various technologies available and those expected to emerge in the future.

Many companies have selected a database solution, sometimes a customer database and sometimes a database which also embraces product, financial and sales elements.

Customer databases are particularly useful – as a repository of all pertinent information about existing and prospective customers – in the sales, promotion and customer services areas, and are frequently used as a targeting device for direct selling. The chapters in Section 3 cover aspects of database marketing.

A specialised form of marketing database is the Geographic Information System (GIS). Such systems combine customer information with 'map-based' data. Some customer databases include spatial information, such as the postcode, without including a visual map-based presentation. GIS which use a combination of mapping techniques and spatially-matched data are increasingly used in applications such as planning capacity in public utilities or siting a new supermarket. Section 4 describes GIS' rationale and techniques, while Section 5 describes some of the most commonly available sources of geographic data, from postcodes through to ordnance survey and road maps.

Finally, the last Section gives various examples of users' experiences in applying IT to their marketing function, and the business benefits which have accrued. These include examples from the finance, publishing, academic recruitment and retail sectors.

Janet Chapman
June 1994

1
The Main Issues: A Review

1 Current practice and future trends: an overview

Professor Clive Holtham
Bull HN Professor of Information Management
City University Business School

1. INTRODUCTION

Marketing is often presented as a highly rational process, with the emphasis on being logical, orderly and systematic. To take just one example, Kotler and Armstrong (1991) define the marketing management process as an essentially rational process:

- Organising the marketing planning process
- Analysing market opportunities
- Selecting target markets
- Developing the marketing mix
- Managing the marketing effort.

Yet there are limits to this rationality. Daily, weekly, monthly we see marketing disappointments or disasters. These have often been subject to lengthy applications of the rational marketing management process. In some cases, these problems are despite the information produced, in others because of poor use of the information.

However, even in the USA textbook definition of marketing, there is explicit recognition of the essentially human-centred nature of the process:

> "A social and managerial process by which individuals and groups obtain what they need and want through creating and exchanging products and value with others." (Kotler and Armstrong, 1991)

Marketing, as with all management processes, including information technology management, operates in a real world where both consumers and managers are subject to uncertainty, feelings and attitudes. Of all the management disciplines, marketing is the one where human emotions, values and personal goals all interact together in the most heady brew.

To be fair to those who are engaged in the promotion of a more rational approach to marketing, they can and do recognise the limits to pure rationality. For example:

> "management scientists should not expect that introduction of a marketing model will change the cognitive disposition of some of the potential users." (Larreche, 1975)

A commonly held view on current practice in marketing information systems theme can be summarised as:

- companies mostly collect and store data on a product basis
- there is generally now far too much data available
- there is insufficient information, particularly that organised on a customer basis
- marketing people are not arguing strongly enough for the right data to be made available in the right format.

These are important themes which are developed further here.

2. A HISTORY OF OPTIMISM

There has been a strong streak of optimism about the use of information and information technology in marketing, and this optimism has been present in many aspects of IT. In relatively early days, Harper (1961) confidently suggested that:

> "To manage a business well is to manage its future; and to manage the future is to manage information."

In one of the early texts on IT and marketing, Hugo (1967) argued that:

> "Managers will be increasingly freed from routine work and will be able to concentrate on what are currently considered marginal aspects of their work. Management should thus become increasingly creative – an art as well as a science."

In 1968 Kotler was speculating on the potential to create what he described as a 'marketing nerve centre':

> "companies have it in their power to make substantial improvements in their marketing information systems – and can ill afford to neglect them."

Moving on a decade, the positivism continued:

> "There is no doubt that the 1980s will see a profound transformation in the

working environment of marketing and sales management, and it seems safe to predict that among the most successful companies will be those who have decided to make efficient use of information systems as a control tool." (Graf, 1979)

"The development of improved information-communication capabilities seems likely to yield substantial benefits in terms of more effective and efficient marketing." (Buzzell, 1985)

It is not only analysts who have an optimistic view. A marketing practitioner, Michael Patrick, senior manager of market analysis of S.C. Johnson suggested:

"The ideal system would allow us to do the filtering of information and then to format and graph it in such a way that our marketing decisions are made obvious." (Coultas, 1990)

3. ARE MARKETING INFORMATION SYSTEMS DIFFERENT?

It can be argued that there is no need for focussed analysis of marketing information systems as they are simply another type of functional information system like accounting or personnel systems. But accounting and personnel are ultimately focussed on the internal administration of the organisation. So too are many elements of marketing systems but, crucially, they are also a major source of data on customers – and it is customers that are central not only to marketing administration, but above all to business strategy.

As Shaw and Stone (1988) have pointed out, computerised systems enable the organisation to stay close to the customer:

"by recording and keeping an electronic database memory of customer, prospect and all communication and commercial contacts, to help improve all future contacts and to ensure more realistic planning of all marketing."

A financial information system imports only a relatively small amount of information from outside the organisation. A marketing information system will import very large quantities not only on the organisation's own products, but also on competitors'. It will import data not only on the physical product and its price, but also on the nature of campaigns, offers, promotions, etc. Intelligence gathering is involved in tracking the 'softer' types of information will be drawing on external information sources, either manually or electronically, e.g.:

- From recruits and competitors' employees

- From people who do business with competitors
- From published material and public documents
- Observing competitors or analysing physical evidence.
  (Flax, 1984)

However, it needs to be borne in mind that not all companies utilise marketing information equally. For example, in relation to market research, OASiS (1989) found that:

- 50% of companies used published market research reports on a frequent basis
- 37% regularly commissioned market research studies
- 29% made regular use of press extract databases
- 25% frequently had access to externally structured market research databases
- 45% hardly ever or never used on-line services.

4. BENEFITS

Marketing systems can be subject to 'overselling' by vendors or analysts. Here is an example of such a perhaps overly optimistic approach:

> "...investments in marketing and sales automation systems hold tremendous potential for productivity improvements. Marketing and sales costs average 15% to 35% of total corporate costs (not just production costs). So a focus on marketing and sales provides a welcome lever for boosting productivity. Moreover, the importance of marketing and sales services is growing. According to the US trade representative and the National Association of Accountants, manufacturers' service activities account for 75% to 85% of all value added. This means that the price a product can command is less a reflection of raw materials and labour than of marketing-related services like selecting appropriate product features, determining the product mix, and ensuring product availability and delivery.
>
> In cases we have reviewed, sales increases arising from advanced marketing and sales information technology have ranged from 10% to more than 30%, and investment returns have often exceeded 100%. these returns may sound like the proverbial free lunch, but they are real."
> (Moriarty and Swartz, 1989)

However Moriarty and Swartz also give more specific examples:

> "Marketing automation investments by a $7 billion electronics manufacturer and an $8 million custom printing company each produced a first-year return

of more than 100%. The electronics concern installed a sales support system for more than 500 salespeople. Sales rose 33%, sales force productivity rose 31%, and sales force attrition dropped 40%. The reduced attrition alone produced savings in recruiting and training costs that paid for the company's $2.5 million investment in less than 12 months. At the custom printer, an $80,000 investment in a minicomputer and telemarketing software returned a 25% increase in sales and attained payback in less than 6 months."

A more specific example of benefits relates to a Fortune 500 manufacturing company, for whom the turnover rate of its large field sales force was translating into sales declines in most of the US and Europe:

> "So the firm attacked the problem by equipping its 7000 member sales force with sales automation tools, including customer intelligence input screens, input procedures and on-screen custom reporting capabilities. The upshot? The return on its $35.7 million investment in the sales system was pegged at $325.4 million, measured in increased revenue per territory." (Mayros, 1990)

A specialised use of IT in marketing can be shown by looking at yield management in airlines. British Airways offers three broad classes of travel on a flight from London to New York – first, club and economy. But within these more than 60 different types of fare will have been offered for sale, each of them usually determined by the degree of restriction and lateness of booking. The techniques of transferring seats between categories is known as yield management, and is shrouded in considerable secrecy (a rare example of discussion is contained in Williams, 1987).

Yield management of this sophisticated type simply could not be done without computers. The basic input of data comes from the reservation system, with analysis being carried out in two stages, the first to undertake the filtering and presentation of the data, the second to implement the profile of seats by category in the reservation system. Seats are frequently shifted between category right up to the moment of departure.

5. MARKETING INFORMATION SYSTEMS

At a general level, Kotler and Armstrong (1991) define a marketing information system as consisting of:

> "people, equipment and procedures to gather, sort, analyse, evaluate and distribute needed, timely and accurate information to marketing decision makers."

Buzzell (1985) groups the use of IT in marketing into three areas:

- Automation of transactional systems
- Better/more effective communications
- Measurement and analysis.

A helpful categorisation is that of Wolf (1984), who distinguishes the ultimate purpose of the system, as shown in Figure 1.1.

In relation to more specific purposes, there are some types of marketing information that are important sub-categories of the above three areas. For example, *marketing decision support systems* (MDSS) and *database marketing*: collating data in the organisation to build up a comprehensive picture of a customer, and then using that data in a wide variety of appropriate ways.

Looking at the subjects in a contemporary conference on IT in marketing, one striking feature is the sheer range of topics and technologies covered – very much greater than in other business IT areas such as finance and accounting:

- Data quality systems
- Database marketing
- External information sources
- Geographic information systems
- Marketing decision support systems
- Multimedia in marketing

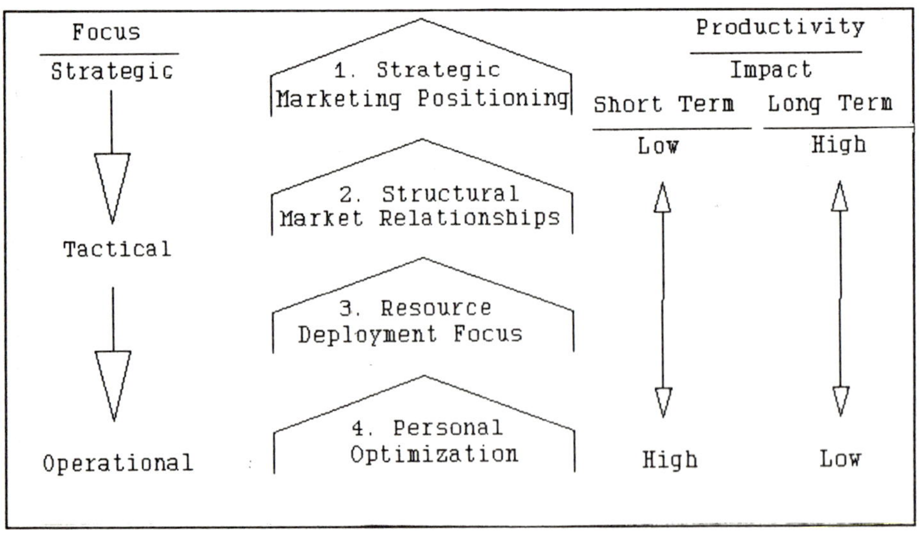

Figure 1.1 Marketing productivity (James A. Wolf, 1984).

- Spatial analysis systems
- Systems for analysing risk exposure
- Telemarketing
- Transactional analysis for managerial decision making
- Using knowledge based systems to interpret marketing data.

This is a very broad range of subjects, and even then it does not cover areas such as the impact of new broadcasting and telecommunications media, IT in sales administration, marketing data collection, store scanning systems, etc.

In a recent US survey of the use of IT for marketing applications Higby and Farah (1991) measured the use of IT in marketing and users' scaled satisfaction levels, 1 standing for strong satisfaction, 6 for strong dissatisfaction. Their results are summarised in Figure 1.2.

6. PROBLEMS

Marketing information systems suffer from problems that are generic to most types of system. Jobber (1977) identified the main problems in marketing systems as:

- Poor quality and inconsistent data
- Defined managers' information needs
- Educating users in the potential of systems
- Technical computer related problems,

and Blyth (1987) observed:

	Use (%)	Satisfaction*
Customer profile analysis	65	3.0
Sales forecasting	63	2.9
Budgeting	58	2.7
Inventory control	49	2.8
Order processing	48	2.7
Pricing decisions	45	2.9
Competitive analysis	43	3.2
Price quotes	39	2.8
Sales force analysis	38	3.0
Statistical analysis	31	2.7

Figure 1.2 Use of IT in marketing activities (Higby and Farah, 1991). *: 1 = high, 6 = low.

What are the main obstacles in helping marketing exploit IT's potential more fully? (ranking 1 = most important)	IT Managers	Marketing Managers	Joint
1. Poor appreciation at board level of potential of marketing information and information management	1	2	1
2. Poor training for marketing staff in IT	3	1	2
3. Difficulty justifying major IT expenditure on strategic grounds	2	4	3
4. Poor understanding of marketing's requirements by IT departments	4	3	4
5. Hardware and software shortcomings	5	6	5
6. Lack of a vehicle for joint IT/marketing planning	6	7	6
7. Rapid pace of technological change	8	5	7
8. Rapid pace of change in competition	7	8	8

Figure 1.3 Obstacles to exploiting IT in marketing (Source: Business Intelligence, 1990).

> "Our problem is not one of data, rather it is one of information. We have too much of the former and too little of the latter."

More specific criticisms relate to the speed of take up of systems, and were identified by Shaw (1988):

> "surveys show that marketers are being both slow and unimaginative in their use of IT hardware and software."

And by Moriarty and Swartz (1989):

> "Despite the proven worth of this technology, few companies have automated any part of their marketing and sales functions. Even fewer appear to understand the significant strategic benefits that can accrue from marketing and sales automation."

Higby and Farah (1991) concluded from their study, already summarised in Figure 1.2, that:

> "The ratings appear to be low, which suggests there are many opportunities available for improving marketing information systems in most firms."

7. THE ENVIRONMENT FOR MARKETING AND ITS INFORMATION SYSTEMS

Account also needs to be taken of the changing marketing factors in the UK (e.g. see Blyth, 1987):

1. The impact of retailer concentration and retailer as brand on product choice.
2. Product proliferation, the disappearance of traditional product field boundaries, and its effect on product positioning.
3. Targeting by lifestyle and psychographics rather than traditional demographics.
4. Sharply increasing advertising time costs.

These changes both increase the need for flexible and responsive marketing information systems, but also make it more difficult to implement them.

8. PHILOSOPHIES OF MARKETING INFORMATION

In strategic terms, it is useful to analyse the contrasting philosophies to the use of marketing in IT. Some research has been done quantitatively on this area (OASiS, 1989) (see Figure 1.4). Organisational use of marketing IT is grouped into one of several categories, ranging from 'Production Orientated' to 'Information Integration'.

From carrying out research into the strategic impact of IT in a variety of sectors (e.g. Dockery, 1991), it may be more appropriate for presentational purposes to symbolise the current situation in terms of a bi-modal distribution. There are a relatively small number of organisations that are using IT successfully in a strategic sense. These seem in particular to have different attitudes towards IT throughout the organisation than those organisations that are less successful in the strategic application of IT. The shorthand used to describe this is that the more successful organisations have created an 'IT culture' (Holtham, 1988).

Mapping the bimodal distribution onto the specific issue of IT and marketing demonstrates the alternative philosophies.

1. *The Strategic Marketing Approach* – IT is seen as central to successful business strategy, and as an essential and central component of the wide marketing management process. There is substantial use of IT at all levels of the organisation and at the top there is a clear understanding of the significance of IT and of the ways through which it can be exploited.
2. *The Discrete Approach* – The marketing function is seen as a series of parallel tasks, each of which may in fact be extensively computer based. Data may

'The Non Performer' (7%) ● Nil information gathering ● Unaware 'One-Man Bands' (24%) ● Limited market research ● Limited customer records ● Complacency 'Orchestral players' (58%) ● Reasonable level of information-gathering ● Spread of 'instruments' ● Good intentions re integration	● Frustration! 'Conductors' (11%) ● Higher-level, co-ordinating role ● More information, more sources ● Internal integration, centralisation ● Higher degree of satisfaction 'Composers' (0.5%) ● Internal and external market data integrated ● Shared access ● More utility value ● Co-ordination and control

Figure 1.4 Approaches to Marketing Information Systems (OASiS, 1989).

flow from one part of the function to another, but this is typically seen as an *ad hoc* exercise. The major gap is likely to be between the *ad hoc* market research systems and the ongoing operational systems of the organisation. The extent of top managerial understanding of the significance of IT may be patchy. It is typically perceived as an administrative tool and as an overhead, rather than a strategic platform.

9. MOVING TO THE STRATEGIC USE OF IT IN MARKETING

The important question which is commonly asked at this point is: 'How do we as an organisation move from the discrete approach to the strategic marketing approach?' There are a growing range of consultancies who will offer methodologies and products to enable this move to take place. It would be wrong to write off all such approaches as essentially pragmatic (even those that emanate from business schools). However, to return to the symbolism of the bi-modal distribution, such approaches are more likely to lead to a shift to the right within the 'Discrete Approach' curve, than to enable the jump to be made across the two curves.

Drawing on City University Business School research into IT in financial services, it was concluded that:

> "the IT function was not always at the fore of the development process, as in some cases it was the marketing function which was the driving force behind the process....marketing gave the impression of being the catalyst behind the IT department's drive to deliver systems." (Dockery, 1991)

If, as suggested, a key characteristic shown by organisations in the strategic management group is the development of an 'IT culture', this in fact hinges on the way in which the organisation is managed as a whole, as well as its specific attitude towards, and capability in, IT.

Although Moriarty and Swartz (1989) provide a helpful overview of marketing and sales productivity (MSP) systems, it is difficult fully to accept their unadorned argument that:

> "Early adapters of MSP systems have gained superior competitive advantage." (p. 108)

They do go on to point out, however, that MSP systems cannot by themselves work miracles, and will not compensate for inadequacies elsewhere; that inappropriate MSP systems can be positively harmful to the organisation, e.g.:

- Poorly implemented voice processing system
- Use of telemarketing in inappropriate areas or in conflict with other direct or channel sales
- Overdomination of thinking by information about the existing customer base. There are many practical and organisational problems which make organisations feel wary about extending beyond this base, but in the type of environment for marketing indicated above by Blyth, to focus on apparently 'hard' data about only existing customers could be a serious if not fatal weakness.

10. MARKETING DECISION SUPPORT SYSTEMS

Marketing professionals have been active users of decision-support software, not least because of the volume and complexity of the raw data they have had to deal with. A good example of use of Marketing DSSs in industrial marketing is General Electric (Lillis and McIvor, 1985). In smaller organisations, and in at least some larger ones also, much marketing analysis is carried out on a spreadsheet (West, 1987). But this cannot by itself currently cope with the volumes of data available in consumer marketing.

One of the problems with the development of machine-readable bar codes on products sold in supermarkets is that there has been a massive increase in the volume of data available for marketing purposes. Schmitz, Armstrong and Little (1991) describe how Ocean Spray Cranberries, a fruit processing cooperative, uses expert system software called CoverStory to extract from raw data the "brands and markets which are currently newsworthy and identifies marketing factors that may be causing changes in those brands and markets."

Ocean Spray uses the InfoScan syndicated database from juices, which has about 400 million numbers covering up to 100 data measures, 10,000 products, 125 weeks and 50 geographic markets. The database, which takes up some 10 gigabytes of disk storage, is held on mainframe, with 11 PCs being located in the marketing and sales function to analyse and present the data. This is done using the pcEXPRESS decision support system.

A series of marketing variables that experience has shown are important for driving sales and market share are selected from the database. These commonly include:

- Displays – percent of stores (weighted by size) that displayed a brand or item
- Features – percent of stores (weighted by size) that ran a feature advertisement on a brand
- Distribution – size-weighted percent of stores that sold a brand
- Price Cuts – percent of stores that sold a brand at a price reduced below a threshold, such as 10%, from the regular price
- Price – several alternative measures can be used.

Within CoverStory a series of rankings are built up to analyse the most significant changes. The rankings depend upon scores that relate to the market, causal factor and size change. The results are presented in word processed format that has the appearance of a report written by a marketing analyst. It uses sentence templates, typeface variations, graphics and sidebars to make the report visually interesting, and also to highlight the marketing facts contained in it.

According to Schmitz, Armstrong and Little:

> "CoverStory is very much a decision support system rather than a decision making system. The user can adjust all major system parameters such as who competes with whom, what weights to use for the marketing factors, and how much information is to be reported."
>
> "Ocean Spray's marketing DSS is used every day in planning, fire-fighting, and updating people's mental models of what is going on in the company's markets...the DSS has made it possible for a single marketing professional to manage the process of alerting all Ocean Spray marketing and sales managers to key problems and opportunities and of providing them with daily problem-solving information and guidance."

11. IMPROVING CUSTOMER SERVICE

Rochester (1990) indicates that:

> "organisations are using information technology to improve their customer service strategies in three ways:

- personalizing service
- augmenting service
- transformation products."

Hanan and Karp (1989) emphasise the central significance of customer satisfaction, and draw out what they describe as 'the Big Eight' factors which promote this:

Product-related Factors
1. Value-to-price relationship
2. Product quality
3. Product benefits and features
4. Reliability

Service-related Factors
5. Warranty
6. Response to and remedy of problems

Purchase Factors
7. Sales experience
8. Convenience of acquisition.

There is a significant overlap between marketing strategy and business strategy – some commentators indeed argue they are one and the same thing. Most of the modern approaches to business strategy lay a heavy emphasis on the customer (as marketing strategies have almost always done). If the relationship with the customer is seen as the central dominating theme of an organisation, whether in the public or private sector, then the question needs to be asked about every existing and proposed IT system: 'How does it help us improve our relationship with the customer?'

This is a question that has all too often escaped the IT project appraisal process.

Even approaches such as Electronic Data Interchange (EDI), that hold potential for improved customer service, particularly in the business-to-business environment, are not necessarily being implemented with service in mind. MIT researchers reported an exception for Office Technologies Corporation, since "unlike the other cases we studied, those EDI applications are all designed to become part of a broad range of services that ultimately will enhance customer support." (Benjamin, De Long and Scott Morton, 1990)

Barabba and Zaltman (1991) make a powerful case for setting up what they describe as an 'inquiry centre'. They define this as the:

"ideal state of mind within a company for effectively and efficiently reconciling the voice of the market with the voice of the firm."

"The inquiry centre describes a particular way of learning about the market place and using the resultant knowledge. While the term 'centre' denotes an organisational unit, it is as much an attitude, ethic, or creed as it is a formal entity. Of course, all firms and their divisions or departments and individual employees have ways of learning about their markets and of using the information: but few take the trouble to check how well their learning systems work and whether they can be improved. The inquiry centre concept fosters the development of a corporate-wide attitude essential in becoming a market--based organisation."

12. DATABASE MARKETING

In the authoritative text on the subject Shaw and Stone (1988) define database marketing as:

"An interactive approach to marketing, which uses individually addressable marketing media and channels (such as mail, telephone and the sales force):

- to extend help to a company's target audience
- to stimulate their demand
- to stay close to them." (Shaw and Stone, 1988)

"we use 'database marketing' to mean a new way of doing business, a re-definition of marketing management which leads to a new way of defining the relationship between a company and its customers." (Shaw and Stone, 1988)

One of the problems with the proliferation of words in both IT and marketing is a real risk of overlap if not duplication. Kotler and Armstrong (1991) define marketing research as:

"The function that links the consumer, customer and public to the marketer through information – information used to identify and define marketing opportunities and problems; to generate, refine and evaluate marketing actions; to monitor marketing performance; and to improve understanding of the marketing process."

One of the challenges of database marketing is that it needs to draw on a wide variety of internal data sources:

- Customer files
- Order records
- Service reports, complaints
- Merchandise return records
- Sales force records
- Application forms
- Enquiries
- Warranty cards
  (Shaw and Stone, 1988)

However, ensuring corporate access to such departmental records is not necessarily a trivial issue, and implementing database marketing can be a major challenge if not threat to at least parts of an organisation.

13. MANAGING THE CHANGE TO A STRATEGIC USE OF IT IN MARKETING

Based on CUBS research into IT strategy in financial services – a number of key areas for action to implement strategic change initiated by IT issues includes:

- Engage top management
- Build information base of customers
- Compete through people
- Search for new market opportunities
- Manage IT initiatives as a change process
- Develop good products
- Re-invent key aspects of the core business, using IT to support.
  (Dockery, 1991)

One specific example of the potential impact of change is on the sales function:

> "Sales representatives call on buyers not only to get orders, but to provide customer services, obtain information, expedite deliveries and so on. If many of the routine processes of placing and processing orders are handled via electronic systems, how will the other dimensions of the buyer-seller relationship be handled?" (Buzzell, 1985)

The impact of an IT-based marketing strategy can impact at all levels of the organisation. Olympia and York, who built the Canary Wharf development in London's Docklands, have based their sophisticated marketing campaign around a fully computerised system. However, a key part of this system is that all contacts with the top managers who form the target group are logged. The actual experience (Burdus, 1990) is that very senior managers can find it hard to adapt to this rigor, and may simply forget to log lunch and dinner meetings with target management. So IT does not only impact on more junior staff.

14. SKILLS

The marketing profession is not homogeneous. On the one hand there are the top few dozen companies involved in consumer marketing who have considerable expertise in marketing, and relatively sophisticated techniques and systems, though there is often considerable secrecy surrounding those systems.

At the other extreme are the host of small firms who have no marketing professional and who may be very product orientated, and where marketing is often seen as part of the sales role.

In reviewing the skills needed, Blyth (1989) argued that:

> "The level at which market research operates within large corporations is often low, with some exceptions, and the reason for this is, I believe, the lack of a focus on information as a totality, rather than the specific benefits of market research. The implications for the industry in the longer term are vast. It is my view that to reap fully the values of the skills they have built up, market researchers need to become increasingly information managers. By that I do not mean getting wrapped up in information technology....Rather what I mean by information managers is taking the discipline acquired by the structuring and ordering of research data and applying it to the wider business context of total management information: designing the structure, interfaces and maintenance of corporate information systems which are relevant to all functions and to all levels of the organisation."

In a study carried out in the early 1980s by CIT research:

> "the future opportunities are enormous for those who can think in terms of active, and indeed interactive media, and narrowcasting rather than broadcasting. To survive in this brave new world, however, there is a need for a new breed of marketing and media professional – someone who can think in terms of segmentation, specialist/minority groups and interactive media rather than delivering mass audiences in predictable volumes to fixed and pre-ordained time-slots; someone who understands the changing role of information and communications technology without losing sight of the marketing mix, however it develops. In short we need broad multi-disciplinary skills able to combine electronics, marketing, media, research, information technology,

advertising and telecommunications. Those organisations recognizing this will be able to tackle the new media with confidence." (CIT Research, 1981, p. 78)

15. MANAGEMENT EDUCATION, IT AND MARKETING

What is the role of those involved in management education?

- Teach the theory and ignore the messy real world
- Teach the messy real world and develop an opportunistic, pragmatic, atheoretical and contingent approach to problem solving.
- Construct an abstraction of the real world which minimises the messiness, and enables satisfying and coherent intellectual models and theorems to be tested and deployed.

It appears like avoidance and lack of decisiveness to suggest that a mixture of all these is needed. But it is particularly important in relation to the use of IT, and for the interaction between IT and marketing.

Our ability to prescribe solutions is circumscribed by:

- external environmental issued faced
- internal culture
- individual goals and values
- structural and technological histories
- current performance and problem perception.

The state of development of theory and of practice of IT and marketing does not yet permit – if it ever will – the application of close ended finite approaches. However much the technology suggests that universally valid solutions are emerging, this is an over-optimistic suggestion.

16. THE IMPACT OF TECHNOLOGICAL DEVELOPMENTS

Although the primary drive for more effective use of IT in marketing must come from the imperatives of the market, of the customer and of the marketing professional, there also needs to be consideration given to the impacts that technological developments are having or could have in this area.

In some cases, technologies have been developed specifically for marketing purposes. In the case of market research, there is a whole battery of specialist technology aimed at the task of data collection.

Gold (1990) contrasts existing data collection technologies:

- Paper diary to television viewing
- Television station records
- Store audits
- Paper purchase diaries

with new data collection technology:

- Television metering
- Commercial recognition technology
- Retail scanner data
- In-home scanners
- Store scanners with household IDs.

He particularly sees significance in the correlation of technologies, in what he describes as 'Linked Multiple Technologies':

In-store:	retail + household
In-home:	household + set-metering
In-home:	household + person-metering
In-home:	TV collection
In-store/home:	retail + household + TV metering
In-store/home:	switching + TV metering

One of the areas to which some attention must be given is the increasing use of small and mid-range systems relative to large mainframes. Eventually, these smaller systems will probably be linked in seamlessly integrated networks using the client-server model, Open Systems Interconnection, standards-driven operating systems and document-exchange standards. But present day reality is rather more prosaic – and many machines, even where physically connected, are unable to interwork in any significant fashion. The reduction in size of the basic unit of computing is likely to mean that it is more difficult to exchange and share data than when the data is held on a single, centralised system.

The decentralisation of IT is being paralleled in many organisations by a decentralisation of management and a reduction in the number of levels of management. It remains to be seen whether there is a fundamental change taking place, or whether it is more of a rejection of the centralised approach which has been commonplace in the last two decades.

But marketing analyses and the promotion of a customer-centred approach require the ability to draw together readily data from a wide variety of sources. In the absence of a single mainframe holding all core data, an alternative must be found. One method is to create a central database which is fully geared to massive data storage and high speed analysis of that data, rather than the somewhat different needs of, for example, on-line transaction processing. Niche hardware and software vendors have moved into this area.

For example, Ratners the jewellery chain use IBM minicomputers to coordinate the point-of-sale data from their Ratner and Zales branches, and an ICL mainframe for their H. Samuel shops. Data is downloaded from these systems into a Teradata parallel-processing database computer, which processes the data at very high speed to produce detailed marketing information. Managers can then access the database direct from an Apple Macintosh*.

17. TECHNOLOGICAL DEVELOPMENTS THAT MAY BE EXPLOITED IN MARKETING

Some of the other areas of technology with particular impact on marketing are summarised below:

- Electronic Data Interchange (EDI)
- Voice/data integration particularly the Integrated Services Digital Network (ISDN)
- Executive Information Systems (EIS) – complex to simple needs
- Voice processing
- Multimedia
- Geographical Information Systems (GIS)
- Customer tracking – Correspondence Tracking and Executive Issues Management System (CIMS)
- Expert Systems/Neural Networks.

No amount of investment in hardware or software can outweigh the significance of the non-technological aspects of systems development, including relationships. Of particular concern here is the key relationship between the marketing and the information systems professionals:

> "It is important to recognise that establishing linkages between the marketing function and IT department creates potential for ongoing improvement in the development of products and future business performance." (Dockery, 1991)

---

*Editor's Note: The Ratner's Group is now the Signet Group, Ratner branches now Kudos and Sacquis, and Zales branches now Ernest Jones. Teradata is now owned by AT&T.

18. CONCLUSION

The use of IT in marketing potentially involves a very diverse range of applications and technologies. In practice, these are often implemented in an *ad hoc* way, and there is often an inadequate use even of readily available and accessible approaches. There are various barriers to more effective use, but one of the main ones is the lack of skills in managing information and technology.

There appear broadly to be two contrasting philosophies relating to the use of IT in marketing:

1. The discrete use approach.
2. The strategic marketing approach.

There also appear to be very few organisations adopting the latter approach, mostly because very few have the resources, and this means above all the skills necessary for implementation.

To make fundamental improvements in IT for marketing to achieve its strategic potential involves much more than the sophisticated computerisation of customer records. It needs a widespread philosophical change. It needs IT-aware and marketing-aware top managers in all disciplines. It needs a fundamental commitment to re-analysing systems to provide a customer orientation.

REFERENCES

Barabba, V. P. and Zaltman, G. (1991) *Hearing the Voice of the Market: Competitive advantage through creative use of market information*, Harvard Business School Press, Boston, MA.

Benjamin, R. J., De Long, D. W. and Scott Morton, M. S. (1990) 'Electronic data interchange: How much competitive advantage?' *Long Range Planning*, **23**(1), pp. 29–40.

Blyth, B. (1989) 'The management and evaluation of marketing information', *Market Research Society Conference Paper.*

Burdus, A. (1990) 'The impact of IT on marketing', *Paper to Hoskyns/City University IT Business School Conference*, London, UK.

Buzzell, R. D. (ed.) (1985) *Marketing in an Electronic Age*, Harvard Business School Press, Boston, MA.

CIT Research (1981) *Advertising, Marketing and the New European Media*, CIT Research, London.

Coultas, C. A. (1990) 'Marketing is sold, but not satisfied', *Computerworld*, 21 May, p. 103.

Dockery, E. (1991) 'The strategic use of information systems technology in banking firms and building societies', *City University Working Paper*, No 117, April.

Flax, S. (1984) 'How to snoop on your competitors', *Fortune*, May 14, pp. 29–33.

Gold, L. (1990) 'High technology data collection for testing and measurement', in ESOMAR, *How to Cope with Data Overload*, Amsterdam, Netherlands.

Graf, F. (1979) 'Information systems for marketing', *Marketing Trends*, **2**, pp. 1–3.

Hanan, M. and Karp, P. (1989) *Customer Satisfaction*, American Management Association, New York.

Harper, M. Jr. (1961) 'A new profession to aid management', *Journal of Marketing*, January, p. 1.

Higby, M. A. and Farah, B. N. (1991) The status of marketing information systems, decision support systems and expert systems in the marketing function of US firms', *Information and Management*, **20**, pp. 33–48.

Holtham, C. (ed.) (1988) *Executive Information Systems and Strategic Decision Support*, Chapman & Hall, London.

Hugo, I. St. J. (1967) *Marketing and the Computer*, Pergamon Press, Oxford.

Jobber, D. (1977) 'Msarketing information systems in US and British industry', *Management Decisions*, **15**(2), pp. 297–304.

Kotler, P. (1968) 'A design for the firm's marketing nerve center', in S. V. Smith, R. H. Brien and J. E. Stafford (eds.), *Marketing Information Systems – A new era in marketing research*, Houghton Mifflin Co, Boston, MA.

Kotler, P. and Armstrong, G. (1991) *Principles of Marketing, 5th edn.*, Prentice Hall, Englewood Cliffs, NJ.

Larreche, J. C. (1975) *Marketing managers and models: a serach for a better match*, INSEAD Research Paper Series, No. 157.

Lillis, C. M. and McIvor, B. J. (1985) 'MDSs at General Electric: Implications for the 1990s from experience in the 1970s and 1980s', in Buzzell, R. D. (ed.) (1985) *Marketing in an Electronic Age*, Harvard Business School Press, Boston, MA, pp. 89–106.

Mayros, V. (1990) 'Have I got a system for you!' *Computerworld*, May 21, pp. 97–102.

Moriarty, R. and Swartz, G. S. (1989) 'Automation to boos sales and marketing', *Harvard Business Review*, **67**(1), pp. 100–108.

OASiS (1989) *The Management of Marketing Information*, OASiS, Maidenhead.

Schmitz, J. D., Armstrong, G. D. and Little, J. D. C. (1991) 'CoverStory – Automated news finding in marketing', in Holtham, C. (ed.) (1988) *Executive Information Systems and Strategic Decision Support*, Chapman & Hall, London.

Shaw, R. (1988) 'Make the database more commonplace', *Marketing Week*, September, pp. 55–59.

Shaw, R. and Stone, M. (1988) *Database Marketing*, Gower, Aldershot.

West, A. (1987) *Spreadsheet Marketing*, Gower, Aldershot).

Williams, I. (1987) '"dark science" brings a boost to aitline profits', *Sunday Times*, November 22, p. 94.

Wolf, J. A. (1984) 'New concepts in improving marketing productivity', *Information Industry Insights*, **5**(4).

2 Marketing intelligence for intelligent marketing

Michael J Baker
University of Strathclyde

1. INTRODUCTION

In recent years it has become increasingly fashionable to talk of accelerating technological change, increased international competition and environmental turbulence. Taken together, these trends are seen as calling for a radically different approach to business and management than that which has prevailed for the better part of this century. The application of information technology (IT) to marketing problems offers the potential for such a radically different approach.

Evidence to support the claim of turbulence is all around us. In very simplistic terms, in the advanced industrial economies of the world it is attributable to two major forces: the potential for exponential increases in supply, driven by new technology, and the slowing down in the growth of demand as population growth falters and even goes into reverse in some countries. One of the most vivid examples of the pace of technological change was provided by the late Chris Evans in his book *The Mighty Micro* (1979). In reviewing developments in electronics for the period between 1955 and 1980, Evans attempted to compare these developments by explaining what would have happened in the automobile manufacturing industry if similar changes had occurred. Three criteria were proposed – cost, efficiency and size. According to Evans, if the world's automobile industry had reflected developments in micro electronics then during this 25 year period, it would have become possible to build a Rolls Royce car for £1.35, drive it round the world on half a cup full of petrol, and park six of them on the head of a pin. As we all know, in the field of microelectronics, these trends have continued to accelerate exponentially with the result that our ability to process and manage data has grown out of all recognition.

Similar trends are to be seen in other areas of technological change which, in addition to permitting increasingly sophisticated ways of satisfying basic needs, have also resulted in a marked increase in our overall supply capability. Now, while the world's population overall has continued to grow exponentially too, purchasing power is largely concentrated in a small number of advanced industrialised economies where population growth has slowed, if not gone into reverse. Ultimately, markets are people and it is the aggregated demands of these people which constitute the markets available to intending suppliers. The outcome of an accelerating supply capability and a stable demand capacity have resulted in the recession which has dogged the world's economy in recent years. In turn, the consequences have been equally inevitable. Faced with a stagnant or declining market relative to ever-increasing supplies the intensity of competition between suppliers has changed out of all recognition.

Creation or access to suitable databases will be essential to competitive success in the 1990s and beyond. Clearly, IT is an enabling innovation which allows many tasks to be done more easily, more quickly, more efficiently and, possibly more effectively. In *Research for Marketing* (1991) I cite Alan Melkman (*The Marketing Handbook*, Thomas, 1989) who proposes four broad areas of IT application, as shown in Table 2.1. These may be described as follows:

1. Enhancing operating efficiency: "...those marketing activities which are already carried out in one form or another within the company. Typically, these include maintenance of customer records, budgeting, preparing and making presentations and analysing sales statistics, scheduling meetings and so on."
2. Changed methods: "...enabling the Marketing Department to carry out internal functions which were not possible before." This will usually start with an extension of applications in the first quadrant such as using databases for segmentation and positioning studies, more sophisticated forecasting and modelling, better and faster communication with a field sales force, etc.
3. Enhancing customer service: this will be made possible by better and faster communication with customers, the application of CATI to obtain timely and relevant data on changing market needs, etc.
4. Marketing innovation: the use of video cassettes to make sales presentations and demonstrate product use, access to and use of large on-line databases such as DataScan, Information Line and Dialog; direct mail services, market

Table 2.1 An IT applications framework.

		Marketing activities	
		Existing	New
Focus of activity	Internal	1 Enhancing operating efficiency	2 Changed methods
	External	3 Enhancing customer service	4 Market innovation

identification studies such as Pinpoint, Acorn and Market Location, EPOS (Electronic Point of Sale). It has been incorporated in electronic banking systems such as HOBS, and it can only be a matter of time before other financial service institutions follow suit. Similarly, the growth of cable and satellite television is likely to increase the growth of telemarketing.

Melkman's four areas of IT application illustrate the likely sequence which organisations will follow in exploiting the potential benefits of IT. A constant and recurring theme of this book is that increased competition has resulted in much greater awareness of the value of timely and relevant data. In parallel with other changes, these have helped to accelerate the take up of IT. Amongst these changes may be numbered:

- The availability of much less expensive hardware.
- The availability of much more sophisticated software.
- Greater user friendliness in both.
- Growing familiarity with visible applications and all the output of IT-based systems, e.g. detailed retail receipts generated by EPOS systems, access to and use of Automatic Teller Machines (ATM), extensive use of word processing, etc.
- The availability of more skilled and trained manpower.
- The establishment of specialist service and software houses.

2. COMPETITIVE STRATEGIES

As a result of the intensification in competition, much time and effort has been given to documenting the nature of competition and identifying those strategies which offer the best prospect of survival and success for firms in a competitive environment. It is now widely recognised that there are only two basic strategies available to the firm – cost leadership and differentiation. For much of recorded history cost leadership has been the dominant strategy on the grounds that, with a basic need to satisfy, the consumer will invariably prefer a lower cost product as offering better value for money. Further, faced with an ever-growing population, the challenge facing producers was to create ever-increasing volumes of output to match the available demand. To do so called for standardisation, and the economies of scale and experience which are associated with mass production, mass distribution and mass consumption.

Without a doubt, the epitome of the pursuit of cost leadership as a competitive strategy was Ford's development of the model 'T'. At the turn of the century public interest in and demand for automobiles was apparent for all to see. At that time, however, motor manufacturing was essentially a craft industry with a large number of specialised suppliers producing cars in small batch quantities. Because of the small scale of production and the high labour content, cars were very expensive and beyond the purchasing power of most consumers. It was this that Ford recognised as a marketing opportunity. The demand for motor cars was obvious – the challenge was to create a car at a price which would put it within reach of the average consumer. Thus, Ford set off with the ambition to produce a car which he could sell for $500. To do this called for a radical change in manufacturing methods and the single-minded pursuit of the economies of scale. It was Ford who conceived of the potential of mass assembly linked to the development of specialised suppliers who would provide many of the sub-assemblies and components required in the construction of a car.

By 1919 Ford had over 60% share of the American automobile market which had grown out of all recognition since the introduction of the model 'T' 10 years earlier. More important, the model 'T' was selling at $258.

Since the rediscovery of the marketing concept in the mid-1950s, Ford has frequently been held up as the archetypal production-oriented manager whose disregard for customers is epitomised in his statement that "you can have any colour of car you want so long as it is black." The reality, of course, is that Henry Ford, like every successful entrepreneur, was by definition marketing-oriented. In 1909 when he introduced the model 'T' he understood perfectly what the market wanted – low cost personal transportation. The fact that Henry Ford was subsequently overtaken by General Motors was due to the fact that he failed to recognise that his own actions had changed the nature of consumer demand, and he had not changed his product to reflect this.

In the period immediately after the First World War, General Motors was Ford's main competitor in North America. Given Ford's dominant market share it was clear to the General Motors' management that they could not hope to compete with them on price alone. Denied the possibility of cost leadership, General Motors had to resort to our other core competitive strategy – product differentiation. General Motors recognised that Ford's low cost automobile had created a whole new market of committed customers who were familiar with the product, but could think of many ways of improving it to meet their own personal needs. Not only that, customers would be prepared to pay more for products which met their particular needs, and it was this that provided General Motors with the opportunity to create a range of complementary models catering to a variety of consumer tastes.

General Motors' product differentiation strategy represented the first step in a movement away from macro marketing, which deals with mass or aggregated markets, to their disaggregation through producer led product differentiation, to market segmentation in which producers start by seeking to assess customer needs and then work back from the market place into the organisation, seeking to match its strengths with identified market opportunities.

Market segmentation is a process by which the total market for a given product or service is sub-divided into a number of comparatively homogeneous groups with similar interests based upon distinctive characteristics in terms of factors such a demography, geography, psychology, perceived benefits, etc. Market segmentation offers a useful compromise between the extreme approach of both the economist and the behavioural scientist, as indicated in Figure 2.1 taken from Baker (1992).

In the marketing literature it is widely agreed that for a segment to merit specific marketing attention it must satisfy a number of conditions. It must be:

1. Measurable.
2. Accessible.
3. Substantial.
4. Unique in its response.
5. Stable, in the sense that its behaviour can be predicted in the future.

Over the past decade or so, the trend has increasingly been towards finer and finer resolution of market segments and the emergence of what has been referred to as 'niche marketing'. One of the earliest proponents of this concept was Philip Kotler (1980), who sees niche marketing calling for much greater specialisation than that involved in normal market segmentation strategies. In his view, "an ideal market niche would have the following characteristics:

> 1. The niche is of sufficient size and purchasing power to be profitable.
> 2. The niche has growth potential.
> 3. The niche has been bypassed or neglected by major competitors.
> 4. The firm has superior competencies to service the niche effectively.
> 5. The firm can defend its position against an attacking major because of the goodwill it has built up.
>
> The key idea in nichemanship is specialisation. The firm has to identify a viable form of specialization along market, customer, product or marketing-mix lines. At least ten specialist roles are open to a market nicher:
>
> 1. *End-use specialist.* This firm decides to specialise in serving one type of end-use customer. For example, a law firm can decide to specialise in the criminal, civil or business law markets.
> 2. *Vertical-level specialist.* This firm specialises at some vertical level of the production-distribution cycle. For example, a copper firm may concentrate on the production of raw copper, copper components or finished copper products.
> 3. *Customer-size specialist.* This firm concentrates on selling to either

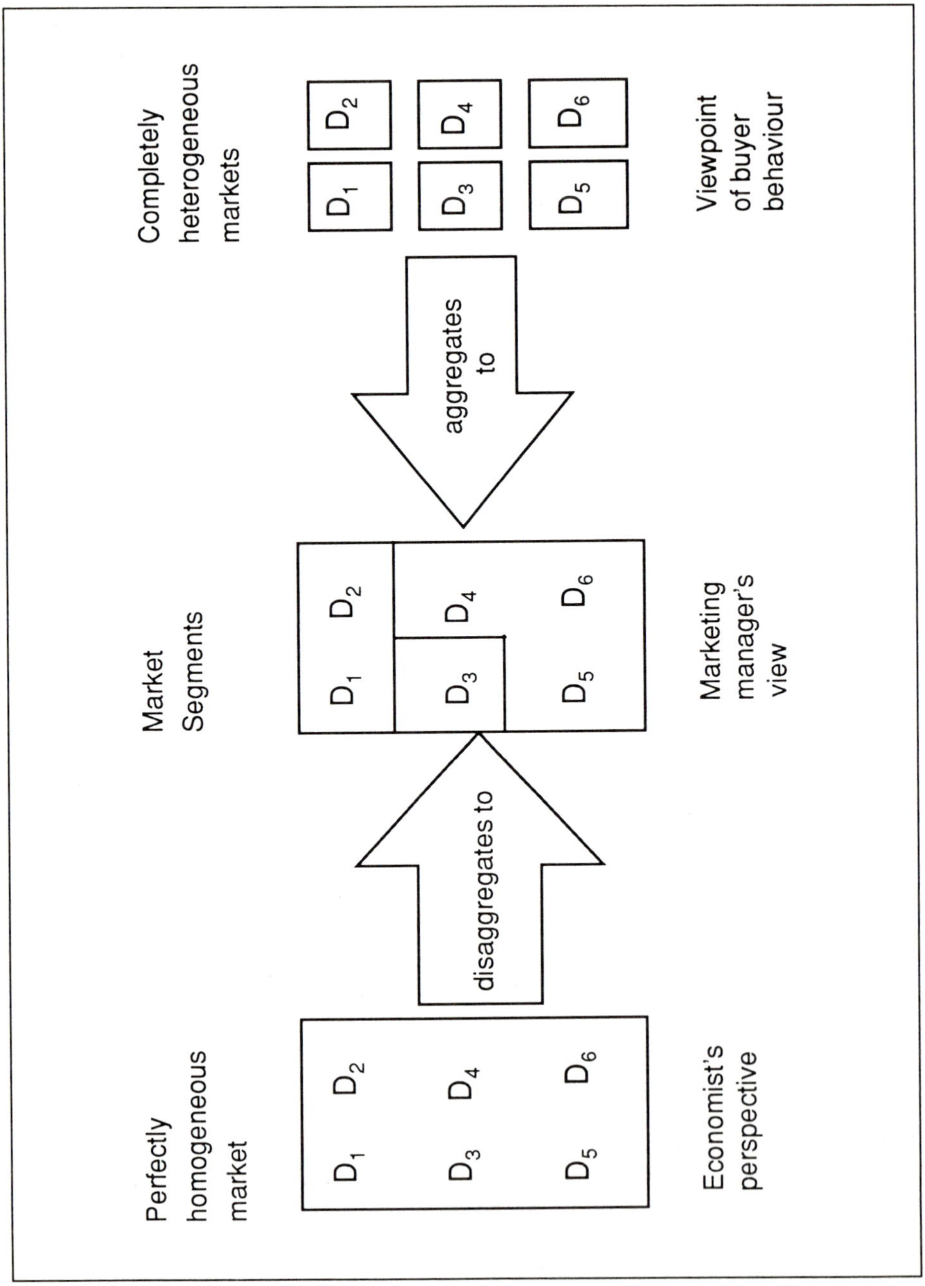

Figure 2.1 Alternative perspectives of the total market.

small, medium or large-size customers. Many nichers specialize in serving small customers because they are neglected by the majors.

4. *Specific-customer specialist.* This firm limits its selling to one or a few major customers. Many firms sell their entire output to a single company such as Sears or General Motors.
5. *Geographic specialist.* This firm focuses on the needs of a certain locality, region, or area of the world.
6. *Product or product-line specialist.* This firm produces only one product line or product. Within the laboratory equipment industry there are firms that produce only microscopes, or even more narrowly, only lenses for microscopes.
7. *Product-feature specialist.* This firm specialises in producing a certain type of product or product feature. Rent-a-Junk, for example, is a California car rental agency that rents only 'beat-up' cars.
8. *Job-shop specialist.* This firm stands ready to make customised products as ordered by the customer.
9. *Quality/price specialist.* This firm chooses to operate at the low or high end of the market. For example, Hewlett-Packard specialises in the high-quality, high-price end of the hand-calculator market.
10. *Service specialist.* This firm offers or excels in one or more services not readily available from other firms. An example would be a bank that takes loan requests over the phone or dispatches an officer to deliver the money at the client's home or office."

From the foregoing discussion it is clear that we can distinguish three distinct stages in the evolution of marketing practice in the present century. Gunter and Furnham (1992) define these as follows:

- Mass marketing: In mass marketing, the seller mass produces, mass distributes and mass promotes one product to all buyers.
- Product differentiated marketing: The seller produces two or more products that exhibit different features, styles, quality, sizes and so on.
- Target Marketing: The seller distinguishes among many market segments, selects one or more of these segments and develops products and marketing mixes tailored to each segment.

In Gunter and Furnham's view, rising real incomes and the move away from traditional class determined patterns of behaviour will further increase the significance of market segmentation. Clearly, the application of IT provides the technology to facilitate this trend.

Gunter and Furnham go on to explain that target marketing calls for three steps:

1. *Market segmentation*: the act of dividing a market into distinct groups of buyers who might require separate products and/or marketing mixes. The company identifies different ways to segment the market and develops profiles of the resulting market segments.
2. *Market targeting*: the act of evaluating and selecting one or more of the market segments to enter.
3. *Product positioning*: the act of formulating a competitive positioning for the product and a detailed marketing mix.

There are four commonly used bases for segmenting consumer markets. The first two can be broadly subsumed under *Physical Attribute Classification*, and the others represent forms of *Behavioural* or *Psychological Attribute Classification.*

Physical Attribute Classification includes: (i) *geographic segmentation*, which refers to the dividing of an overall market into homogeneous groups on the basis of population location and has been used for hundreds of years; and (ii) *demographic segmentation*, which refers to the dividing of an overall market into homogeneous groups based upon characteristics such as age, sex and income level. Demographic segmentation is the most commonly used method of subdividing total markets.

Behavioural Attribute Classification, on the other hand, includes (i) *Product use and benefit segmentation*, which focuses upon product purchase behaviour and the benefits the consumer expects to derive from a product or service. These segmentation bases can be important to marketing strategies, provided they are significantly related to differences in buying behaviour; and (ii) *psychological segmentation*, which utilises profiles of consumers developed either from standardised personality inventories and from analyses of the reported activities, opinions, interests and lifestyles of individuals.

To generate the data required for target marketing of this kind, organisations need good marketing intelligence. In turn, this depends upon marketing research.

3. RESEARCH FOR MARKETING

The importance of good intelligence as a basis for strategic decision making has long been recognised by the military. The maxim 'time spent in reconnaissance is seldom wasted' can be traced back to the writing of Sun Tzu, the Chinese strategist, whose *Art of War* was written four centuries before the birth of Christ. Indeed, the whole thrust of Sun Tzu's philosophy, which is reflected in more recent writers such as Clausewitz and Liddell Hart, is centred on the securing of competitive advantage through superior knowledge and understanding. In the world of business, numerous recent studies have pointed to the fact that there is a strong positive association between competitive success and involvement in marketing research.

During the 1980s there was a constant stream of advice on how organisations might improve their competitiveness. While this advice ranged from the rigorous to the anecdotal in origin and methodology, it was virtually unanimous in its conclusion that a key factor in sustaining and improving competitiveness is sound market intelligence. Such a finding should be no cause for surprise, for as long ago as 1964 a study by the National Industrial Conference Board in the USA into the causes of new product failure found that the most frequently cited cause was 'inadequate market analysis'. In addressing the question of how to improve success rates, 65% of the respondents spoke of the need to set up a proper organisation for the task. The next most frequently cited reply (52%) was 'provide better market research'.

In *Marketing and Competitive Success*, Baker and Hart (1989) report that throughout the 1970s market research was frequently associated with higher export performance (Rollason, 1971; British Institute of Management, 1975; ITI Research, 1979). Such findings were confirmed in a study carried out by Baker and Abou-Zeid (1982), where 86% of companies with a Queen's Award for export achievement carried out export market research. The most popular method of conducting market research was to use salesmen, while agents and government sources were less popular means. The main use to which the information was put was in selecting the foreign markets, while other uses were providing market information and identifying the required adaptation to suit the needs of these markets.

Cross-national comparisons have also highlighted the importance of market research to competitive success. For example, Connell (1979) describes how innovation in Japanese firms is typically initiated by sales and marketing personnel in the light of identified customer needs. This, along with other factors which emphasise customer interaction and interdepartmental cooperation in product development, distinguished Japanese firms from British firms.

Recent empirical work in the UK also lends weight to the argument that market research plays an important role in successful companies' marketing operations. Takeuchi and Quelch (1983) quote examples of successful companies who constantly monitor product quality from the buyers' point of view. The market research tactics involved include:

- conducting customer satisfaction surveys
- tracking and recording all complaints and problems
- having a questionnaire completed by all customers returning goods
- carrying out extensive field tests on new products
- analysing warranty claims
- assessing the condition of goods received by administering a questionnaire.

Alexander (1985) shows that the use of qualitative market research by three companies (studied by her in some depth) generated information which was used to move beyond existing product concepts and to translate market requirements into innovative, successful designs. In the study by Walsh and Roy (1983) into the practices and policies of winners of the Design Council Awards, all award-winning companies paid attention to market research, and many ideas for new market opportunities, as well as design evaluation, came from market or customer research. Finally, Hooley and Lynch (1985) report that successful companies made much greater use of all types of market research than did less successful ones. Table 2.2 summarises the types of market research used by both high-fliers and also-rans.

Despite Hooley and Lynch's claim, the table shows a surprisingly low usage rate of market research. This finding was confirmed by Baker and Hart (1989). As can be seen from Table 2.3, while above-average companies made significantly greater use of market research than below-average companies, the highest recorded level was 69% for external sources and only 52% had an in-house market research capability.

Numerous reasons may be advanced for this low take-up, amongst which the most frequently encountered are:

- it is too technical
- it is too subjective
- it is just common sense.

According to Curry (*The New Marketing Research Systems*, 1993), a great deal of marketing research consists of one or a series of *ad hoc* studies designed to solve a particular problem or to address a single major issue that might consist of several related sub-issues. He claims that many executives think about the research function in this way, and that the key components of this view may be characterised as:

- The role of marketing management is to solve a series of independent,

Table 2.2 Frequent use of market research techniques (Source Hooley and Lynch, 1985).

Laboratory experiments	Sample	High-fliers	Also-rans	Significance (t)
Sample size	1504	175	1329	-
Customer surveys	26.9%	33.7%	26.0%	0.05
Qualitative research	24.7%	30.9%	23.9%	0.0
Field experiments	18.5%	26.9%	17.4%	0.0
Laboratory experiments	12.4%	20.6%	11.3%	0.001

Table 2.3 Market research in above- and below-average companies (*significant at the 5% level) (Source: Baker and Hart, 1989).

Research type	Above-average companies	Below-average companies	Variation
In-house	52%	31%	+68%*
External	69%	47%	+47%*

isolated problems.

- The research function is, therefore, time-discrete. A project starts, is executed, and ends.
- The data necessary to solve one problem are separable from (or are more useful if separated from) the data needed to solve another problem.
- Different managers have different responsibilities and hence must use different approaches and different information to solve problems.
- Marketing as a business function should be separated from finance and manufacturing.

The mainstay of marketing research of this kind was, and is, the sample survey designed to elicit the attitudes, opinions and behaviour of consumers with a view to defining market segments of sufficient size and substance to merit the development of a tailored marketing mix. As Curry puts it, this form of mass marketing:

> "was epitomised by majority strategies, efforts by manufacturers to find the largest group of people with similar needs and buying habits who could be attracted to retail outlets by messages in the mass-media and convinced by replicates of mass-produced items. Economies in production, media buying, and central warehousing drove this approach, which thrived on a 'bigger is better' rationale. Mass marketers sought compromise in product design, channel selection, and sales message to reach and sell to a few demo- or geographic collectives."

The advent of the computer and information technology is changing this. According to Curry:

> "the ideas compiled in current research texts – the 10 steps in research projects; simple random sampling; mail, telephone, and personal interviewing; hypotheses testing, and regression analysis – are dinosaurs. They represent a project philosophy that no longer makes sense, they require expertise that is often irrelevant, and they focus on technical issues rather than business problems."

Three major kinds of shift can be identified which herald the emergence of a new research order. The first of these shifts derives directly from the new technology which makes it possible to collect, store and use disaggregated data in integrated databases. Second, new methods of data capture such as article numbering and electronic point of sale equipment, make it possible to create a dynamic research system directly accessible to the manager without having to go through the intermediary of a market research specialist collecting indirect and often static data by means of *ad hoc* surveys. Third, the primary emphasis in marketing research to date has been 'to reduce areas of uncertainty surrounding business decisions'. Today its role has become more proactive and concerned primarily with identifying business opportunities.

These trends and developments in IT have brought marketing full circle. The origins of marketing can be traced back to the first 'commercial' exchange when an individual recognised that they could improve their standard of living by exchanging surpluses of products, of which they had a sufficiency, with other people with surpluses of other kinds of products. To facilitate such exchanges markets evolved as central places where people could exchange their surpluses with one another. The existence of markets encouraged people to specialise in the knowledge that they could increase their productivity and then exchange their surpluses for other kinds of products which could be produced more efficiently by others.

In turn, task specialisation led to the division of labour and industrialisation which were to create the mass markets and mass consumption described earlier. At the same time, however, the concentration of manufacturing and the pursuit of scale economies resulted in both the physical and psychological separation of producer and consumer. No longer were suppliers interacting closely with the users of their output and it became necessary to close this information gap through marketing research of the kind described earlier.

As well as reducing uncertainty surrounding business decisions this kind of marketing research was fairly effective in defining viable market segments. Given the manufacturing methods which prevailed prior to the electronic revolution, a viable market segment would need to satisfy at least the five conditions specified earlier. Namely, it would need to be measurable, accessible, substantial, unique in its response, and stable in the sense that its behaviour could be predicted in the future. Only if the segment satisfied these conditions would it be worth developing a specific marketing mix for its exploitation. But the impact of the electronics revolution was not confined solely to improved data processing. Linked to manufacturing, computers have made it possible to develop flexible manufacturing systems able to produce almost infinite variety without any significant loss in manufacturing efficiency. As a result, it has become increasingly possible to tailor a formally standardised output to meet the precise needs of individual customers.

This ability has resulted in what Curry calls the "shift from mass to micro marketing." In his words:

> "by 1975 computerised, data-based technology revealed the promise of addressing individual consumer needs and the unsettling consequences of ignoring them. The possibility of directing the advertising dollar to a specific buyer ended the days of shotgun strategies. Marketing could employ more cost-efficient, personal, and accountable techniques and could be guided not only by targeting but also by predictions of behaviour. And the efforts could be scored by an investment mentality that had no trouble with concepts such as lifetime value or relationships with individual human beings. Micro marketing returned the individual to the marketing equation."

The switch from mass to micro marketing did not occur overnight. In simple terms, the 1950s and 1960s were the heyday of mass marketing. Increased competition in the 1970s resulted in a greater emphasis upon segmentation and line extension underpinned by more sophisticated manufacturing and marketing techniques. During the 1970s, however, there was a significant increase in international competition which, by the early 1980s, had caused many producers to concentrate on highly focussed strategies directed towards niche markets. Micro marketing, with its emphasis upon the individual consumer, is a logical extension of this.

4. DATABASE MARKETING

To conclude this chapter, it is useful to remind ourselves that the very heart (and mind) of micro marketing is the creation of a marketing database.

In his book *The Essential Guide to Database Marketing* (McGraw-Hill, 1992), John Davies defines the marketing database as

> "a collection of all available information on past, present and prospective customers, structured to achieve maximum usefulness."

He also offers the more comprehensive definition developed by the National Centre for Database Marketing in the USA, namely:

> "Database marketing involves at least the following elements: 1) managing, 2) a computerised, 3) relational data-base system, 4) in real time, 5) of comprehensive up to date, relevant data on customers, inquiries, prospects and suspects, 6) to identify your most responsive customers, 7) for the purpose of developing a high quality, longstanding relationship of repeat

> business, 8) by developing predicting models, 9) which enable us to send desired messages at the right time, in the right form, to the right people ..., 10) all with the result of pleasing our customers, increasing our response rate per marketing dollar, lowering our cost per order, building our business, and increasing our profits."

Given the existence of a database which satisfies these criteria it becomes possible for management to interact with their marketing information in a much more dynamic way than is possible with traditional project based research. Conventionally, much market research has been of this kind. As Curry (1993) points out:

> "Research projects are either exploratory, conclusive, or performance monitoring . . . ."

Exploratory research is usually undertaken to help clarify a perceived problem, be it a competitive threat or a marketing opportunity, and is intended to help management identify possible courses of action. Conclusive research seeks to evaluate these courses of action and performance-monitoring seeks to establish the success of the chosen course of action once implemented.

Curry points out that the new technology can easily result in a 'data deluge' so that there is a pressing need to manage the database and have a clear view of what is required from it. In support of this view, he cites the president of AC Nielsen's USA market research operation, John Costello, who said:

> "We need more insight, not more data. Technology is not an end in itself. Databases are critical, but know what you're working for first. What happened to knowledge?"

Given one is mindful of this advice, it is clear that IT creates the opportunity to create a marketing research system substantially more powerful than was possible when it depended upon a series of discrete projects linked by basic sampling data of the kind obtained from retail audits and the like. In the past, much data depended on respondent co-operation and was subject to bias. Through the use of electronic data capture accurate data on sales, promotions and distribution can be secured in real time without the conscious involvement of the consumer. More important, such systems may be integrated and analysed directly by corporate management without the need for intermediaries to assist in data collection, analysis and interpretation.

However, in his enthusiasm for database marketing Curry is, perhaps, too dismissive of the value of project-based research. Certainly, the evidence cited earlier would seem to suggest that firms which have used this kind of marketing research have performed better than firms which have not made use of it. Further, as with most management techniques, in the final analysis the benefits to be derived from any kind of research will depend very much on management's interpretation of it and the use to which they put that interpretation.

Without doubt, database marketing is a very powerful and important tool. Its potential, use and benefits will be discussed in great detail in the following chapters and an understanding of them will be critical to competitive success in the future. In and of itself it is not a substitute for the more conventional project-based research which is always likely to be more effective in explaining the *why* rather than the *what* – but it is obviously an essential extension of it.

REFERENCES

Alexander, M. (1985) Creative Marketing and innovative consumer product decisions – some case studies. *Design Studies*, **6** (1) January.

Baker, M. J. (1992) *Marketing Strategy and Management 2nd edn*, Macmillan Education, Basingstoke.

Baker, M. J. (1991) *Research for Marketing*, Macmillan Education, Basingstoke.

Baker, M. J. and Abou-Zeid, E.D. (1982) *Successful Exporting*, Westburn Publishers, Helesnburgh.

Baker, M. J. and Hart, S.J. (1989) *Marketing and Competitive Success*, Philip Allan, Hemel Hempstead.

British Institute of Management (BIM). (1985) *Managing the Export Function: Policies and Practices in the Small and Medium Company*, Survey Report, 26.

Connell, D. (1979) *The UK's Performance in Export Markets: Some Evidence from International Trade Data*, Discussion Paper, NEDO.

Davies, J. M. (1992) *The Essential Guide to Database Marketing*, McGraw-Hill International (UK) Ltd, Maidenhead.

Evans, C. (1979) *The Mighty Micro*, Victor Gollancz Ltd.

Gunter, B. and Furnham, A. (1992) *Consumer Profiles*, Routledge, London.

Hooley, G.J. and Lynch, J. (1985) Marketing lessons from UK's high flying companies. *Journal of Marketing Management*, **1** (1) Summer.

ITI Research Ltd. (1989) *The Barclays Bank Report on Export Developments in France, Germany and the United Kingdom*, Barclays Bank International.

Kotler, P. (1980) *Marketing Management, 4th edn*, Prentice-Hall Inc, Englewood Cliffs.

Rollason, B. (1971) What the successful exporter knows. *Exporting*, November.

Sun Tzu (1981) *The Art of War*, Hodder and Stoughton.

Takeuchi, H. and Quelch, J.A. (1983) Quality is more than making a good product. *Harvard Business Review*, **61** (4) July/August.

Walsh, V. and Roy, R. (1983) *Plastic Products: Good Design Innovation and Business Success*, The Open University Design Innovation Group, DIG-01, August.

3 The management and valuation of marketing information

Bill Blyth
Taylor Nelson AGB plc

1. SUMMARY

The paper takes, as its starting point, the belief that the management and valuation of information in the broadest sense is ignored in both management texts and practice. The need to cost existing information systems is discussed so as to provide the base line for comparison. Suggestions are put forward as to the management and planning of the information function. The concept of an annual information audit is outlined, together with a potential case study based approach for empirically valuing information.

Finally, some of the implications for market research as part of the broader information industry, are discussed.

2. INTRODUCTION

The thoughts in this paper arose over a substantial period of time spent reviewing and planning for the future demand for marketing research derived information services. Clearly, in the future, both manufacturing and services will have to integrate fully internal and external information to be able to react quickly to the complex and changing demands of the market-place. The scale and need for that integration will be increased by the rationalisation of manufacturing, distribution and marketing on a European basis. It will also be increased if Europe follows the US trend towards database marketing.

It follows, therefore, that in part the size and shape of the UK and European market research industry will be driven by the development of users' information systems and the style of management and information investment appraisal they adopt.

At this point there was some intellectual difficulty, because thinking about all the users of AGB data that I was acquainted with; there seemed no pattern or model that I could discern in the way that marketing information – in the fullest sense of the word – was handled from company to company.

Having put the issue, as it were, to one side, it seemed to crystallise for me when I read Peter Drucker's article 'The Coming of the New Organisation'. I would commend this article if only for the perspective it gives on running skill based business such as market research or advertising agencies.

The thrust of the article as I interpreted it is that to survive, large organisations in the future will use fewer, more skilled specialist managers:

> "..... the typical business will be knowledge-based, an organisation composed largely of specialists who direct and discipline their own performance through organised feedback from colleagues, customers and headquarters. For this reason it will be what I call an information-based organisation."

Drucker goes on to attribute this change to a variety of causes: IT, demographic shift, management need. He goes on to define information as:

> "..... data endorsed with relevance and purpose."

He moves on to discuss historical examples of such an approach – the Indian Civil Service – and then to discuss the organisational and management impact. However, whilst struck by the implicit resonance with my own thinking, there seemed an almighty gap. That gap was that information pertinent to such a management style would naturally emerge in some Darwinian fashion, given that all managers are rational men!

It struck me then that, here, as far as market researchers were concerned, was the nub of the matter. Market research is part of the information business all the way from providing unordered data to added value consultancy. But the value and management of information as a totality is overlooked in both marketing and financial management texts.

To produce information as an ordered subset of the available data chaos costs money, sucks in resource and requires top down management firstly to yield its value and secondly be acted upon. Until the value of an information based approach can be demonstrated and acted upon, it will be a Cinderella function subject to short term vagaries of budgeting, personnel changes and fashion.

The level at which market research operates within large corporations is often low, with some exceptions, and the reason for this is, I believe, the lack of a focus on information as a totality, rather than the specific benefits of market research. The implications for industry in the longer term are vast. It is my view that to reap fully the values of the skills they have built up, market researchers will need to become increasingly information managers. By that I do not mean getting wrapped up in information technology.

The problem with many information systems is that they have been designed by IT specialists, for the convenience of the IT specialist, and are run and submerged in layers of pseudo complexity by IT specialists. Rather, what I mean by information managers is taking the discipline acquired by the structuring and ordering of research data and applying it to the wider business context of total management information: designing the structure, interfaces and maintenance of corporate information systems which are relevant to all functions and to all levels of the organisation.

3. INFORMATION MANAGEMENT – AN APPROACH

Another strand in the thinking underlying this chapter has been the repeated observation that so much of the potential value of market research is lost or misdirected because of the lack of organisation and structure in users' internal information systems. Even now it is common for companies not to be able to access sales volume rather than production volume, customers rather than invoicing points, users rather than account holders, customer by customer, levels of repeat business. However, until management understands its own business, the utility of external information is lost. How should that be achieved?

4. COSTING

The first stage is one, I believe, of costing and functional organisation. For most companies, market research is purchased externally and the expenditure on it and the cost of any internal department that manages it can be put into a nice simple slot on a budget. That is not true with internal information. It is my belief that the amount of money spent on internal information will be several times larger than that spent on market research, irrespective of the value of that internal information system, but it's an unidentified cost embedded in the woodwork of functions. That cost needs shaking loose and the value for money observed.

Within any one commercial enterprise there are three primary data sources which one can crudely label:

- finance
- production
- sales.

In part these are to meet external legal requirements in part to manage the business as a totality, and in part to manage the function. Almost invariably, each function has, over time, generated its own information for its own convenience. Managers change its base to suit their own style or to prove a point or obfuscate one. Definitions vary from division to division, or country to country. Data compilation is run on different computers or software systems which don't talk to each other or even if they do, don't have the hooks which enable the data files to intermingle. The cost of the extant systems can be arrived at by detailed analysis once there's a management will. At the same time, a detailed study will identify the congruities or otherwise of the separate systems. Thus the start point is the real cost of current systems in all areas.

5. DESIGN REQUIREMENTS AND CONSTRAINTS

After the cost comes the management philosophy. All information is historic. We need to understand the past to try to improve the chance of getting to where we want to be in the future. However, today, inference about the future for large organisations is generally not based on the insight or clairvoyance of one individual. Rather, it is by systematic analysis of common information across all functions. To be effective requires investment and consistency over time, regardless of people and systems. It is too important to be played around with.

As has been argued previously (Blyth, 1981), information is an historic investment: Guard it! Preserve it! Profit from it! Measure its return over time!

6. AN INTEGRATED INFORMATION SYSTEM

An integrated information system must:

- be integrated in the fullest sense of the word
- be consistent
- be relevant
- possess unassailable integrity.

Such features are self-descriptive. The system needs:

- design
- technology
- management
- reporting lines.

The design should reflect all the time periods of the corporate plan. Every organisation will have its own specific requirements. The key elements, however, must be commonality of definitions, periods, units, at all levels within all functions. In this manner, the use of relational database techniques will enable any transformation of the raw data input as long as the original data model and attributes has been properly planned.

The technology should be as simple as possible and not lead the design. Rather, the design and user requirements should be completed and the technology acquired subsequently.

For this reason, I believe it crucial that the information function manager should not be an IT specialist, but rather a senior manager on secondment from any of the key functions. I further believe that to preserve the consistency (lack of interference), integrity (lack of manipulation), relevance (lack of conflicting requirements), integration (lack of bloody-minded functionalists), the information function should, if possible, report at least as far as policy is concerned to either the chief executive or a senior representational group. The management of the function, with the insight it gives into the total workings of the company, should be regarded as an import career step prior to top management appointment.

7. PLANNING AND VALUING

Having focussed on the design of the information system, the issues to be addressed are the planning of information acquisition and its valuation.

To attain systematic planning of such a complex and often ephemeral matter as information requires discipline and management commitment. Information will be the key to successful management in the coming years, as Drucker says.

To meet this end I believe there is the need for an annual multi-functional information audit alongside the draft annual plan and updates of longer term plans. The basic questions to be addressed:-

- What do we need to know to meet these plans?
- What do we need to know to monitor progress?
- What do we know?
- What do we plan to know?
- What are the gaps?
- How do we fill them?
- How much will it cost?
- Is it worth it?
- Recommendation?

By formally putting an information plan alongside annual and five year plans – by making it an independent function; by putting its reporting lines at the top level of management – it is more likely that the provision of relevant information, including market research, will be better served, and that the true value of that information perceived.

All of this may seem self-evident common sense, but it is not how things work in real life. To take some examples in one market: many hundreds of millions of pounds are being spent developing and marketing new financial services. For the domestic markets does anyone accurately know:

1. The numbers of buyers of insurance policies by type, by value?

2. % share of financial services business by point of sale?
3. Volume shares of the savings market by interest rate band and demographics?

I have taken the financial markets because the investments are so great and the gaps so large but other examples are available, e.g. there is no objective quantified system for valuing brands for accountancy purposes.

Against the overall corporate plan all information needs can be planned and some assessment made of the value at least in the sense of 'what is the risk if I don't have this information?' It should be stressed that at this level one is talking about a mix of data, information and application; for example, not just wanting sales data but also wanting a retail site performance model for target setting.

However, as stated earlier, information is historic and we use it to learn from the past. That is just as relevant to the way we have used information as in the way we have managed any other aspect of our business. It is also a task that is rarely done. In an information oriented business the way it is used will only be improved by feedback, by evaluation and culture change. It is also only in this way that its value can be truly assessed.

To this end, as part of the activity prior to an annual information audit, a complementary exercise should be the information value contribution case study. What is envisaged by this is the systematic evaluation of actual outcomes against previous plans – say 1 year, 3 year and 5 year. This should be done in an independent objective fashion, and not as a witch-hunt. The effects of exogenous shocks have to be allowed for. However, beyond that I believe it should be possible for a small project team to examine what was known, how it was used to plan, and where, with insight, the variances from predictions occurred, and why.

The conscientious management should not be content to rest on its laurels. The question to be asked is should we/could we have done better? By this we are not looking purely with the benefit of hindsight with which one always could have known better. Rather, how much of what we should have known could we have known at that point in time. Why didn't we bother to acquire that information? What are the lessons of the past for today?

From case study approaches it should be possible to put a cost on wrong decisions and missed opportunities caused by a lack of information or inadequate information, and contrast these costs with the cost of attaining that information. At the same time, redundancies in information could also be identified, which can contribute to cost savings in the system as a more focussed information set arises that is consistent with the decision making style of the organisation.

8. THE IMPLICATIONS FOR MARKET RESEARCH

The implications of such a model for market research are myriad. They relate to the services provided, their pricing, skill support, staff training, marketing, industry structure and, last but not least, attitude.

9. ATTITUDE

Whilst it is now a truism to say that market research is part of the information industry, the survival of market research will require us to go a lot further than this. Information is not an end – it is a means to an end. To optimise the achievement of the aim, we must see ourselves as being part of that aim. That requires a far greater understanding, on behalf of research suppliers, of a client's business, Market research as part of that totality of information cannot restrict itself to marketing as a function, but must cover all inputs to marketing; product/service quality, customer satisfaction, employee attitude, as well as advertising development and evaluation, and sales monitoring. In addition we will require broader business skills and experience than hitherto exhibited by most market research suppliers. The absence of such skills as reflected by the historic management of market research agencies themselves has been sufficiently commented upon elsewhere for me not to need to address them in detail here.

However, to achieve such an attitude and skill change will require investment in human resource and the technology to optimise the value of these skills which are going to cost so much.

In this area the commitment to training and support systems shown by leading management consultants is an example to the industry. It can only be achieved, however, by being able to charge for human resources at realistic standalone rate cards, not just as an absorption on top of the sale of relatively cheap semi-skilled non-unionised part time labour – fieldwork!

Nevertheless, within the area of the application of information to marketing, the skills of market researchers are generally much greater than those of accountancy or IT driven consultants. The presentation of those skills is poor, however.

10. MARKETING

To achieve the synthesis required between those skills and supporting clients' business, not only will market research agencies need closer understanding of the way clients' businesses work, but they will need a closer involvement in it. To ensure consistency of approach, relevance and effectiveness, I foresee a split between major full service agencies and technique specialists. Over the next five years I believe we will see a move towards more and more research being handled on an account basis, similar to the advertising agency, with guarantees about the avoidance of business conflict on the one hand, and minimum incomes on the other. This will favour a small number of larger units who can afford to spread the load of the bigger skill base and develop non-competitive client bases. The need for checks and balances on the evaluation of the efficiency of specialist inputs, in my mind, will inhibit the level of cross-referral from horizontally integrated marketing services business. House buyers don't want estate agents doing surveys on properties they are selling! This trend will be accelerated by the growth of integrated international planning and the need to avoid employing armies of multilingual data reconcilers.

At the top of the business, change has already occurred and is continuing to occur as reflected in the changes in ownership of major agencies – A C Nielsen, IMS, AGB, NMRA, MRBI, over recent years. Here the barriers to entry and the investment of IT systems are getting greater and greater. The growth of EPOS data and the capture of consumer-based data via smart cards, passive systems or other electronic means is leading to an explosion of data, but not as yet the corresponding investment in basic empirical analysis. Repeat buying behaviour theory is over 20 years old, but is still the only fundamental advance in consumer analysis. The data explosion will lead, I believe, to the substantial use of expert systems designed to filter the raw data bases automatically. Again, such a trend is already beginning, particularly in the US.

Earlier papers (Bowles and Blyth, 1985; Blyth, 1987) have touched on some of the problems and opportunities this particular aspect of data explosion will bring.

Overall, within 15 years the industry will have changed beyond recognition, as will the skill profile of those employed within it.

11. CONCLUSIONS

The concepts outlined here will take time and energy to develop practically. That is perhaps a task to report back on in two or three years. However, irrespective of that empirical work, I believe that the concepts outlined above provide a different perspective when considering and planning for the future of our industry.

2
Which IT Solution?

4 A practical guide to developing integrated marketing information systems

Miles Faulkner
Manager, Marketing Information Consultancy , OASiS

1. INTRODUCTION

The purpose of this chapter is to discuss the problems of communication between marketers and information technologists. Whilst the 'hybrid' concept is currently very popular, I would suggest that it is really the lack of a common vocabulary or frame of reference which is the underlying cause of so many systems development and support problems.

This chapter looks at this issue and how to overcome it, as well as giving some practical tips about how to develop successful Marketing Information Systems.

2. SO MANY OPTIONS!

This book includes discussion of some of the latest techniques in data analysis and supporting technologies. Marketers today are faced with a huge number of such techniques and competing software products. Where should you start? How do you ensure that you are getting the best out of your current systems, before looking at new applications? With so many data sources, how do you ensure consistency and rigor for purposes of comparison and accuracy? This bewildering array again demonstrates the need for a common level of communications between marketing and IT personnel.

3. GETTING BACK TO BASICS

There is a common misconception about the difference between an 'Information Technology solution' and the role of software and hardware. Computer software and hardware are in fact potential solution mechanisms, and are not solutions in themselves. Without, for instance, adequate data and correctly specified business processes, the technology is meaningless.

Many organisations skip crucial stages in problem definition because of the urge to select a package which, on the surface, appears to have many attractive features. The implementation of the package can then often be forced upon an IT department by users unwilling to invest in the necessary requirement definition phase due to urgent needs or a lack of understanding of the consequences. The response from the IT Department can then be a system specification which is hastily constructed, and based on little, if any, contact with users. This fatally flawed partnership is like a cancer for many systems developments.

4. THE COMMUNICATIONS GAP

OASiS has conducted a significant amount of research into this field and discovered very few practical success stories, with marketing systems being one of the areas which suffer most. The results of this research have invariably found poor communications between business management, and the IT function as a principal cause of systems development nightmares. There is an urgent need for a common framework which both business and systems managers can 'buy into', to provide a platform of understanding. This is not just the classic systems development lifecycle so familiar to information technologists, but instead a commonsense set of steps, fully understood by both parties, and with mutually agreed performance measures.

5. BUYING A HOUSE

Because there are so many technical terms in computing, many business managers either 'tune-out' in meetings with systems staff, or struggle through them and inevitably misunderstand, despite their efforts. Many business managers, conversely, undervalue the potential of systems analysts and do not give them the time or the resources necessary to design effective systems. The solution is not simply to find a team of elusive 'hybrids', but to make an effort to speak the same language.

If business users and systems developers are not speaking the same language, users will not be able to communicate their needs effectively. This lack of communications is like buying a house without seeing the inside – and then discovering that you need a few extra rooms and that all your furniture needs to shrink six inches. The worst crime of all is that some organisations actually invite the estate agent in to tell them exactly which house they want. This is done because they believe that the agent knows more about their needs than they do! Of course, large computer systems are more complex than houses, but you would be surprised by the similarities.

Houses are never built without a blueprint, designed by an architect. This blueprint principally reflects the structural needs of the buyer – such as the number of rooms, a big kitchen or a small kitchen. The size and number of rooms is reflected in the actual design of the house, which in turn reflects on the materials in which it is to be built. Naturally, there are cost considerations, but these are simply compromises after fitness for purpose has been considered. Note that the sequence is logically dependent. One often looks at second-hand houses and ready made new houses to see examples of how needs can be satisfied – but even then you don't just buy the first one you see, because there might be something more appropriate elsewhere.

Continuing with the house analogy, computer technology (hardware and software) is only the material holding the house together – the thinking behind the design of the house is far more important. If you were given a brick, a wall or even a room, would that tell you the type of house you could really have?

The process of designing and building systems should be simple (even if the contents are complex). Most of all, business managers should clearly understand the series of steps needed to generate their half of the equation, the user requirement. Both parties must agree a 'best practice' set of steps and the level of detail and investment, in time and resources, required at each stage, which is effectively the basis of a contract between the service provider and the user. An *ad hoc* approach, even within a well documented project plan, is liable to break down as it is unlikely to be thorough and proven.

6. A PRACTICAL FRAMEWORK

So far, I have described the type of problems which are encountered when developing Marketing Information Systems, and the need for a common understanding between marketing and IT people. OASiS has developed a framework for developing such systems which will provide a platform for this understanding. Figure 4.1 represents an overview of this approach.

The framework begins with a thorough definition of the requirement, which is then translated into applications prototypes and finished systems. Particular features of the approach include the initial definition of 'best practice' marketing processes, as well as the use of *key decision nodes*. These decision nodes are set stages of the development, at which pre-defined outputs should be provided and goals achieved. All parties should then agree the best way forward.

Another important feature of the OASiS approach is its modularity. When developing a marketing system, the users' requirements are normally translated into a series of 'applications' – different areas of functionality which together form an integrated system. There may a large number of potential applications, across a wide range of technologies. In this situation, a modular approach is very successful because it allows individual applications to be developed very quickly, using 'prototyping' to ensure that the resulting system meets user needs most effectively. Prototyping involves creating 'mock-up' models of the applications which allow

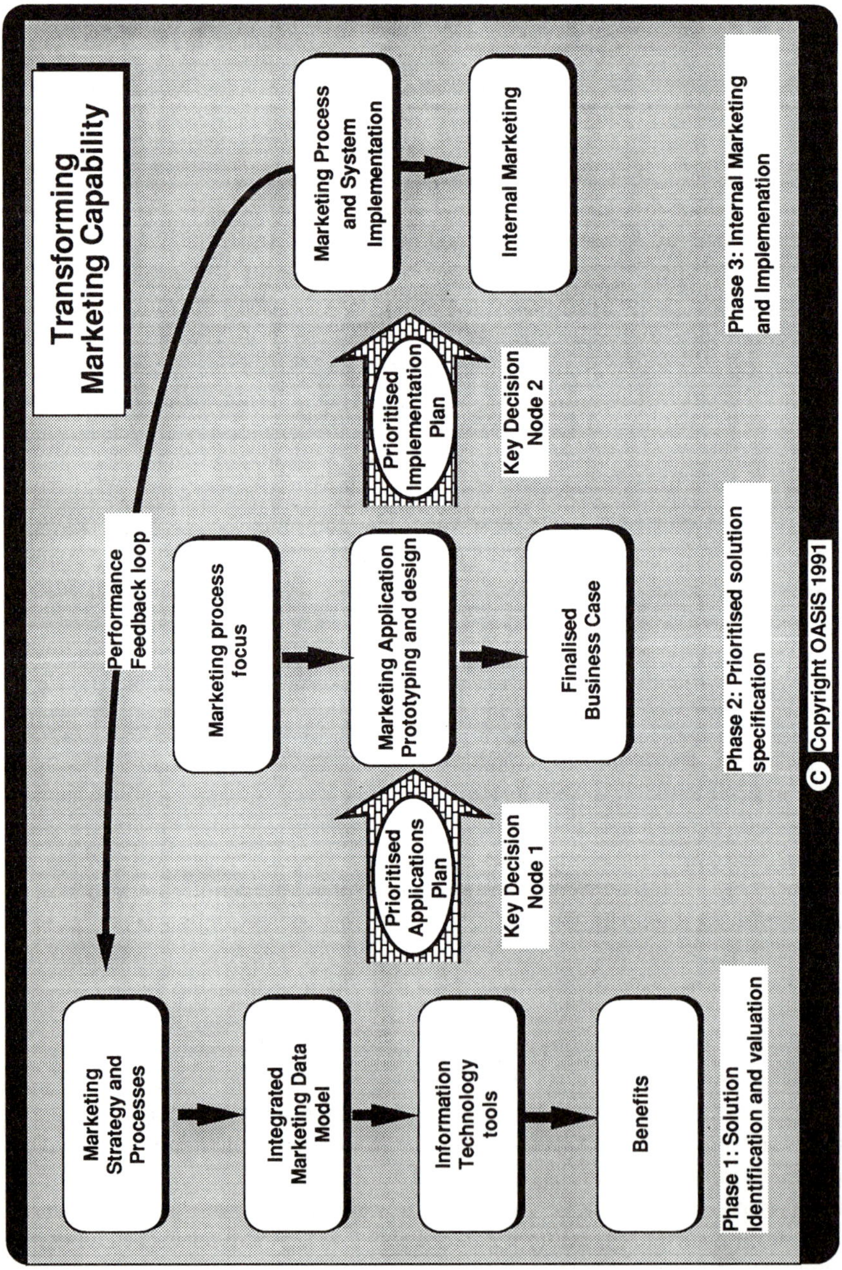

Figure 4.1 Transforming marketing capability.

users to experiment with the system, instead of having to deal with the cost and difficulties of changing a finished system. By developing applications individually, business successes can be achieved very rapidly. This approach also allows development lessons to be feed back into further modules.

The approach distinguishes three critical phases. First, the top level, open-minded view which creates the 'big-picture'. This stage is then processed through the first key decision node, where an applications plan is developed. Second, more detailed work is conducted on the applications chosen for implementation. Finally, the applications are implemented and internally marketed to users. Within each stage of the process there are a number of specific methodologies for conducting the work, and user managers need to ensure that they are clear on the necessary inputs and outputs. Note that Invitations to Tender should typically only be given out after Phase 2, when all the required functionality and performance benchmarks have been defined.

At the end of the day, there are many system development frameworks. We believe that simplicity and focussing on business needs will always win through. Even more importantly, the approach you choose should have an 'action' orientation. Experiment with prototyping as early as possible – this will encourage analysts to be daring and to learn through inexpensive mistakes. Above all, when both IT service providers and users have a common set of expectations and quality standards, the chances of success increase significantly. An understandable and agreed development framework will move most organisations a long way down that track.

7. SOME PRACTICAL TIPS

This chapter has been concerned with outlining a simple but useful framework which enables all parties to have effective input to information systems. OASiS has wide experience in developing such information systems for major companies worldwide, and the following are some practical tips which have been found to be useful in the past.

- Look at package software to collect ideas about typical applications. Develop a full specifications of needs with a significant level of detail, before any Invitation to Tender (ITT). There is nothing wrong with packages. They are, in fact, often the most cost effective solution – however, they should be evaluated against a rigorous specification.
- Always develop requirement definitions independently from software houses or computer manufacturers selling packages. Use internal staff or third party consultants who are not in the software sales business.
- Insist of a fully documented plan for every phase of the project and make the

timescales demanding – typically between three and four months to determine an applications prioritisation plan.

- Focus early on the full set of benefits, both quantifiable and strategic, to justify the investment of the whole programme and charge only the recoverable, quantifiable benefits against business units for budgeting and control purposes. Spend as much time considering the hurdle rate criteria or IRR percentage as determining the benefits themselves. Do normal corporate investment standards apply to information systems projects?
- Develop paper based analysis as fast as possible and use example software to create prototypes straight away. Our experience indicates the 'frailty' of much paper-based analysis before software is used to test its practical viability. Ensure that there are plenty of high quality, business-oriented workshops, with constant feedback to users.
- Check that the latest technologies are reasonably represented in your application set; for example, relational databases, decision and executive information support systems and, where appropriate, text databases. Most marketing systems will require a wide range of applications, and you must be sure that you have taken advantage of all the available technology options to find the most effective solution.

5 Marketing systems that are fit for purpose

Robert Shaw
Managing Director, Shaw Consulting Ltd

1. INTRODUCTION

"In five years time there will to be two types of company. Those who use the computer as a marketing tool and those who face bankruptcy."
Warren MacFarlan, Dean of Studies, Harvard School of Business (1988)

Five years ago, Computer Aided Sales and Marketing (CASM) crawled out of the technological swamp and roared very loudly. People were ready. The 1980s had been a difficult decade. For five years, the empty words 'Information for competitive advantage' had echoed round the halls of management. Then CASM arrived. In 1988, at last, there was a tangible technological investment which offered hope of short-term returns and longer-term strategic advantages.

Now the bubble has burst. CASM was never a panacea. Warren MacFarlan and many other CASM enthusiasts must surely regret their naive optimism.

Investment in CASM is heavy. It accounts for over 15% of IT expenditure today – over £1.5 billion in the UK. Yet there is general agreement that CASM investment is not good enough. Over 50% of sales and marketing managers believe that too little is invested. Most are dissatisfied with their systems. (These figures, and those which appear later in this paper, come from the Shaw Consulting survey of CASM users.)

2. PROBLEMS WITH INVESTING IN NEW TECHNOLOGY

Sales and marketing people are not the first to have problems with IT investment. Accountants, production and distribution managers, designers, warehousemen, secretaries – many people adopting IT for the first time have suffered problems. Indeed, many people replacing systems for the second, third or fourth times are still having problems.

Placed in context, it is hardly surprising that CASM creates almost as many problems as it solves. Relative to other technologies, it is very new (Table 5.1).

Certain problems are common to all new systems, including CASM:

- Wrong system for wrong purpose

Table 5.1 Evolution of computers and their applications

	# computers	Hardware	Software	Applications
1950	10	Valve machines	Machine code	Accounting
1960	1000	Mainframes/batch	Assembler	Accounting
1970	10,000	Minis/on-line	Flat files/COBOL	Operational
1980	1,000,000	Personal computers	RDBMS/4 GL	Management
1990	100,000,000	Portables/networks	Spreadsheets/WP	CASM

- Users and IT disagree
- Technology fails to deliver.

3. WIDE CHOICE OF SYSTEMS

Choosing something new is always difficult, and CASM is no exception. Ignorance or lack of knowledge is a widespread problem in such a new area. DP staff generally do not have a good understanding of sales or marketing. Sales and marketing staff have a limited knowledge of IT.

The problem is compounded by the wide choice of applications. Sales and marketing users typically choose several applications, as Figures 5.1 and 5.2, from the survey, clearly indicate.

Knowledge of the applications that are available will not, of itself, guarantee

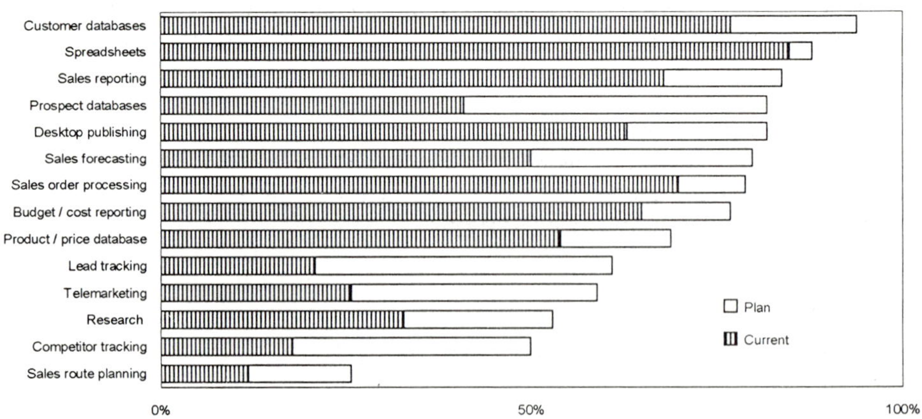

Figure 5.1 Percentage of users with specific sales applications

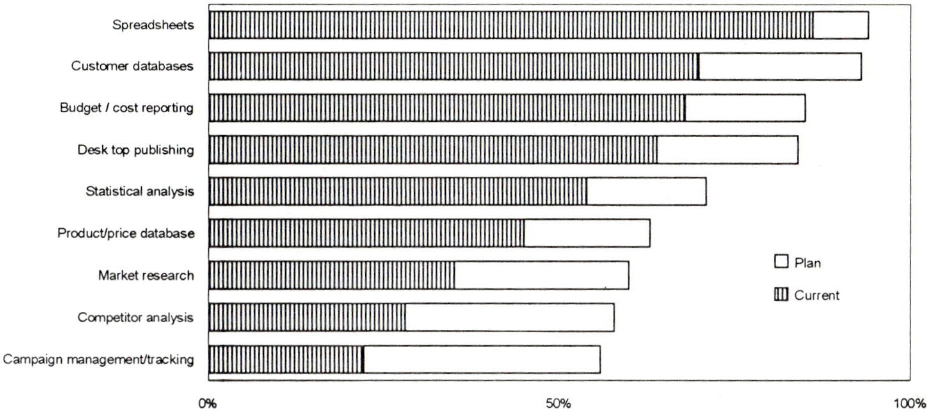

Figure 5.2 Percentage of users with specific marketing applications

success. In the USA, where knowledge of CASM is far more widespread, studies by 'The Conference Board' show a mixed pattern with some CASM successes but many failures.

4. MAKING THE RIGHT CHOICE

The potential opportunities for sales and marketing are numerous; some are complex; many are costly. Their successful exploitation needs a selective and pragmatic approach.

Those actually responsible for sales and marketing need to take the lead in choosing the right systems. Often they are assisted by external specialist consultants who can:

- Provide clear guidance on the opportunities
- Bring experience of the feasibility and benefits of alternative options
- Provide a framework to equip sales and marketing to select and implement the most suitable information strategy

4.1 Opportunities

Sales and marketing need a clear understanding of the opportunities that are available. This will require:

- Appreciation of the dependence of sales/marketing on information

- Experience of the opportunities which are being exploited by your competitors and by sales/marketing in other industries
- Knowledge of the package solutions currently available.

4.2 Feasibility and benefits

The opportunities are numerous and not all are possible or justifiable. Opportunities must be reviewed in the terms of feasibility and benefit. This involves:

- Knowledge of which technologies are feasible today (or soon will be)
- Experience of what they cost
- Understanding of how much benefit they will really yield.

4.3 Vision and ownership

Sales and marketing management need a framework to visualise what is feasible and justifiable, and to equip them to control the planning and implementation of what they require. This will be achieved through a process which involves:

- Presentation of only the key business information issues (formal training of technology is kept to a minimum).
- A logical series of decision-making steps in which non-technical management can plan the direction and speed with which information systems are developed to support their business.

5. BUSINESS INFORMATION STRATEGY PROCESS

The business information strategy process provides a comprehensive method for the management team to tackle the key issues which will influence the direction and momentum of information systems development. It is driven primarily by

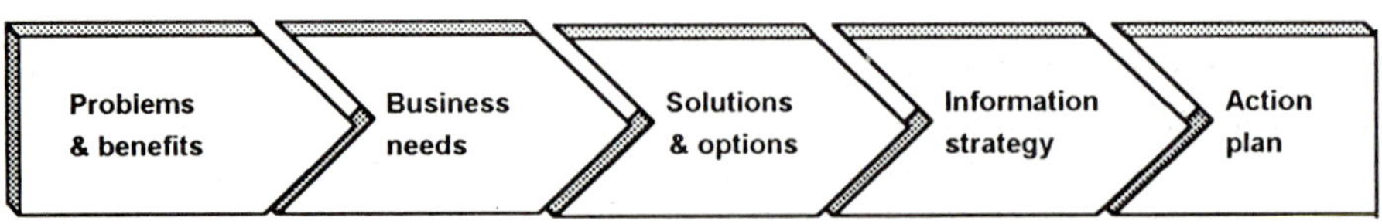

Figure 5.3 The process.

business needs rather than by technical developments. It identifies ways in which information systems can fulfil business needs and improve performance. Specifically, it involves:

- Aunanimously agreed list of business problems and the quantitative benefits of solving them.
- The activities that sales and marketing need to perform, which they cannot do now, that are dependent on information systems development.
- The information systems solution and options required to support the business needs.
- The benefits and costs of implementing all or some of the information systems.
- The action plan for moving forward.

The process is implemented within and by sales and marketing at its own pace. Managers attend five meetings, for which some preparation is required. At each meeting, reports will be reviewed and decisions will be taken to produce the desired outputs.

The duration of the process will be dependent upon the commitment given to it by the Task Force. If the Task Force is prepared to meet as information is gathered and reports are prepared, a Sales and Marketing Information Strategy could be completed within two months, with detailed action plans soon after.

5.1 Step 1: Information requirements

The first step produces a listing of the main profit opportunities that depend on information systems development.. The task force determines the business problems associated with each of the main marketing processes. Typically, there will be 8–12 problems in total. For each problem, the task force estimates the profit opportunity that will be realised through solving it. They also estimate the extent to which the profit opportunity depends on information systems development. This procedure ensures that the systems requirements are tied to business needs.

5.2 Step 2: Information gaps

The second step expands each business problem into more detailed business needs. The task force identifies the activities they need to perform, which they cannot do now, that will contribute to the delivery of the benefits. They produce a list of business needs that is necessary to delivering the benefits and complete. Typically, there may be 50 business needs.

5.3 Step 3: Solutions and options

The third step looks at the solutions and options available to meet the needs which were identified in step 2. The task force reviews the current IT environment:

- IT Strategy
- Existing systems
- Competitor initiatives in the use of IT
- Future developments in IT.

Possible causes of gaps and opportunities for filling them are considered. Technical opportunities may include:

- New IS developments
- Packages systems solutions
- Existing system enhancements
- Sharing of systems

Organisational opportunities may include:

- Improved training
- Changes to distribution lists, access security networks
- Redefinition of roles and responsibilities for creating or manipulating information.

All opportunities are reviewed in step 4.

5.4 Step 4: Business information strategy

The purpose of step 4 is to build an information strategy. Preparatory to step 4, technical and organisational reviews are developed for each opportunity. These provide further detail regarding each potential project, including business and technical specifications and cost-benefit cases. The reviews are used to gauge the suitability of a project for inclusion in the strategy.

Priority and management approval will depend upon the degree of support that the project provides for sales and marketing's key success factors and the cost-benefit analysis. The agreed technical and organisational projects are combined and constitute sales and marketing's information strategy.

5.5 Step 5: Action plans

In step 5, detailed plans are developed to implement the information strategy, and ensure that the agreed actions are taken. Work performed during this step is built into an action plan consisting of a series of defined projects, either technical or organisational. Preliminary timings for each project are also set. Corporate procedures to manage and monitor projects are adopted. Results of the monitoring are fed back into the next planning cycle.

6. MANAGING THE TECHNICAL RISKS

Having chosen the right system for the right purpose, the remaining problem is to select technology that works effectively today and in the longer-term. Two types of risk are associated with technology decisions:

- Specific problems to CASM
- General technology risks.

7. CASM PROBLEMS

There are over 300 suppliers of CASM in the UK. None is perfect. Many are very imperfect. It is always best to review several suppliers before selecting one. This review is best conducted through a formal Invitation to Tender. A carefully written ITT will yield responses which are well structured and which can be compared with out too much effort.

Several problems crop up with monotonous regularity in CASM packages, and should be avoided at all costs. They are associated with:

- Address clean-up and de-duplication
- Mass data updates
- Data integrity checkers
- High data-volume performance
- End user reporting and analysis
- Statistical analysis
- Distributed databases and interfaces.

7.1 Address clean-up and de-duplication

Duplicates occur in all sources of sales and marketing data. Duplicate names and duplicate addresses are the most problematic. Most CASM software packages do not provide any tools, or adequate tools, to solve the duplication problem.

Usually it will be necessary to purchase additional software to solve the problem. This will do two things:

- Addresses will be cleaned up and formatted to a UK standard
- Duplicates will be identified and where necessary eliminated.

7.2 Mass data updates

Periodically, it will be necessary to change the codes on various records. This happens for various reasons, such as when territory boundaries change, or when product codes are modified. Most packages lack the tools to deal with these problems. Additional software may be needed to solve this problem.

7.3 Data integrity checkers

Many CASM packages are poorly designed to deal with data integrity. Problems start to occur when customer records are deleted, and the corresponding contact or order details remain on the database. Invalid codes are permitted to be recorded on some CASM packages. Data integrity is an area that must be addressed in any ITT.

7.4 High data-volume performance

Databases run slower the bigger they become. Many packages grind to a halt when data volumes grow. Volume performance must be examined in the ITT. Do not accept blanket assurances from suppliers that 'it will be alright on the night'.

7.5 End user reporting and analysis

Many CASM packages do not provide any, or adequate, tools for producing reports. Sometimes it is possible to purchase additional software to produce reports.

7.6 Statistical analysis

Similar comments apply to statistical analysis. Be careful to differentiate between suppliers' claims that their software includes statistical analysis, as opposed to analysis being supported, but by other packages.

7.7 Distributed databases and interfaces

Data often has to be distributed between multiple locations and systems. Care must be taken to ensure that data transfer between systems is planned in a systematic way. It is too easy to ignore this issue and end up with a mess of data flows between systems (Figure 5.4).

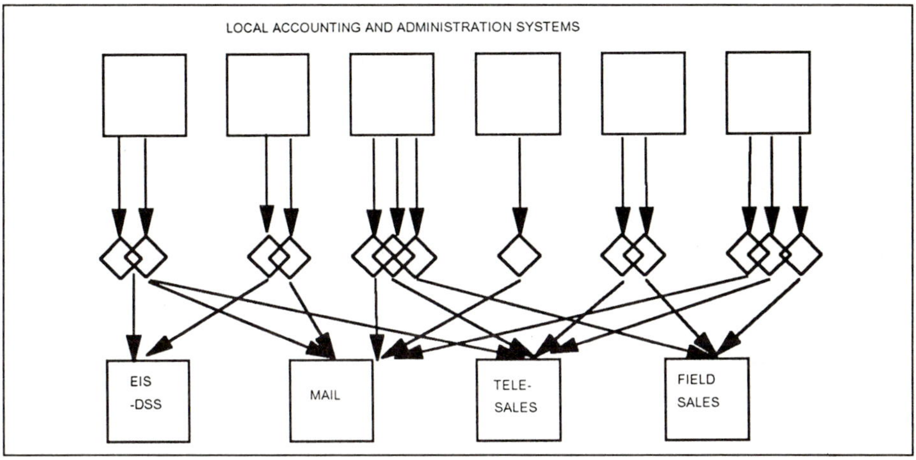

Figure 5.4 Incremental interfaces – 'spaghetti junction'.

It is easy to see how such an arrangement will be costly to develop and maintain. The solution, at present, is to develop a common database which draws data from all sources and is available to distribute to all applications requiring data (Figure 5.5).

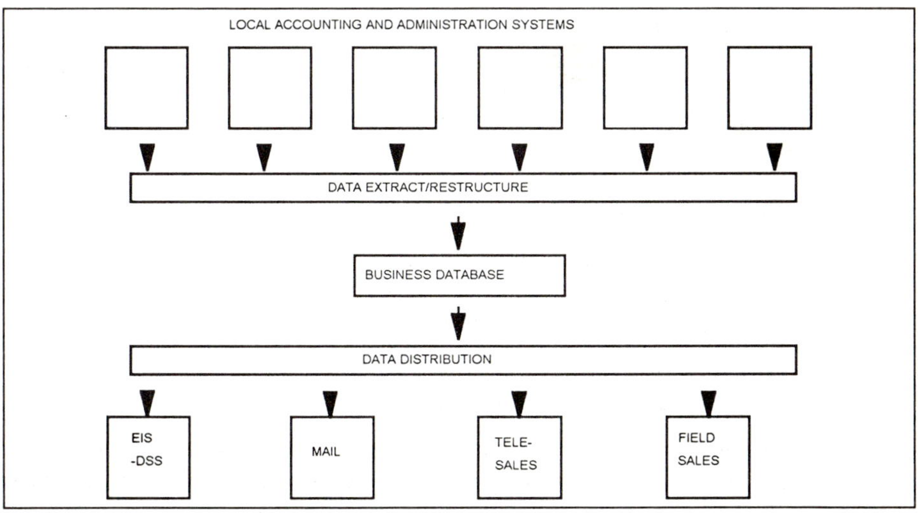

Figure 5.5 Streamlined interfaces – database solution.

There are two factors to consider in looking at the database solution:

- Functional requirements to maintain integrity of data updated at different locations
- Technical requirements of a Data Base Management System (DBMS).

The functional problem arises when two or more locations have the right to update the same record. For example, field sales may wish to update a customer's address, and at the same time telemarketing may wish to record an enquiry. Unless the software has suitable in-built intelligence, either the address update or the enquiry will be overwritten. At present there are only a very few CASM packages with the ability to resolve this problem.

The technical problem is addressed in the next section.

8. TECHNICAL FUTURES

Every aspect of IT today is in a state of major change – many technologies are in crisis. No decisions should be made without taking account of these factors. Although nobody will succeed in precisely forecasting the outcome of many of these technical changes, equally there are many technologies which, put simply, should be avoided at all costs. Critical areas are:

- Databases – Microsoft vs. Borland vs. the rest
- Beyond relational
- Lotus Notes and others
- Beyond the notebook
- Pen interface
- Advanced telephony
- Fax modem standards.

8.1 Databases – Microsoft vs. Borland vs. the rest

Relational databases (RDBMS) have been in fashion for several years, and there are several dozen suppliers on the market. It is becoming clear that the most important aspect of RDBMS is SQL. The SQL language has become the *de facto* standard for accessing databases. Many tools are now available, as package add-ons, which use SQL to access the package's database.

The golden rule is only to choose a package based on an RDBMS which uses a widely used version of SQL. Good choices are Oracle, Ingres and Sybase. However, the game is changing with the entry of Microsoft into the database market, and Borland's acquisition of dBASE when Ashton Tate collapsed. Microsoft and Borland are currently players at the PC end of the database market, but as

PCs become more powerful it is certain that Microsoft, Borland and a few others (perhaps Novell) will become important players.

8.2 Beyond relational

Even though SQL is likely to remain important over the next five years, possibly longer, other aspects of database technology will change. Most importantly, Object Oriented Data Base Management Systems (OODBMS) are seen to be the critical new development.

8.3 Lotus Notes and others

New families of database products are also evolving out of what was traditionally not a database area: document processing. Lotus Notes is the most important of these. It combines the ease of use of spreadsheets, and the openness of electronic mail, with the power of a database. This technology needs to be reviewed alongside the traditional RDBMS.

8.4 Beyond the notebook

Hardware is evolving fast. The portable market has been the fastest growing recently, and it has attracted massive R&D funding. Research coming out of Xerox Palo Alto Labs suggests that the traditional notebook machine is not an ideal solution. It is likely that a wide range of portable devices will evolve in the next couple of years.

8.5 Pen interface

The pen is being widely heralded as the input device of the future. Microsoft's development of Pen Windows is going to be significant in boosting the growth of this area.

8.6 Advanced telephony

Communications technology will also have a major impact on CASM. In particular, technologies such as Call Path will revolutionise Call Centres and Telemarketing Units.

8.7 Fax modem standards

Image and data transmission are also evolving fast. Just as the fax machine suddenly exploded on the business scene a decade ago, so too will the new datacomms technologies. Battles between rival standards are at present hindering this area. However, there are strong indications that an effective standard is emerging, and therefore the fax modem should be on the CASM developers' shopping lists.

6 Best of breed – choosing a business solution for sales and marketing

Andy Blair
IBM (UK) Ltd

1. FUNCTIONAL REQUIREMENTS OF SALES AND MARKETING PACKAGES

The following is a list of functional areas to be considered when reviewing software packages or system requirements. Not all will be required for every system implementation.

1.1 Marketing database

The style and flexibility of the database is critical to all DBM and SA applications. Simple flat-file databases may be acceptable for a few simple applications where all the data can be predefined for a transaction (such as outbound telemarketing), but hierarchical databases are normally considered a minimum for most functions. Relational databases are required where complex relationships are needed between the objects in your data model. Most marketing databases need to have complex designs if they are to reflect the complexity of your relationships with your customers.

1.1.2 Marketing database creation and tailoring

No package provider can possibly provide all of the specific marketing data you will need for your business. Therefore most packages allow you more or less flexibility to add data elements to the core data (name and address) that they define. The ease with which you can create and change the database design is an important factor. Warning: many packages will not allow changes to the database once it is defined.

1.1.3 Code table control

Data in the database can only be used analytically if it is in a predefined coded format rather than in free-format text. A central control of all allowable codes is highly desirable to ensure consistency of information. However, new marketing campaigns will inevitably lead to the need for new codes. These should be capable of being added to the validation tables of the system without requiring users to log off the system.

1.1.4 Mass data change tool
Occasionally you will need to change one value throughout your database to another (e.g. when London telephone numbers changed from 01 to 071/081). Tools are sometimes available to allow this.

1.1.5 Import of external list into base database
Tools should be available to reformat data arriving from other databases. Reformatting should allow you to convert from one coding system to another using user defined cross reference tables.

The more sophisticated packages provide utilities that will recognise similarities between addresses coming in and those already on the database to prevent duplicates being created.

1.1.6 Export of list for external fulfilment house
If you wish to export data to other computer systems (e.g. laser printing bureau) you will need to be able to format the data suitable for that system to read. Most fulfilment houses are very flexible in their ability to accept different data formats.

1.1.7 Database security
Your marketing database can be one of the most valuable assets that the company possesses. It is certainly of exceptional value to your competitors. Therefore, you may wish to impose strict security controls on who can view the database at all or who can view or update parts of the database. These functions are controlled by the facilities of the DBMS (Database Management System) used by the package. Many packages use one of the standard DBMSs, and you will quickly learn what is possible within each DBMS environment. (See also Data Security Access Control later in this document.)

As well as company imposed access control over the database, you may wish to allow end-users to control others' access to their data (this is particularly useful where teams of people need to access the same data.)

1.2 Data entry

1.2.1 Data entry screen design tool
Different user applications often require different items of data to be available on a single screen (e.g. marketing questionnaires with many multi-choice questions.) Some packages provide facilities to allow the user to design the data entry screens. Remember, however, that you will usually want to validate data entry against a set of rules, and the screen designer should allow you to do this.

1.2.2 Data entry deduplication search database
When adding new companies or people to a database you need to ensure that they

are not already there. A name/address search is required to stop duplicates. Be careful of searches that only look at the start of the name line for companies. Think about what you would do presented with 20 screens of companies starting with 'The'. However, usually, the more flexible the search, the slower it will be.

1.2.3 Data entry abbreviated input based on Royal Mail PAF file

Allows the keying in of the postcode only to generate the address from the Postcode Address File provided by the Royal Mail. Useful for high volume addition of addresses to save time or to increase accuracy of postcode and addresses on the database for mailsort discounts.

1.3 Target list management

Database marketing is all about creating targeted market segments call Lists. Most DBMSs allow you to create different lists for different purposes. There should be no limit to the number of lists you can create.

1.3.1 Multi list duplication

Having created your lists it is better if you can merge them together rather than having to re-extract a new list using different criteria. The merge tools should allow adding lists together and taking one list from another. All list merges must automatically suppress multiple occurrences of the same person (de-duplication).

1.3.2 Database statistical analysis and profiling utilities

The extractor tools defined above will normally give some facilities in this area. Purpose built statistical packages are available for marketing databases to analyse data using multi-variance techniques.

1.3.4 Marketing campaign management and coordination

Facilities to asses the planning of marketing campaigns and their individual elements. Needed where lots of direct marketing campaigns are running concurrently.

1.3.5 Campaign cost analysis

Project planning tool to allow costing of campaigns based on database of previous costs. Also allows comparisons of planned response rates and sales against actuality.

1.4 Telemarketing

A word often misused. Most telemarketing packages also provide sales support functions. Most general purpose marketing packages provide some telemarketing functions. All TM applications require very fast screen response times – a two second pause is perceived as a long time from the other end of a phone! Inbound TM requires different system support from outbound TM. Be careful in defining requirements in this area; just because a telephone is used it does not mean that full TM functions are required.

1.4.1 TM script design tool

Scripts are a means used by TM packages to prompt the operator to follow a predefined path through a telephone conversation. The more sophisticated packages use conditional logic to vary the path through the script based upon the data entered by the operator. Packages should allow insertion of data from the database into a script screen, branching to be dependent on multiple variables, hotkey facility to choose from a list of all screens for unstructured inbound conversations.

1.4.2 TM call management

Ability to provide a supervisor to allocate calls to different telemarketers. For inbound TM, ability to use an ADC (automatic call distribution system) to share TM workload. Most packages can use simple modems to provide automatic dialling of numbers stored on the database.

1.4.3 TM digital switch control

More sophisticated packages can interface with digital telephone exchanges to control call rerouting and analyse statistics from the exchange. Important to ensure that your internal exchange is compatible with the telemarketing package before assessing these functions.

1.4.4 TM call statistics, cost and workload analysis

If setting up a high volume telemarketing centre these features can be very important by enabling efficient management of the resources.

1.5 Mailshot management

The control of mailshots from your database requires that all communications that are sent are automatically logged by the system. You may need security features that allow the owners of customer relationships (e.g. salesmen) to veto the sending of letters to their territories. if not using mailsort a variety of sort orders for mailshots and audit reports should be provided. Picking lists should be supported for enclosure of brochures and inserts. If you are intending to run your own automatic mail stuffing machines, understand the printing requirement for the control of these machines. Ensure label output formats are suitable for your needs.

1.5.1 Text/data merge

Most packages will have their own embedded word processor. These are very low in function, often not even including spellcheck. Look for compatibility with mainstream word processing packages that your organisation already uses. Ensure that data from the database can be embedded in the letter text over and above the name and address data.

1.5.2 Mailsort

Mailsort and Presstream allow considerable discounts to be received when mailing letters via the UK post office. The process relies on the vast majority of your addresses being correctly postcoded. Special mailsort codes are then applied to your database based on postcode, and these are used to sort the mailed output into batches. These batches have to be bagged by you with the correct labels and audit reports attached to each bag. Packages often offer mailsort coding, but this will not satisfy your bagging and labelling requirements. Normally it is cheaper to have your mailings mailsorted by the printing company, unless you are planning to set up a large print shop in house.

1.6 Advertisement management

Basically a project control feature to allow you to keep control of complex TV and press advert slots and to review results by medium.

1.7 Marketing event management

Marketing events include seminars, exhibitions, training courses, etc. Very few packages support the management of these events. When evaluating software bear in mind the possible need to charge for the event.

1.7.1 Enrolment and attendance processing

For limited capacity events you will need to enroll attendees and issue confirmation letters. As people arrive they need to be logged as attending on the database. Many exhibitions at which you may have a stand offer barcoded badging facilities for recording attendance – do you wish to be able to automatically record the results of the interests captured in this manner? Do you wish to record the evaluations of attendees? If your events are held in sites away from your marketing systems, can you download the attendance process to a portable PC?

1.7.2 Event facilities management

Project management tool to help you ensure that all the facilities (catering, presentation aids, guest speakers, etc.) are all there on the day of the event.

1.8 Regular marketing publication subscription management

Ability to register people on the database to regularly receive your company's newsletter.

1.9 Response management

The ability to record the responses to all marketing communications is vital to assessing the effectiveness of a campaign as well as acting as trigger for the next action in the campaign. The ability of software to handle complex questionnaires with many data entry fields and then post the data thus collected in the correct place in the database is highly variable. See also 'Data Entry'.

1.10 Sales automation

Sales automation refers to computer systems that are designed to support the salesforce in handling their one-to-one sales situation as well as allowing sales management to control the activity of their sales force.

1.10.1 Sales territory allocation

The system should be able to allocate customers on the database to individual salesreps or teams. The number of allowable criteria is an important limiting factor here. Geography (by postcode) is normally supported, but industry classification code, geography by map reference or distance by road, individual nomination, and others may be required.

1.10.2 Sales lead distribution

Leads collected from campaign responses or telemarketing need to be distributed accurately and swiftly to an appropriate salesrep to follow-up. If a closed-loop lead management process is required, then the system must ensure that no lead is forgotten or deleted and all leads must be monitored through to completion.

1.10.3 Deal monitoring/diary management

Once the lead has been given, a salesrep may need to follow it through all stages of the sales cycle using a notepad and diary system. Consideration should be given to possible interface needs, like corporate email or diary management systems.

1.10.4 Sales product support functions

The salesrep or telemarketer often needs product support on-screen. These can usually be provided by user tailored help screen functions.

1.10.5 Proposal/tender document creation

Pre-formatted proposals, tenders, or offer letters are often required with the system calculating costs or choosing paragraphs of text based on data provided on the nature of the deal to be struck.

1.10.6 Sales forecasting

Using the status of leads forecasts of sales success can be automatically generated. Care should be taken that the software package you are assessing handles this area in a way your sales management can support.

1.10.7 Portable computer data upload/download control

Most sales forces are often on the read visiting customers. They may need the facility of carrying some or all functions with them in a portable computer. Some packages support this requirement while some do not. Care should be taken when reviewing upload and download controls.

1.11 Reporting

Reports are the life blood of database marketing and of sales and marketing management. They allow the user to view the progress of his marketing efforts. All reports should be viewable on screen as well as being capable of being printed. There are two types of report; pre-formatted reports where the application defines what you can see, and *ad hoc* reports that allow the end-user to construct the report contents and format.

1.11.1 Pre-defined reports

Most packages have some reports available as pre-formatted reports. These can usually be selected from a reports menu. Some variability can often be introduced at the time of running the report, such as changing the sort order of the report or the selection criteria of the contents of the report.

1.11.2 Ad hoc reports

User-definable report writing systems are very important in containing the cost of writing user reports. Marketing system users are more demanding in this area than any other type of computer system user.

1.12 Documentation

Comes in two forms: printed technical and user manuals for system administrators and users; and on-line help text to help the end-user while using the system.

1.12.1 Manuals

Documentation should be easy to read and have excellent Contents and Index sections. Most printed documentation is only used for reference purposes, hence the importance of the Index. A good tutorial booklet (possibly supported by audio or video cassette) is a very important feature to get the user started quickly.

1.12.2 On-line help text

Few end-users will want to carry reference manuals around with them particularly if they are using a portable computer. On-line help is therefore the only practical way of learning the system. Help can be primitive (where the user is always confronted with the same help contents page regardless of which screen he accesses the Help from), or 'context sensitive', where the screen or even the individual data element control the Help text that the user sees.

2. TIPS ON REVIEWING FUNCTIONAL REQUIREMENTS

Using the function list as a starting point the following tips will enable you to define requirements more precisely.

2.1 Define your terms

Come to an agreement with your colleagues about precisely what you mean by various marketing terms. A lot of time will be wasted if a consistent mental image is not available for such terms as 'telemarketing'. Remember that these terms will be used in presentations to senior management when requesting funds and that their image must be the same as yours.

2.2 Weight functions

Score each functional area according to its importance in your plans. Get all of the key players to agree the weighting you are giving to each function. This is probably best done in a single short meeting where you together define your terms and weight functions.

2.3 Keep requirement group small

Depending upon the extent of the project, many departmental managers may wish to get involved. Keep the number of different specifiers as small as possible.

3. COMPUTER REQUIREMENTS OF SALES/MARKETING PACKAGES

Your organisation will undoubtedly impose certain constraints on the type of computer system you need to run your sales an marketing systems. The following is a list of systems areas to be considered when buying packages.

3.1 Computer hardware

Software packages are developed to run on specific types of computers. Sometimes this can be a major limitation in that the computer that the package runs on is not one that you wish to use. Increasingly, packages run on more than one platform, and most developers are actively 'porting' their software to different platforms. Beware of 'vapourware' – the promise that a package will be available on the platform of your choice 'in a few months time'. Your IS department will have very strong views on which computers you can use to fit in with their strategies.

3.1.1 Computer size

For PC-based systems you will be told by the software vendor what size of machine you will need. For minicomputers you will also be told about the size needed to support various numbers of users. Normally, for mainframe packages you will be sharing the computer with other existing applications, so your IS department will have to calculate your requirements. This latter problem may also occur with large shared mini computers.

3.2 Computer skills

Remember that the more complex the computer environment, the more need there will be for specialist staff to support them. Your IS department will help you here but insist that you use computers that they understand. If you decide to ignore them, or have no current computer support, be very careful about budgeting for the people and skills you will need to support the computers.

3.3 Computer operating system

The operating system is the program that runs on the computer to control the basic functions of the machine. Software packages have to work with the operating system and, like the hardware, will be limited to the operating systems they can be run under. Again, your IS department will have strong view on which operating systems are acceptable.

3.4 Number of users

The number of users you wish to support will obviously affect the size of computer system you will need. Don't just count the direct sales and marketing staff, ask IS about the number of support terminals they will need, and also consider the need for secretaries, administrators and planners who may need to get at information in the system.

3.5 Response times

For some marketing applications such as telemarketing response times at the terminal are absolutely critical to the effectiveness of the system. Get guarantees from your own IS people and the software vendor on this issue. If possible, see the response times at a company using the software you would like under the same technical constraints. Always take a technically competent person along with you on these visits. Be exceptionally careful if you are planning to have terminals on a network into your main database.

3.6 Interfaces to other systems

You will almost definitely need access to information from other systems, such as your billing or stock control applications, in your marketing database. If this information is only needed very irregularly then the data import features of your package may be sufficient. If you want data on a regular or very frequent basis then you will have to have some interface to the non-marketing systems to collect the data and make this available to your marketing system. Take these interfaces into account (and who is going to design, code and implement them) before you plan your system.

3.7 Data security access control

The marketing database is a vital asset to any company and must be secured against unauthorised disclosure under the terms of the Data Protection Act. Access control in packages varies from non-existent to very comprehensive. You might need to set up security so that people within your company can only get at segments of the database on a 'need to know' basis. You must also ensure that the computer system security features are set up to match those required by the package. This can be a problem if you are sharing a computer with other users.

3.8 Backup and recovery

A computer is a machine and requires maintenance and sometimes repair. You must take these costs into account when costing your system. You must also take backups (copies of the database on disk or tape) to ensure that if anything goes wrong you do not lose all that data you have been carefully collecting. Who is going to do this and how often? Who will write your security and backup procedures for you? How long can you afford the computer to be off the air before it becomes critical to your operation?

4. TIPS ON REVIEWING COMPUTER REQUIREMENTS

4.1 Get yourself technically involved

You should not attempt to become a computer expert but at least take the time to understand the technical issues your package suppliers and internal computer people are wrestling with. On the other hand, don't let the computer issues divert you from your business directives.

4.2 Appoint your project manager early

This person should work for marketing but have a good experience of computer systems and how to run computer related projects. He should manage the project implementation and coordinate the actions of hardware and software suppliers and your own IS group.

4.3 Get IS involved early

If you have an IS department get them involved early. You may have a hard time persuading them that you need to buy in a package rather than have them design one in-house, but if you point out the marketing skills required in their organisation to understand marketing systems, they will almost always admit that they would have great difficulty acquiring them. It is easier to have IS on your side than fighting you; and essential if you want to use their financial systems or networks to get at corporate information. You can analyse the functional requirements but they will be needed to analyse the systems environment needs.

4.4 Get hardware integrator

If you are using a complex hardware environment such as a PC LAN then get an experienced hardware integrator to set the LAN up for you. You may find that your own company's IS people can do this or even the package providers, but if not – get in a professional.

5. PACKAGE SUPPLIER REQUIREMENTS OF SALES AND MARKETING SYSTEMS

We have reviewed the functional and computer requirements of your marketing system and now we must look at the package provider to complete the picture.

5.1 General company health

No different to assessing the health of any company you intend buying complex equipment from – but don't forget it, computer companies can go out of business just like any others.

5.2 Previous and reference sales

Obviously the more sales to your type of company the better. Ensure that the systems they are selling are recent and not all sold in a batch about three years ago with no recent sales. Ask to see a reference site, and talk to their managers and supervisors about how the system 'feels' to the user. When choosing a reference site, choose one that is doing the highest priority items on your functional checklist. If necessary, go on several reference visits to see different functions being used.

5.3 Technical support skills and resource

Ensure that enough technical support is available to answer all the questions your staff will have during the first few months. Ask to go to the company premises and meet their support team. Some companies have no technical support in the UK for packages from abroad; they rely on support from the developing country. Is this going to be good enough for you?

5.4 New releases of software

Applications constantly develop more and more function over time. How are new releases of software handled by the package provider? How often do they come out? How much influence will you have on which way the development goes? What is the cost of these upgrades?

5.5 Maintenance agreement

What is the cost? What response time guarantees are there?

5.6 EDUCATION

All but the simplest packages require that the user staff be educated to use them effectively. How much will this education cost? Will the company provide 'teach the teacher' style education?

5.7 COSTS

There is a great difference in cost between the highest and lowest in any range of software. Ensure that you have not bought a Rolls Royce when a Maestro will do! Remember to take into account *all* the costs when looking at prices – software, hardware, software and hardware maintenance, people and space, education, interface software development, etc.

6. TIPS ON PACKAGE SELECTION

6.1 Create shortlist of packages

Based on the weighted functional review, computer review, and company review, draw up a shortlist of package suppliers for review by the requirements group.

6.2 View packages and vote on functional strengths

Brief the suppliers on the environment you are anticipating and then invite each in turn to demonstrate their products before the specifying group. Try to get the highest function package viewed first as this will spark off ideas in the audience about the possibilities open to them. Have a score card available for each group to score each of the functions you have already decided upon. Have a round table discussion after each demonstration to record unquantifiable views of the package. After all packages have been seen, draw up the weighted scores and you will then have a good idea of the outstanding package. Hopefully, as you have democratically assessed the packages together, the specifiers will all agree on the outcome.

7 Which database and what can it do for me?

Robert Shaw
Managing Director, Shaw Consulting Ltd

1. INTRODUCTION

American research shows that the name and other details of every US citizen are processed by computers 40 times every day.

Computerisation has filled the world with data, yet most data provides a very fragmented picture of the customer as an individual. Most businesses fail to capitalise on the data explosion despite all the improvements in information technology. Why?

'Database', like 'strategic' and 'lifestyle', is just another buzzword in business, and I have to admit that sales and marketing are as bad as anyone else at picking up new words. However, 'database' has to go down as one of the most overused and misused words in sales and marketing.

Database marketing still commonly requires the assembly of a good quality mailing list. Up to the mid-1980s, the gurus of direct marketing preached three factors necessary for effectiveness: list, offer, copy. Today, the word list has been replaced by the term 'database'. However, the thinking has rarely advanced very far beyond this.

Most direct marketing advertising agencies say they practise 'database' marketing. List people have become trendy. They now rent 'databases'. Service bureaus are self-styled 'database' processing companies. Analysts and consultants offer 'database modelling'. Research agencies sell information on 'databases'. Printers supply electronic 'databases'. A plethora of relational 'database' software is available for computers, large and small alike. 'Database marketing' means too many things to too many people.

What's missing from most existing 'database marketing' systems is management information, e.g. performance statistics, market segment sizes and results, channel effectiveness, survey results and other types of summary information. The addition of these missing ingredients to the database takes fusion way beyond the realms and capabilities of 'database' marketing.

Some marketers may still be inclined to dismiss such concepts as just fancy new names for direct marketing, market research and segmentation. But those with an eye for the future see it as much more than that.

2. WHAT ARE MARKETERS ACTUALLY DOING?

The Sales and Marketing Systems Report is a study of what is currently being used, and what is planned, by over 500 direct marketing managers in the UK (see Tables 7.1 and 7.2).

The overall picture, summarised in the tables, revealed higher current dependence on external direct mail printing services, but an otherwise consistent emphasis on internal facilities.

Over the next two years, there will be dramatic growth in direct marketing systems. The primary focus is on in-house resources. There is also likely to be some increase in bureau activity in certain areas.

Overall, the in-house facilities predicted to develop most over the next two years are:

- Direct response tracking: + 22%
- Telemarketing databases: + 21%
- Out-bound telemarketing: + 18%
- Direct mail databases: + 17%

Direct mail printing

Direct mail printing was one of the more stable and established areas. Letters are both printed by external bureaux and in-house. In most sectors, external bureau

Table 7.1 Current use of direct marketing system (1991 data).

	In-house	Bureau
Direct mail printing	39	42
Direct mail databases	53	25
Direct response tracking	31	13
In-bound telemarketing	29	9
Out-bound telemarketing	26	13
Telemarketing databases	23	12

Table 7.2 Planned use in two years (1991 data).

	In-house	Bureau
Direct mail printing	44	42
Direct mail databases	70	23
Direct response tracking	53	15
In-bound telemarketing	40	10
Out-bound telemarketing	44	15
Telemarketing databases	44	14

printing is more commonplace. Financial services is the exception – they often make use of their extensive in-house printing facilities for direct mail.

Direct mail database

Databases today are predominantly held in-house. Only about 50% of companies have such databases, and there will be substantial growth, both in bureau and in-house facilities.

Participants seemed to be generally unhappy with the service which database bureaux provide. Slow turnaround times, lack of skills and unfathomable pricing were some of the complaints. Also, security was an issue for some, particularly in financial services.

Direct response tracking

The tracking of direct response campaigns is a very hit-and-miss affair at present. Currently under 40% of participants track their direct response campaigns.

Most tracking is carried out in-house. Financial services seem to be further ahead than other sectors in their tracking of campaigns.

2. WHAT IS A DATABASE?

In their current enthusiasm for 'database' marketing, marketing and sales management often pass over the question of what a database really is. Their use of the word certainly differs from that of computing professionals, who use 'database' to describe certain kinds of software which provide linkages between different items of information.

A *database* can be properly defined as follows: a collection of related data stored together, with the minimum of duplication and providing a common pool of information to serve one or more applications. Hence the database is the information itself, not the software or tools used to manage and manipulate the information.

With database software called a *Database Management System* (DBMS) you can attach data together in relational or hierarchical structures allowing fast and efficient access to particular fields, without having to process the entire file.

In popular terms, the adoption of a database means putting all the sales and marketing organisation's data into one computerised filing system. However, in practice it can also mean assembling a number of separate databases, each serving a group of related applications. It can be perfectly acceptable to have several databases coexisting. Thus we may find organisations with different needs following a variety of approaches:

- A mail order company may have a single database, serving direct mail and

order processing applications.
- A building society may have two separate databases, one dealing with direct mail, and one with mortgage accounting.
- A computer company may have several databases, interlinked, covering direct mail, telemarketing, field sales and order processing.

Obviously, where more than one database is involved, it may be necessary to provide bridges, or interfaces, for data to flow between them.

3. COSTS

The costs of a database accrue from many areas:

- the costs of hardware and software;
- the operational staff costs for designing the new operational databases;
- the time and costs required to convert existing operational systems to work under the database regime;
- the disruption caused to daily operations in moving across to the new database regime.

These costs are prohibitive unless there are substantial benefits of the database approach to operational staff. Under most circumstances, it is wiser to take a smaller step towards a marketing database, before redeveloping the operational systems.

It is often difficult for management to identify the direct benefits to the user from a DBMS approach, especially when most of the arguments advanced appear to be advantageous to the data processing department:

- better use of facilities;
- ease of change and maintenance;
- an exciting new technique to attract and retain the interests of the computer expert.

The first time a sales or marketing manager hears about DBMSs and their advantages are when a proposal from the computer department lands on the desk. Just as he is beginning to learning about computers, he is plunged into a new and baffling area of jargon and expertise that places him once more at the mercy of the technician.

This is not the place to give the reader a layman's introduction to database jargon. However, I do not advise you to place your trust totally with the technicians. You should make sure that they are basing their decisions on sound commercial judgement, particularly with regards to three issues:

- will it provide information to users' satisfaction?
- will it do the jobs that users expect?
- will it be within the capabilities of your people?

Not all DBMSs have the same end-user capabilities. Some systems such as Oracle and Ingres include tools which can be used by end-users to manipulate data and create reports and outputs without substantial help from data processing.

Doing the job means much more than just end-user tools. Capabilities to examine closely are:

- data distribution capabilities;
- multiple operating systems;
- multi-hardware support (where you have several different hardware environments);
- performance of batch and on-line processes.

Several DBMSs are becoming capable of manipulating data held at different locations in a manner that is transparent to the end-user. Additions, deletions and updates, multiple copies and other functions which can potentially lead to data integrity problems of distributed databases, are handled without error by some modern DBMSs.

Where you are using multiple operating systems (such as UNIX, MVS, DOS, VMS, OS/2) or multiple hardwares (such as IBM 30XX, IBM 43XX, IBM AS/400, DEC VAX, ICL, UNISYS, HP, BULL, NCR, Data General, Apple) you need to be careful to ensure that the DBMS you have chosen will work throughout your systems.

Performance of DBMSs is still a problem. Table 7.3 illustrates the payoff between several types.

Table 7.3 DBMS performance comparison.

	Relational	Hierarchical	Flat File
Programmer productivity	High	Medium	Low
Machine performance	Low	Medium	High
Examples	DB2, Oracle	IMS	VSAM
Language	Universal (SQL)	Specific	Specific

As one moves from flat file to hierarchical to relational databases, the speed with which the data processing department can modify and maintain the systems gets better. However, the payoff is reduced DBMS performance.

The performance of a computer system is measured in terms of the time (and hence cost) of performing a given set of instructions, invoked by the applications being run. The time is taken by two activities – storing and retrieving data (essentially, the time taken by the data-retrieval arm in the disk pack – known as Input/Output time, or I/O time) and the time taken performing instructions (known as Central Processing Unit time, or CPU time). The following formulae can be used as first gross estimates:

$$\text{CPU Time} = \frac{\text{Total Instructions/Exchange}}{\text{CPU Speed in Instructions/Sec}}$$

$$\text{I/O Time} = \text{Accesses/Exchange}*(\text{Seek} + \text{Rotation} + \text{Data Transfer})$$

Other factors such as contention elongation are then taken into account in arriving at the figures for on-line response time, and batch processing time.

While you need not perform such calculations yourself, you must ensure that the data processing management have done them before you start to develop your database. Sadly, surprisingly few database developments take heed of such precautions.

4. APPLICATION PACKAGES

A large number of software packages has emerged aimed at the in-house user. Direct mail packages are mainly supplied by bureaux. It should be noted that

Table 7.3 Direct mail packages.

Database Mailman	The Computing Group
Direct Mail Manager	Tranzline
DOMAS	The Computing Group
EZ-Letter	The Computing Group
Face	The Computing Group
Frontrunner	Decision Technology
Listor	Wilford
Mailbrain	UCL
Mailor	Wilford
Marketman	Coggan
MemoBase	MemoBase
Microbase	The Computing Group
Prophit	Acxiom

Table 7.4 Telemarketing packages.

BT telemarketing system	BT
Brock	Co-Cam
Callbox	Oak Telecom
Connect	Mercury Management Software
Connect	Telemarketing Merit Direct
Early, Cloud	Early, Cloud
Edge	Datapoint
Mailbrain Telemarketing	UCL
Marketing Control System	Marketpoint
MSM	Diskus
Open	CDS
Overlord	Programmes Know-How
PAT	Prime Computer UK
Pro.File	Pippbrook
Tel-ALL	Pulse Train
Tel-Athena	Alpha Numeric
Telemagic	Equinet
TOPCAT	Independent Software Marketplace

there was widespread distrust of bureaux as suppliers of software. Participants made negative comments about 'spaghetti code' and thought that a 'proper software house' would be a better source of packages.

Telemarketing packages are quite different, and most of the more established ones have come from the United States. There is a range of substantial packages capable of handling multiple campaigns and handling hundreds of thousands of calls. Brock, Edge, Early Cloud and TelAthena are some of the market leaders.

PC telemarketing packages have also emerged. Rather similar in scope to many of the lead tracking packages, these offer a low cost/low volume alternative for smaller users, or for pilots.

5. IT IN MARKETING – WHAT ARE THE BENEFITS?

Taking the average overall ratings for the range of benefits, it was clear that technology has made most impact in relation to:

- improved customer service
- meeting customer needs, and
- selling more products.

However, it appears (Figure 7.1) that technology has not succeeded in reducing

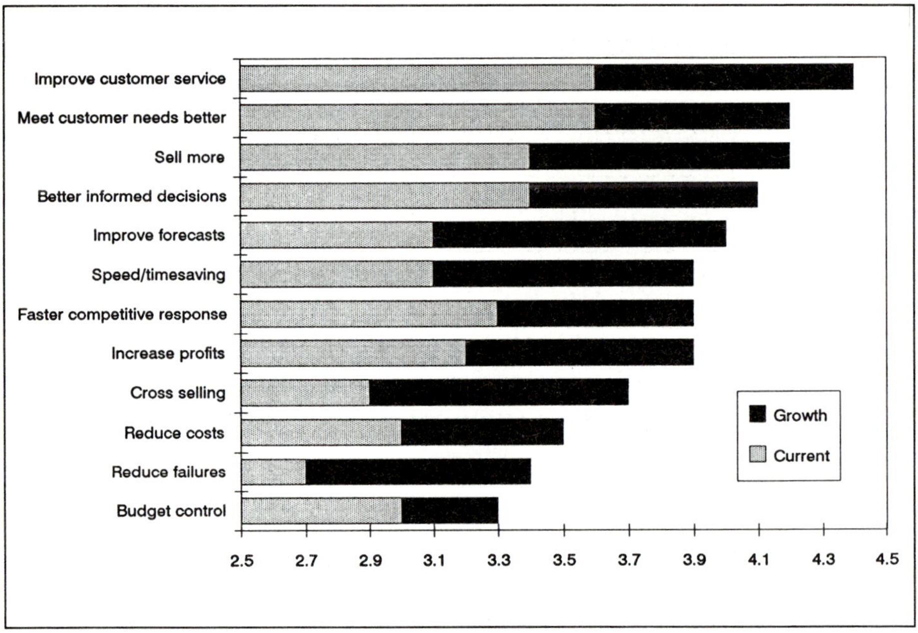

Figure 7.1 Main benefits achieved by participants in the sales and marketing systems report

marketing campaign failures and problems, or in helping to promote cross selling of products – both of which achieved below average scores. Nor has it apparently had a very positive effect on cost reduction or the control of marketing budgets. Both of these factors emerged with average ratings overall in the research, and a similar response applied to achieving faster competitor response, increasing customer profitability, forecasting and speed/time-saving .

Prospects for the future were, however, predicted to be much brighter. In line with the optimism shown in relation to sales, the benefits of technology in marketing were universally expected to increase.

Assessing the impact of IT on business performance in terms of the percentage of turnover which could be attributed to the use of IT was, quite clearly, a difficult concept for many participants to grasp.

On average, the impact was estimated at 26% of 1990 turnover. However, this average conceals a picture of widely differing estimates ranging from 5% or less (29% of participants) to over 70% (20%) of the participants.

The survey demonstrates clearly nevertheless that participants expect the impact of IT on the business to increase sharply over the next two years – by

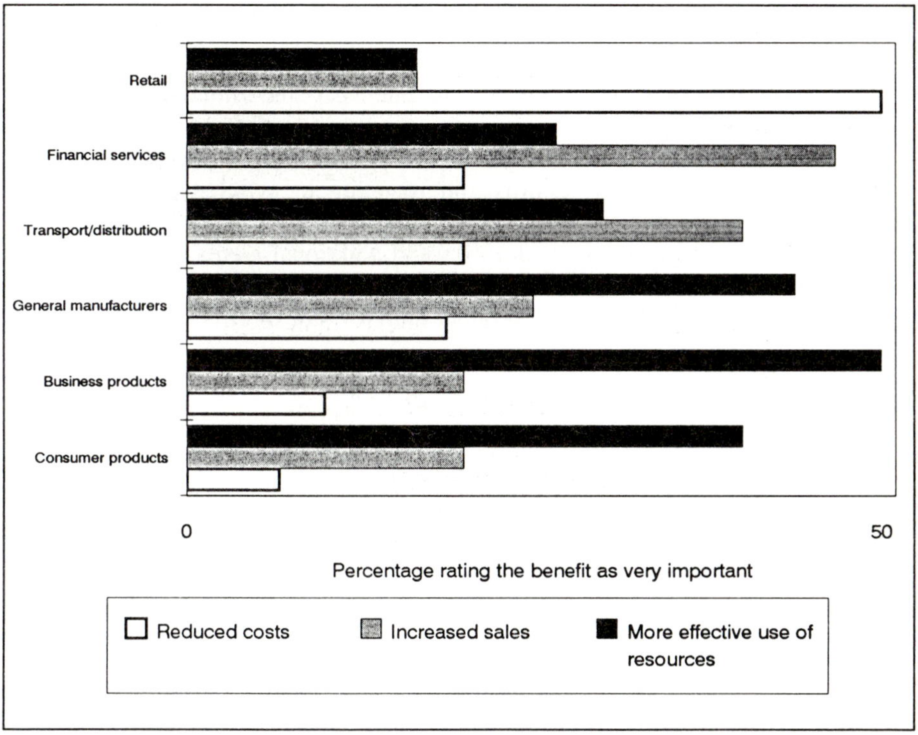

Figure 7.2 Industry views on benefits.

1992, 36% of turnover was forecast to be IT dependent compared with 26% in 1990. Given the difficulties surrounding the valuation, this should be seen more as an indication of the belief in the value of IT than a true measurement of what IT contributes. However, it is a perception across all categories of respondent and industry sectors.

6. VERTICAL AND CROSS-INDUSTRY BENEFITS

Are the benefits of sales and marketing systems vertical, horizontal or something in-between? The type of business transacted can help identify the most promising applications and the resulting benefits.

Our research identified as the most promising classification that of G.E. Miracle, whose classification system is often referred to in marketing textbooks.

6.1 Group one

Companies in this group are selling items of low unit value, with little time and effort spent purchasing, high frequency of purchase, and simple service needs. The primary industry in this group is retailing.

Retailers primarily expect cost reductions from their sales and marketing systems. Removal of duplicate records and targeting to avoid over-contact with direct mail are examples of the benefits they expect. The benefits currently obtained are relatively modest, and only small additional increases are expected.

Group one companies are primarily served by computer bureaux today. The focus is very much on cost reduction rather than revenue or effectiveness benefits.

6.2 Group two

The second group are selling items of medium unit value, which buyers spend moderate amounts of time purchasing. Sales are more occasional, more considered, and involve a more complex service. This group includes consumer products, business products and general manufacturers.

Group two businesses obtain somewhat higher benefits than Group one, and expect more substantial increases over the next two years, as further systems are put in place.

More effective utilisation of resources is the main focus of computerisation for Group two.

Group two companies are supplied heavily by software package suppliers. Sales systems for lead tracking and telemarketing and marketing systems for campaign management and brand management are widely used.

6.3 Group three

The third group are selling items of high, long-term value, which buyers spend a long time considering purchasing. Sales are infrequent, and involve a complex service. This group includes financial services and transport/distribution companies.

Group three businesses expect a much larger benefit than Groups one and two. They also expect this major benefit to come from increased sales of their products.

Group three companies often require custom built software to meet their specific needs. Selling and servicing complex client requirements are not easily met by off-the-shelf packages. Large consulting firms, such as Andersen Consulting, Hoskyns and Logica, are active in this market, providing tailor made solutions.

8 Multimedia information in marketing

Peter Chatterton
Daedalus Consulting

1. THE HIGH-STREET RETAILER

Mainframe and minicomputer systems are extensively used in retailing for sales order processing, stock control, accounts and so on, i.e. in applications that start with the manufacturing of goods and extend along the chain to the sales outlet itself. However, the chain typically stops with the sales assistant. The customer is not allowed to interact with the computing environment.

And for good reason – these computing systems are user 'unfriendly', to say the least.

And yet there could be many marketing advantages to be gained in letting the customer interact with the company computer – their buying motives could be assessed, their preferences evaluated and their shopping habits appraised. But how do you get the customer to yield this valuable information?

The PC has the answer. This recent development which has crept in the back door of corporations (not always with the blessing of the IT department) has features that are quite unique:

- it is immensely flexible and can be tailored to a wide variety of applications
- it is low cost
- it can connect to a wide variety of peripherals
- it is a very powerful computer with potentially very large storage capacity
- it can be simple and consistently easy to operate
- it can now process audiovisual information.

The latter point is the key factor in facilitating the introduction of the customer to the computing environment, enabling the retailer access to those millions of customers who are frightened by the very word computer, or the sight of words and numbers on a screen. For when audiovisual material is presented, the computer can appear to be a TV, not a computer – and a large percentage of those millions of people will have a TV and have long accepted this technology.

And that is why multimedia is important to marketing – in making computers more acceptable to both customers and sales staff, so that they will use the PC as a sales tool:

- to see pictures of products (the entire range)
- to find out accurate and up-to-date product details (prices, technical details etc)
- to explore their interests, without immediate sales pressure and in different languages (a European market)
- to see an extended product range (it may not be possible to stock all items due to limited space).
- to enquire from different perspectives, e.g. by product colour, make, country of origin, design, etc.
- to look at product coordination possibilities – including interior design (matching endless combinations of products, fabrics etc)

In using such facilities, the system can monitor what the customer is interested in, and, with one or two carefully worded questions, can keep track of customer buying patterns.

In so doing, the customer will provide the retailer with valuable marketing data. The marketing tool is thus 'disguised' as a sales aid.

The system can also be used to 'pre-launch' products and gauge customer acceptance and reactions to the products, by displaying the products and details on the screen, without having to go the full length of stocking the shop.

2. AN INTEGRATED APPROACH

Such technology developments are not, in all cases, likely to be used as a sales and marketing tool alone, as it may not be possible to cost-justify such a system in isolation, therefore a strategic plan should aim to integrate the sales and marketing facility with:

- an interactive training tool – training and testing in product knowledge, sales skills, etc – particularly for temporary staff
- a communications tool – communicating between stores and with head office
- a data processing tool – integration with the company sales order processing and stock control systems.

The addition of these extra facilities will assist in a successful integrated approach and will help cost-justify the system, particularly the audiovisual information, which is usually the most expensive item to prepare. It will allow the sales assistant to:

- be more efficient and productive
- be better trained in product knowledge and sales techniques (training in their

own time, at their own pace and in-store)
- have access to up-to-date information (prices, delivery dates, etc.) and thus able to spend more time selling to customers.

3. TELE-SHOPPING IN THE HOME (OR HOTEL, AIRPORT.....)

There have been a number of developments in home-based tele-shopping systems, though none of them to-date has been very successful, for a number of reasons. A major factor is obviously the culture change needed to order (and pay) for products from the home. A secondary factor is that ordering goods from a large database of items can be complex and time-consuming – particularly if it is text-based (as many of the systems are). In some cases, it can be quicker and simpler to go to the shop!

Audiovisual material will play a major role in home-based tele-shopping systems of the future, in making them more acceptable as:

- the system can be made to appear more like the TV in the home
- shopping can be made quick, simple, fun and interesting (for some people, supermarket shopping is all but that)
- the use of pictures can dramatically reduce the number of decisions to be made by the user (more choices can be put in a picture than using text)
- new shopping concepts can be introduced, e.g. shopping by menu.

As with the high street shopping system, the home-based tele-shopping system can thus 'learn' how customers are using the system, their needs and their aspirations – the potential for collating marketing data is enormous, if the system is carefully thought-out.

Whilst tele-shopping is not the answer for all customers, for example, the 'social shoppers', it will increasingly become a major part of tomorrow's retailing, thus providing retailers with unrealised opportunities for targeted selling.

4. THE TECHNOLOGY

Multimedia technology is essentially part of the natural evolution of the PC.

The PC initially processed text and numbers, then graphics, and now audio and video information. Video information is typically stored on a laser disc (which can store 40 minutes of moving video, or 45,000 still slides) and which is played via a laser disc player. A typical interface card that slots in the PC will convert the analogue video signal into a digital format, which can be displayed on a standard VGA (or Apple) monitor. The video fits into screen windows as if it were a normal PC application.

It thus allows the PC to act as if it were an edit suite – a very low cost one!

Audio information can also be brought in from other sources, e.g. compact disc audio or a voice digitising card. The latter is useful as all voice information can be stored on the hard disc, allowing flexibility of using different audio messages, for the same video information.

Alternative technologies do exist:

- storing the video on CD-ROM, though the video quality is not good enough yet to be used in a sales and marketing application
- picture scanning, though the colour content does not always yield a high quality picture.

The traditional keyboard is not the most 'user-friendly' tool to communicate with the PC, so other technologies are used, for instance:

- the touch screen
- the bar-code wand
- the smart card.

A video cassette recorder can be linked to the PC to record the products that the customer is interested in, which the customer can take home to aid decision making.

The PC has such flexibility that it allows these different technologies to be integrated. It is even possible to integrate the standard EPOS facilities into the PC multimedia system, including cash till and credit card reader.

Tomorrow's EPOS system is thus very likely to be PC-based and include multimedia facilities.

5. SUMMARY OF THE BENEFITS

The benefits of using multimedia technology in sales and marketing are:

- information can be gathered from customers under the guise of a sales aid
- 'service' as well as products can be delivered to customers in the high street shop (to compete with home tele-shopping!)
- browsing/buying patterns can be determined
- products can be 'pre-launched' to determine the market
- new opportunities are available to display product coordination possibilities
- customers can quickly locate products that suit their interests
- personalised print-outs and video cassettes can be supplied to customers to aid decision making

- the marketing tool can be combined with a sales, training and communications tool to maximise the technology, effort and information and ensure that tomorrow's sales staff have efficient tools, can communicate quickly, get access to up-to-date information and are well trained.

6. IMPLEMENTATION

Imagination of the possibilities of this technology is unlimited – it is the practical implementation that is not so easy. A successfully integrated system requires all different divisions of a company to work closely together (sales, marketing, training, IT, operations, customer care, etc.). It also requires art and design people to work with programmers and technologists – not always an easy mix! And who is going to coordinate all this? Invariably not the traditional data processing manager. It requires someone with a combination of business and communication skills, blended with highly effective management skills – and who is not afraid of technology!

The prerequisites for such multi-discipline developments to succeed are, therefore:

- the drive must come from the top
- a co-ordinator or champion must be appointed to spearhead all developments.

Such an approach will ensure that budgeting and accounting methods are duly apportioned. It will also ensure that the benefits are recognised as having both short and long term implications.

The coordinator will have to:

- set the plan in the light of the corporate management structure and culture
- plan a long-term integrated approach
- quantify the short, medium and long term effects
- evaluate and monitor the risk to the company
- identify skills requirements and balance internal and external sources
- assess technology on a needs, not on a gimmicks basis
- harness co-operation from all relevant divisions of the company.

Emphasis in this chapter has very much focussed on the development of an integrated technology system that combines sales and marketing, training, communications and data processing. However, the development of the system does not have to include all these facilities at once.

The system can be designed to be modular in concept, so development can be phased. For instance, the sales and marketing tool can initially be developed.

Provided that the system design is well thought out, the training, communication and data processing modules can be added at a later stage, and they can draw on the multimedia database of product information.

When it comes to system design, a much under-rated aspect is the human-computer interface. The design of this *must* come from a multi-discipline approach and the co-ordinator should certainly ensure that the design is not left to the programmers, as with most software developments (the system will be used mostly by non-technical people, not computer specialists!).

7. AND, IN CONCLUSION....

It may sound simple and rewarding to develop multimedia technology in sales and marketing – if well planned and thought out, it can be. But there are lots of hurdles on the way. This chapter provides some pointers in avoiding the major pitfalls, and learning from the writer's experiences in this area.

There is no one in the world who, hand on heart, can say for certain how such technology will be used in sales and marketing over the next ten years. One thing is for sure, though – there is a lot more to it than showing pretty pictures on a screen.

The most successful retailers will be those who really get to grips with how customers shop – who they are, what their motives are, how they can be influenced to change their shopping habits, how their needs can be met and so on. Marketing will therefore be critical in determining how technology can best be exploited.

Technology is thus likely to profoundly change the way we shop in the future, and it cannot be ignored – any more than other information technology developments in retailing. Those retailers who therefore start their learning curves now will gain most from an early competitive edge.

3
Database Marketing

9 From the portfolio to the individual

Marc O'Regan
Information for Marketing

This chapter provides a synopsis of the reasoning behind database marketing together with a list of the key issues to be resolved in adopting the database approach. The next chapter explores the principles in more detail, with practical advice on selecting appropriate data.

1. INTRODUCTION

This chapter considers how database marketing changes the focus of marketing from the customer portfolio to groups of individual customers. Some of the benefits of this approach are explored, together with some of the management issues that are encountered. These opportunities and challenges will be of increasing significance as the use of database marketing develops.

2. THE CUSTOMER-CENTRED VIEW

Database marketing is the best example of how IT is transforming the marketing process. Marketing goals such as the effective segmentation of customers, prediction of their behaviour, and ultimately, the ability to understand and manage each customer relationship have been made more achievable by the adoption of the database marketing philosophy.

Manipulating information to create customer centred views, and using these to drive customer level marketing, has become a key competitive issue for contemporary organisations. Adopting a customer-centred view recognises all the relationships that a customer may have with an organisation, and offers the potential to manage these relationships in new ways.

This approach offers significant planning and control advantages. It also creates important new management issues.

3. CUSTOMER LEVEL PLANNING

Organisations that have several media options available for communications with individual customers can use the history of their relationship with them to determine which option will best meet their business objectives. For example, a financial institution that has an investment product could try to cross sell this product to its current account portfolio. Many such organisations have the choice of using a sales leaflet enclosed in the monthly current account statement, or sending a letter to the customer to tell them about the investment opportunity.

Of the two approaches, the letter is more expensive per contact, but produces a higher response rate. If customers with the best potential for the investment product can be identified, then they can be selected for the letter. If customers whose investment responsiveness is too low to justify the costs of the letter are selected, then contact with these customers will be unprofitable. It may be that the promotion overall is profitable, but that certain sub-groups of customers are loss making. Using the most cost-effective approach will therefore show significant bottom line improvements when summed for the whole portfolio.

Improving the profitability of communications from the organisation to the customer has obvious attractions. Where does the information come from to decide that the customer has higher business potential? Most organisations are obliged by law to calculate whether they are profitable, which can be interpreted (roughly) as the total profitability of their portfolio of customers. Individual profitability cannot simply be estimated by dividing by the number of known active customers into the portfolio total. To achieve a credible estimate, all interactions with the customer need to have costs and revenues calculated or at least estimated to model historic customer value as realistically as appropriate. Sales value alone is an imperfect guide.

Understanding what the historic profit has been is not the end of the story, however. Commercial results just two years ago are a reflection of the effectiveness of the customer management policies, competitive challenges and environmental forces prevailing at the time. Most likely, all of these will have changed to some extent, and, therefore, the objective historic value figure needs to be tempered by a more subjective assessment of what the future will bring.

Organisations with the best information about what is happening at the micro level can make more informed decisions, customer by customer, and therefore maximise trading profit. Marketing decisions might include the timing and nature of contacts made, products offered, and price. Micro level planning leads to better marketing decisions being made than treating the portfolio as a homogeneous mass. However, there is a price; numerous barriers have to be overcome along the way.

4. DIFFUSION OF THE DATABASE MARKETING APPROACH

Industries vary in the extent to which database marketing has been adopted. Mail order, financial services and subscription publishing operations were quick to use information technology to improve product or service delivery. Realising the potential of direct dialogue with their customers led to innovations in customer management, arguably creating database marketing as a distinct management discipline.

Retailers, packaged goods manufacturers and leisure operators are among those now recognising the commercial benefits of database marketing, as environmental change encourages organisations to plan, deliver and record interactions with individual customers.

Falling costs of computing makes database marketing more cost-effective than other types of marketing expenditure. Large volumes of customer information, and new approaches to analysing and using it, are features of this approach. This does not necessarily mean that it becomes the only significant marketing expenditure. But it is growing in importance in a wide range of markets.

5. SEGMENTATION

The concept of segmentation is central to successful marketing. It becomes considerably more meaningful when applied to a marketing database. Segmentation is the process of dividing customers into groups (segments) that have similar characteristics within groups, but very different characteristics across groups. Productive marketing depends upon the identification of segments that allow differences in customers to be acted on profitably.

Organisations without a customer database can either make intuitive assumptions of how their customers differ or, more typically, will contact a sample of customers for qualitative or quantitative research.

Researchers might describe what a sample looks like in either demographic (for example, age and number of children), or psychographic (for example, beliefs and attitudes) terms. Groups will be derived from this information, and marketing strategies designed around them. However, practical application of the segmentation can cause some problems. If, for example, an organisation found that customers who have children are the best segment for a particular offering, then the effectiveness of the strategy will depend upon whether customers with children can be accurately identified.

Building a customer segmentation from database information makes the segments more useful. The information that is used as a basis for defining the segments is the same information that is used to identify customers for communication. Just as importantly, the same information is used to identify the customers in order to track their behaviour and monitor their profitability. Database segmentation is therefore concerned with the use of 'hard' known data on all customers in order to group them.

Qualitative research can be used to describe segment characteristics once they have been formed, but it is important to recognise the distinction between the use of 'soft' qualitative data to define a segment, and using it to describe a segment.

6. A WIDER VIEW

Marketing databases can extend beyond the analysis of existing and past customers about whom information, either on paper or some form of digital storage, is available. Some organisations keep records about individuals (prospects) they would like to have as customers, but they have not yet started to trade with.

The identities of these individuals might be researched from name and address records that have already been collected but not yet used, rented, leased or bought outright. This can be a comprehensive framework such as the electoral roll for consumers, or the list of private and public limited companies available from Companies House. Organisations that are not large enough to afford to do so might assemble a less comprehensive list of prospects (unconverted enquirers or past customers, for example). Prospect databases allow the organisation to record, and act on the results of recruitment activity over time. The number of selling contacts made to a customer can be recorded, and powerful tactical segmentation characteristics like the number of unsuccessful contacts calculated.

Single use rental from a wide range of lists is still the most common form of prospecting, which does not require the up front investment that a prospect database does.

Customer behaviour ('will they buy or not ?') in response to promotions can be most effectively predicted by knowledge of what they have bought before. Considerations such as the household income, or location, of a customer tend to be less important than the fact that a customer has bought very recently, buys very frequently, or spends a lot. This does not apply to prospecting where, by definition, there is no transactional history.

In response to the growing demand for large numbers of qualified potential prospects, data owners in both business and consumer markets have made considerable improvements in the volume, quality and diversity of information available.

Lifestyle questionnaires which collect demographics, interests and brands used by consumers can provide very highly qualified pools of potential prospects. For certain niche products, precise selection of prospects is very important. As consumer behaviour becomes ever more diverse, niche products will remain in the ascendant, and the search for ever more accurate targeting will continue. A number of subscription magazines aimed at people who have retired, or are just about to, were launched in the early 1990s. Age is critical in the selection of prospects for these products, and circulation growth via database marketing is largely constrained by the number of prospect names available in target age groups.

In business markets, credit reference agencies have supplied information to potential lenders (banks and trade creditors) for some time. This information includes financial performance measures such as liquidity and turnover. The same facts are now becoming available to enhance prospect (and customer) records, at prices which are more realistic for database marketing applications. A fact about a company has a higher value when it is used to make a decision about risking a credit limit of £10,000 than when the same fact is used to make a decision about making a prospecting contact with a potential profit or loss that is many times smaller.

7. OBSTACLES TO DEVELOPING DATABASE MARKETING

So far so good, but the sceptical reader may well ask why customer databases have not made greater inroads into marketing. There are a number of management and technical obstacles that have to faced and overcome. Paradigm changes don't happen overnight.

Management and technical issues are the most significant problems. Many large financial services institutions, for example, still struggle to achieve comprehensive customer level views, but this is due more to the Herculean task of fully integrating information systems from different products than a lack of belief in the potential benefits. Mergers and acquisitions add new customers and products, adding to the difficulties for those involved. As well as system integration work, new skills need to be learned, and changes made to the planning process.

Some of the issues that have to be successfully resolved in the earlier stages of database marketing are:

- Successfully recognising, making and gaining approval for the business case for name and address contact
- Selecting appropriate marketing information to hold
    - which products or lapsed customers will be loaded onto the database
    - how often to update information
    - whether to collect, rent or buy the information
- Achieving, and maintaining, data quality
- System performance and efficiency issues
- Recognising the need for new analytical and creative skills to make the most of it, and employing internal or external resource to deliver it
- Which people should product X be offered to?
- What should the proposition be?

As use of the database develops, new issues appear. Once several successful campaigns have been carried out, management need to:

- Make sense of the copious volumes of campaign and database statistics
- Review the time horizons for investment decisions
- Move from planning 'who will get promoted for product X?' to 'which product(s) should customer A get?'

Giving product groups access to customers that will prove most profitable for the organisation as a whole, rather than simply from the viewpoint of any particular product group, is one of the more advanced goals of database marketing management. Few organisations that have product-centred marketing management structures have achieved this goal, or even addressed the issue in a way that will allow better micro level decisions to be made.

8. THE FUTURE

Progression to understanding the value of customers happens at different speeds for each organisation. Issues for the future will vary depending upon where they are on their own learning curve.

Environmental forces that favour database marketing are growing in significance, although EC draft directives on data protection and distance selling pose potential threats to the industry.

Cheaper computing generally leads to more customer information. Consequently, managers face increasing difficulties in making sense of ever more comprehensive pictures of customer behaviour. Fortunately, the root cause of this management problem is also the source of the solution. Cheaper computing also means that faster and more sophisticated analysis is possible. New techniques for using customer information to describe customer dynamics and predict their behaviour (such as neural networks, genetic algorithms and rule induction) are being developed. Such techniques will continue to appear, and generate heated debate over their relative merits, particularly amongst those with vested interests.

Even more importantly for users of database marketing, new sources of data on customers and prospects have become available. Two of the lifestyle questionnaire databases are now under joint ownership, and the first information products based on 15,000,000 different people are now appearing. For about half the households in the country, age, income and other key demographics are available. At the time of writing, this data can be used to drop unlikely prospects from mailings, or as a postcode classification to compete with or supplement census data. Further developments are inevitable.

For the organisation with international interests or ambitions, it is becoming possible to study the characteristics of customers in one national market and use these to identify suitable customers in another using postcodes. Analysis of the postcodes of Dutch customers allows prospects in Spain to be prioritised. Given the lack of a common pan-European data set on which to build the classification, one might have some doubts as to the validity of such a classification, but the point is that a benchmark has been established. The system can be tested, and usefulness evaluated.

All supermarket shoppers see 'money off' promotions on the packaging of items on the shelves. Many of the beneficiaries of these promotions are not buyers of competitive items, but loyal buyers of the product on a regular basis. For these customers the promotion is an own goal, as they cannot be screened out from receiving the promotion. Experiments are being conducted with systems which recognise brands bought by the consumer by barcodes, and issue money off vouchers only to buyers of competitive products. Using technology to target promotions in this way offers the ability to avoid wastage in hitherto undreamed of ways.

As use of database marketing proliferates, there comes a point where it can pay for one competitor to pay a premium rate for exclusive access to a particular item of data, in return for the assurance that competitors will not have access to the data. Several daily newspapers in the UK have found that mailing a free or heavily discounted trial offer to known buyers of competitive titles is a cost-effective way of increasing circulation. Consumer lifestyle questionnaire databases allow publishers to select their rivals' individual customers and make them an offer. Like the barcode driven promotions example, this allows them to avoid wasting their promotional budget on a discount to their own customers who would have bought anyway. News International negotiated an exclusivity arrangement with data owners for the use of the 'Which daily newspaper do you buy ?' question, demonstrating how important a data item can become as a tool for competitive advantage.

The promise of database marketing has not lost its allure. Heinz recently announced that it would transfer all product advertising expenditure (an eight figure sum annually) to database marketing, citing a desire to 'build relationships with individual customers'. Could it be that database marketing has become the way in which customers will be managed in the future?

10 The consumer database as a targeting device

Edwina Dunn
Dunn Humby Associates Ltd

1. TALKING TO YOUR KEY MARKETS

Today, database marketing is usually viewed as the process in which a business uses the computer to collect and analyse customer and prospect information to target relevant sales offers. However, this is only part of the picture.

Businesses need to understand not only how customers behave and respond to advertising (demand), but also how they react towards retailers or agents and competitors (supply).

Furthermore, a business must be able to measure the probable impact of new products or new channels of distribution on customer sales before spending money on fresh marketing strategies. Knowing the answers is vital in building and sustaining market share in the competitive markets of the 1990s.

In other words, the database must be able to record, compare and set out facts which can illuminate all aspects of the marketing process, not just those which relate to direct communication with customers and prospects (such as direct mail and telemarketing).

Knowing where and how to find the data you need is the first priority. If you are marketing high-quality in-car CD players, for example, you will first need to obtain data on where and how quality car makers are spending their advertising money.

Readily purchasable sources such as the typical MEAL chart shown in Figure 10.1 will tell you not only how much the major car advertisers are spending, but the periods in which they are concentrating their advertising and in which publications. So you can begin to draw appropriate conclusions about how and where to market your quality CD player to quality car owners.

Naturally you will also need to know as much as you can about quality car owners. Obtaining the readership profiles of the publications listed in the MEAL chart will tell you a lot about these people (your 'key target groups'), a useful illustration of how one set of data can often point the way to other ways of taking a magnifying glass to your marketplace.

Such readily obtainable sources of facts about your current or future market-

---

* This article was originally commissioned by Royal Mail Streamline and was first published in the *Royal Mail Fact File*.

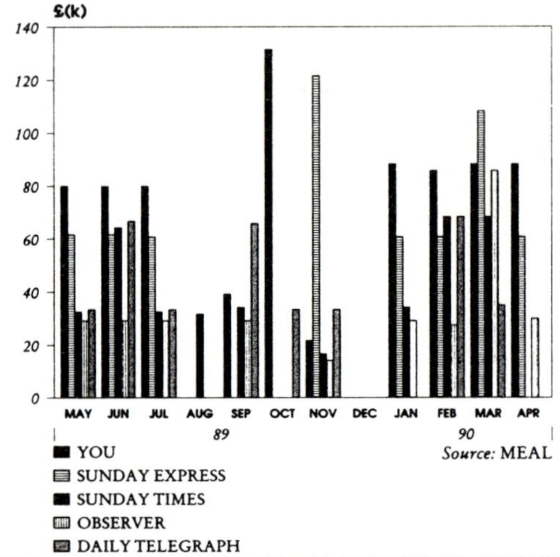

Figure 10.1 BMW expenditure in colour supplements (qualification £300k p.a.).

place will enable you to answer many of the questions that are vital to planning your marketing campaign.

Let us continue to imagine you are marketing that quality in-car CD player and see what kind of answers we can 'buy' in the data marketplace. There are three basic questions:

1. *Are the public buying this type of product and what do they think of it?*
   Answers to this type of question can be obtained through market research. Research on broad product categories (e.g. in-car entertainment) can be obtained through syndicated panels such as Target Group Index (TGI) from the British Market Research Bureau.

   Research on your specific CD player can be conducted directly through questionnaire surveys and 'focus groups' of typical purchasers to gauge reactions to the product, its pricing, your advertising approach and other factors.
2. *Who are out main competitors, what are they doing and how much are they spending?*
   Again, there are commercial sources for this type of information, including Neilsen Marketing Research and (for media spend) British Rate & Data (BRAD).
3. *Which people should we target and where can we locate them?*
   Basically you are asking "Who, where and how many?", and the answers will

come through sources like CACI Ltd and Pinpoint Analysis. These large databases will tell you how groups of people live, work and play in the different areas of the UK and how many of them comprise your target markets.

Such information will be helpful to your marketing, but there are a number of important points to remember. Marketing data of this type tends to be 'fuzzy', compared with the more precise data used in traditional computer applications, such as accounts and pay-roll.

A marketing database will typically aim to define 'good' customers or prospects in a variety of ways. A 'good' customer selected for one product may be someone who has purchased £100–£150 worth of your products in the last six months. For another campaign, 'good' prospects might be defined as people of certain social or lifestyle characteristics (as with out in-car CD player example).

The marketing or database manager will usually handle this situation by defining 'good' within acceptable ranges or grades. The objective will be to focus on the people most likely to react positively to the marketing message (i.e. buy as a result). This part of the data gathering process will aim to identify the 'suspects' who can be converted to prospects and customers, through effective marketing.

2. HOW THE DATABASE INFORMS THE MARKETING PROCESS

It would be easy to convey the impression that database marketing is all push-button mechanics, with no impact on the creative and intuitive aspects of marketing. In fact, database marketing provides a vital creative marketing resource: the database can store and output *decision aiding data* to help make the planning decisions.

As testing and advertising proceeds, response monitoring will add *decision qualifying data* about which key groups are reacting best to the campaign, further refining the decision aiding data available to the marketing team (Figure 10.2).

Used in this way, the marketing database allows us to build accurate 'models' of different situations. To do this we can qualify the 'bought-in' data from various sources by comparing them with customer data. We can then apply calculations to project the sample sizes for testing and the number of responses we will need to make the campaign profitable.

The database can therefore help us to build a picture of our marketplace in five essential areas:

1. *Identify marketing opportunities and customer needs*
   - Define key target groups, segmenting by:
     - Geographic data (where they live)

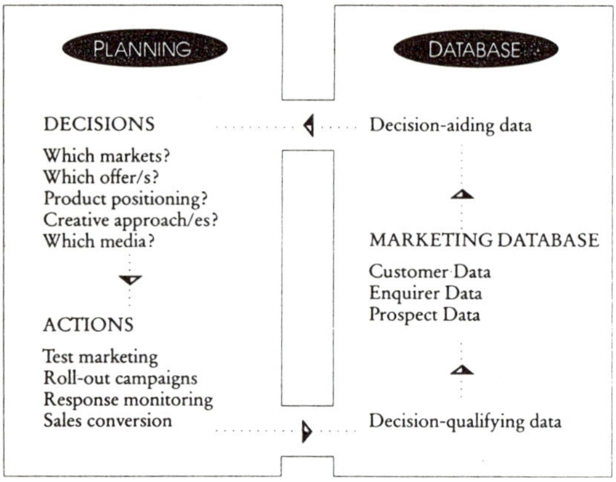

Figure 10.2

   - Demographic data (types of people/neighbourhood)
   - Lifestyle data (purchasing and leisure preferences)
- Find out how your own and competitors' products are selling
- Break your market down into easily identifiable segments
- Look at the whole picture and identify your opportunities

2. *Manage your new and existing products*
   - Explore new avenues for existing products and brands
   - Introduce new products and test to target markets
   - Research, test and set price levels for optimum profit

3. *Improve and extend distribution so that more people can buy*
   - Identify new outlets and assess their potential
   - Manage existing outlets to improve distribution and sales
   - Ensure competitive representation at outlets
   - Motivate wholesalers, agents, dealers or retailers to stock and sell your products.

4. *Advertise and promote your products and where to buy them*
   - Find out which media give you best coverage of your markets and test to response
   - Position your products to appeal to your key markets
   - Identify and test response incentive offers
   - Agree and produce advertising/promotional campaign

- Review response and sales conversion and measure them against your projections.

5. *Ensure successful and profitable trading*
   - Plan the marketing effort to ensure optimum results
   - Control the marketing effort to meet your objectives

3. SOURCING THE DATA TO TARGET YOUR CUSTOMERS

Designing a database to help us to do the kind of things we have just described will give us a powerful 'engine room' for our marketing operations. To make it work, we must fuel the engine with the right data from two main areas.

Data on your *current customers* will be essential in telling where to look for more people like them (your key target groups). Data on where and how we can contact your *key target groups* will help to analyse groups of suspects and focus on the 'prospects' most likely to become new customers for your products.

We therefore have the potential to create a powerful direct marketing database containing data on *both areas* and organised in such a way that each part of the database can 'converse' with the other. The customer data will help to profile the 'prospects' we are looking for, while responses from prospecting promotions can be used to update the customer file.

In this section, we therefore deal separately with the two main areas of *in-house* customer data and *external* market data. What to look for, who are the main sources and how to combine in-house and external data so that you can sell to your current and future customers economically and effectively.

4. CREATING A PROFITABLE CUSTOMER DATABASE

Most companies have some or all of their customer addresses computerised. They may come from a variety of sources, most frequently from the accounts database used to bill customers for goods or services. For this reason, the data may need to be processed or enhanced before it is suitable for marketing and typical sources include:

- *Enquirers* who have expressed an interest or requested information about your products or services. May include name and address, area of interest and some basic information on the customer.
- *Current Customers*: information on existing customer may be available, typically from a store credit card billing system or from information held on previous purchasing records and advertising promotions.
- *Dormant and lapsed customers*: in addition to current records, data on

previous customers going back several years may be available. Data on such dormant and lapsed customers can be revitalised through inclusion in mailing programmes and there are companies offering services which include verifying names and addresses.

- *Promotion Respondents*: coupons and telephone enquiries from advertising or store promotions are a valuable addition to the database, since these can help to identify potentially responsive groups.
- *Customer Recruitment*: developing a brand or store loyalty club can help to establish a list of active customers. Both manufacturers and stores have become increasingly aware of the need to know the customer and have conducted profitable loyalty club promotions, yielding a bonus of detailed information on who is buying what and why.
- *Guarantee Cards*: these can be a source of detailed customer information. Customers who have purchased a consumer durable, such as a washing machine, are usually willing to write down why they chose the product, their occupation and even age group. Most guarantee cards now contain a registration section which includes a 'questionnaire' element to gather in this information in a consistent format for datacapture.

4.1. Troubleshooting with in-house data

Not all of your sources of in-house data will start out by being fully accurate or 'clean'. The original material may have a number of flaws. Normally, these can be corrected, but it is important to be aware of the potential pitfalls.

4.2 Gone aways

About 10% of the population move each year. As a result, names and addresses which are not used on a regular basis become old and out-of-date. The extent to which this is a problem will vary.

The rate may be much higher if your customers tend to be highly mobile people, such as younger singles or professionals moving quickly through a series of 'life-stages'. Some databases may contain names and addresses stemming back over several years. These files can be 'cleaned' by cross-reference with other files, as we shall see later.

4.3 Personal data

Some personal data may be collected from application forms or guarantee cards, including details such as age, job, income level or family status.

However, individuals inevitably age, marry and change occupation, completely altering their lifestyle. This is a significant factor in the 'ageing process' of your customer list and frequent customer promotions are needed to help track these changes through responses.

Designing the database and your promotional response devices to bring in fresh information will help to ensure that you promote the right products to match changing lifestyles.

4.4 Decentralised data

You may have several individual sources of customer addresses within the company. Credit account records, delivery records and customer enquiries will all be in different forms, often for the same customer. Duplication will therefore be a problem when attempting to merge several data sources. The solution is to have the resulting list run through one of the 'merge/purge' programs available from data processing bureaux and mailing houses.

4.5 Data protection

If you are holding large amounts of personal data and intend using it for direct marketing purposes, you will need to examine the various provisions of the Data Protection Act as they may affect your company. If you are not already registered under the Act, you will need to check with the Office of the Data Protection Registrar as to whether you are required to do so and how the intended uses of your customer data may be affected.

5. ADDING POTENTIAL PURCHASERS TO YOUR DATABASE

Having looked at how we can fuel the database with facts about our *actual* purchasers, we can run to the much more problematic area of adding *potential* purchasers – the customers of tomorrow.

As already noted, by getting it right we have the potential to create a powerful direct marketing database containing data on *both areas*. We can organise the customer data in such a way that it will help to profile the 'prospects' we are looking for, while responses from prospecting promotions can be used to update the customer file.

The customers who have already bought from you are clearly your best 'prospects' – the people most likely to buy again. It therefore makes sense that finding the prospects who are most like your customers is a good way to qualify groups of potential purchasers. So let us look first as some of the ways in which you can put your existing customer records to good use in this way.

5.1 Customer profiling

Data on individual customers can be analysed to see what main groupings comprise your key potential purchasers. It may be, for example, that 20% of your customers account for 80% of your sales. A closer look at the make-up of that 20% of high-value customers by social and lifestyle characteristics will give you a clear lead towards finding groups of *potential* high-value customers. This is achieved by comparing a sample from this segment of your customer file with a cross-section of the population, using one of the Neighbourhood Segmentation systems we will be looking at a little later.

5.2 Market penetration

The most profitable groups within your customer file can also be cross-checked against market size information. A good example of this is where geographic considerations are important. The percentage of high value customers falling within each area can be compared to a national figure on the number of homes, types of neighbourhood and purchasing patterns in the same areas. Areas which contain an above average percentage of these high value customers can then be selected as having a potentially high penetration for your product or service.

5.3 Defining market segments

By comparing customer data with information from one of the commercial companies selling Neighbourhood Segmentation data, you can identify which segments of the population are most likely to contain a worthwhile percentage of people 'similar' to your most profitable groups of customers.

To see how you can put these processes to work, we shall return to the in-car CD player example. As a first priority, the company's marketing department have combed existing customer sales records and data from guarantee cards. This has enabled them to identify their 'most active' file, in this case comprising customers accounting for the highest percentage of turnover.

6. IDENTIFYING YOUR 'MOST ACTIVE' CUSTOMERS

To achieve a similar customer profile for your products or services, you will need to have set down all of the salient facts in a logical sequence. You can then draw the appropriate conclusions as to which of your customers represent your own 'most active' file. Let us follow the in-car CD marketing team a little further and see how to go about it.

A useful format to follow will be a briefing document about your products or services. This could include the following components, adapted to your situation:

- Product positioning
  Description of Product or Service, Main Features, Main Benefits, List of Disadvantages, Main Competitors, Advantages/Disadvantages versus Main Competitor, Key promises you can make to clinch the Sale.
- Target market
  Current Customers (Type, Number, Orders over 12 months, % of total), buying Decision Maker(s), Financial Authoriser(s), New Customer types to prospect for, Geographic location and Customer Profile (with exclusions).
- Campaign objectives
  Sales, Financial and Budgetary, Marketing
- Offer strategy
  Means of persuading Customers to respond/purchase, How to make offer easily available, Follow-up and conversion strategy and methods, Response conversion monitoring methods.
- Marketing strategy
  Primary Contact, Secondary Contact, Sales conversion, Response Monitoring (quantitative and qualitative).
- Timescales
  Campaign stages to intended Launch Date.

Completing such a briefing document will give you the basis for setting down the facts which identify your own 'most active' customers; this is the essential preliminary to finding more people like them.

As you can see From Table 10.1, the in-car CD marketing team can now extract an initial 'raw' profile from a variety of facts summarised in their 'Target

Table 10.1 In-car CD Player/Quality Car Market/£185 RRP incl VAT.

CUSTOMER TYPE	NUMBER OF CUSTOMERS	TOTAL VALUE OF ORDERS £	PERCENT OF TOTAL
Single male/female	8,000	1,480,000	18.82
Married:			
18 - 25	3,500	647,500	8.24
26 - 30	5,560	1,028,600	13.08
31 - 45	10,590	1,959,150	24.92
46 - 60	14,850	2,747,250	34.94
TOTALS	42,500	7,862,500	100.00

NOTES:

1. Most customer profiles can get this far on data from sales records in order to calculate the financial breakdown.
2. Guarantee cards with a personal details section my yield age-bracket, marital status and other data.

Markets' section of the Brief. In this example, sales records and information from guarantee cards are indicating that the two older groups of married people account for just under 60% of sales.

One inference might be that these are the groups with an increasing amount of disposable income, with a lifestyle compatible with the product. However, this initial conclusion needs to be thoroughly checked at the outset to ensure that no expensive mistakes are made later.

Your own raw profile of 'most active' customers should emerge in the same way, given a systematic approach to analysing your customer records and a reasonable expenditure of midnight oil! So what happens next?

7. PROFILING YOUR 'MOST ACTIVE' CUSTOMERS

The next step will be to talk to the people at one of the neighbourhood segmentation systems, such as CACI Ltd, Pinpoint Analysis or CDMS. They will take the key segments you have identified and profile each of them separately, showing for example:

- Regular Buyers vs Infrequent Buyers
- High Spending Customers vs Low Spending Customers

The result should be a print-out for each segment showing which neighbourhood types have the highest concentrations of your 'most active' customers.

Being able to identify these key segments will enable you to make planning and budgetary decisions in a far more informed way. For example, the print-outs may show that you can reach 30% of all the 46–60 year olds by selecting neighbourhoods with a high proportion of this age group. The print-outs may also show that to reach your target 30% you will have to mail 50% of the population. However, you will save the cost of mailing the remaining 50 people in every hundred that the database has helped you to exclude.

The degree of *market penetration* will then be worked out by comparing your customer segments with the information on one of the large consumer databases.

For the in-car CD player market, this might typically show the purchasing patterns for 'home entertainment' as a category and 'in-car entertainment' within that category. Matching the customer profile to areas with the highest indices for 'home entertainment', 'home ownership' and 'car ownership' will identify areas with the highest market penetration for the in-car CD player.

Finally, you can work out how this information plays out in terms of the *market segments* identifiable through the database system. The database profile will have told you that you are twice as likely to sell in-car CD players to home-owning, two-car families in good neighbourhoods with a high percentage of home entertainment purchasers. These neighbourhoods can then be identified by appropriate types as coded by the database system you have selected to work with. You can then use this data to help in planning your marketing activities in a number of ways. If your in-car CD is being sold through selected dealers and you wish to extend your network, you can negotiate and establish new outlets in areas with high sales potential.

Each of the companies offering neighbourhood segmentation systems have the ability to identify areas with high concentrations of your 'best' or 'high value' types of customer. Advertising to promote your product can benefit from using the additional profiling data to refine media selections. And of course, you can complete the circle by printing out the addresses of people living in the selected areas for use in mailings to generate dealer showroom traffic and sales!

As you can see, the end product of these activities is twofold. You will have collected a considerable body of knowledge about your marketplace, and you will have reached the point at which you can quantify and list the people most likely to become your next customer.

8. FOCUSING IN ON YOUR POTENTIAL PURCHASERS

As already shown, it is possible to get to know a great deal about the great wide world in which our products will be looking for buyers. It is a world about which we can discover more and more, with a frequently bewildering variety of marketing facts available on computer. Facts which we can combine with customer data to paint a picture of *who* our potential purchasers are, *where* they are to be found and *how many* of them there are, nationally, regionally or in your local TV area.

To understand more of how this happens, let us take it a stage further by looking inside the typical commercial marketing database. This will help us to make the kind of selections illustrated in the previous paragraphs.

Today's commercial segmentation systems (such as ACORN, PiN or Super Profiles) combine two basic sources of data. Raw data, which describes people by where they live (Census Statistics), and researched data (Market Research Surveys) on what they like to buy and how they like to live.

The *raw data* will typically comprise basic statistics from the 10 year official Government Census. This provides detailed information on small areas or neighbourhoods (known as Enumeration Districts), but not about individuals. This data is linked, via the postcode, to other raw data such as the electoral roll. The electoral roll is collected every year by each local authority to register adult voters. Altogether, there are 43 million adults registered to vote each year, and the electoral roll contains each person's full name and address.

9. THE POSTCODE SYSTEM AND DATABASE MARKETING

A further element of raw data – the postcode – is needed so that this vast mass of names and addresses can be conveniently divided up into accessible units, to enable the market research data to be applied. Let us see how this essential aid to direct marketing works.

The postcode system is applied to marketing databases for three main reasons:

1. The postcode is a way of recognising and analysing small groups of households. For example, it links the address system to the census database. Researched information can be applied to help choose areas with high concentrations of good prospects. In fact, postal geography is increasingly used for building and managing specific sales territories.
2. Having accomplished that, the postcode then achieves its original purpose of enabling mailings to be accurately addressed and delivered to the selected areas.
3. Substantial postal discounts can be secured by advertisers through the Mailsort system, which is based on the postcode*.

10. BUILDING A PICTURE OF YOUR POTENTIAL PURCHASERS

Building an accurate picture of your potential purchasers is an essential element of providing the 'decision aiding data' we mentioned as an important basis for our campaign planning. If you were starting out to construct a prospecting database from scratch, you would therefore need to apply a variety of marketing data to the 'raw material' of your postcoded address file to build the required picture of your potential purchasers.

In fact, this has already been done by a number of companies who have developed segmentation systems, giving you a wide choice of options as to the degree of detail you build into the picture. The type and amount of detail available will vary according to the system you choose, so it is useful to review the basic types of marketing data and how they help to add essential colour to the picture by helping to segment your market into recognisable groups.

10.1 National census data

The Government Census collects a massive amount of information on every

---

*Editor's Note: Details of the postcode structure and the way in which it can be used to reference marketing catchment or penetration areas are described in the chapter 'Postcode geography: Current situation and future developments'.

household in the UK every 10 years. The last census was taken in 1991 and published in 1992. The Census Office (OPCS) releases only statistical information to protect the privacy of individuals. Nevertheless, when properly distilled, census data contains elements that provide a great insight into the way people live, particularly about the neighbourhood in which they live or do business.

This vast array of data on virtually every household in the UK can thus help to qualify the raw data we have described above, by telling us broadly what types of people live in which districts. The original intention of the census is to provide details of population characteristics to help the Government and Local Authorities plan the allocation of resources. Commercial consumer databases will therefore further qualify this basic data in a variety of ways described below, to home in on specific types of purchaser.

The census is also helpful in providing a basic 'selection grid' which has been adapted and developed for direct marketing. Under the census system, the United Kingdom is divided into 130,000 Enumeration Districts (ED) containing an average 150 households. The ED has become the basic selection unit for a number of databases incorporating census data. When combined with the postcode system, the ED will thus enable you to select the addresses of groups of potential customers, each averaging around 10 postcodes per ED.

10.2 Marketing surveys

Sample surveys carried out by market research companies enable you to paint a more detailed picture of your target market. Survey data particularly help those companies who do not have any customer names and addresses.

Basically, these surveys are conducted to establish current consumer attitudes and buying patterns across a range of products and services. This data can then be used to create and update the demographic profiles held by the major commercial neighbourhood systems. Potentially, this enables you to identify market segments with a high percentage of heavy users of your type of products and services. For this to happen, your product type has to be one of those measured on one of the market research panels. You can then rent prospect names and addresses falling within these same segments on the electoral roll or other rented lists.

There are a number of examples of surveys of this type. BMRD Target Group Index (TGI) analyses consumer purchasing habits across 4500 brands and services from over 500 products fields. National Readership Survey, published by JICNARS, is a detailed analysis of the readership of major national newspapers at all levels. Specific consumer usage trends are covered through the Audits of Great Britain (AGB) surveys for a range of products and services.

Individual product groups are also increasingly covered by surveys regularly commissioned by specific industry sectors. The textile, paints, beer and wine markets and DIY/home improvements industry are among those who regularly contribute to the body of available consumer data.

11. MARKET SEGMENTATION SYSTEMS

There are a variety of segmentation systems on the market. They apply the different types of data already described to provide a choice of selections at three levels.

1. *Neighbourhood Segmentation Systems* are among the most popular, since they enable the advertiser to use a fine-screen selection. The basic unit is usually derived from the census ED, each comprising an average 150 households and covering around 10 postcodes. Each ED is then given a code based on what is known about the neighbourhood from the available census, survey and market research data. The main systems include:

    - ACORN from CACI Ltd
    - PiN, FiNPiN from Pinpoint Analysis
    - DEFINE from Infolink
    - Super Profiles from CDMS

2. *Postcoded Systems*: As already discussed, the postcode system is applied to all major databases to aid area selections and addressing. However, CCN Marketing have taken the concept of classifying neighbourhoods down to the postcode level. The average unit is thus as small as 15 homes, and their system is called MOSAIC. The data which is available at the postcode level includes credit searches and changes of address. However, a major element of the data used in MOSAIC is only available at the ED (i.e. 150 household) level.

    As a result, postcoded systems like MOSAIC differ from the other neighbourhood systems, but the finer level of geographic selection may not always show significant gains over other types of system.
3. *Lifestyle Segmentation Systems:* The systems we have outlined so far classify everyone in the UK based on 'where they live' and a variety of market research data on large groups of people.

    Lifestyle systems, in contrast, are *as described by themselves*. The lifestyle systems only collect information on people who volunteer facts about themselves – usually around 5–10% of the population.

    NDL's Lifestyle Selector is one of several such databases, and is based on a bank of over two million consumers who have actively supplied their own information through detailed questionnaires. Regular questionnaire mailings are used to update the information and add new names to the database at an average rate of around 100,000 addresses each month. In a typical sample of respondents, 60% have already bought by post, 40% by phone and each has recently made a major consumer purchase.

CACI Ltd have developed a household segmentation system, ACORN Lifestyles. This system overlays estimated age and marital status – modelled from first names and surname patterns – to subdivide the homes in each ACORN type into 'lifestages'. Strictly speaking, this is not lifestyle data as it is inferred data based on probable age scores (from first names) and probable household composition (from surnames).

Several of the companies with lifestyle databases have begun to develop segmentation systems which are based on clusters of respondents rather than individual respondents, and the first of these is PERSONA from CCN Marketing. Again, strictly speaking, this is no longer 'lifestyle' data as the behaviour of the many (the total address file) is inferred from data measured against the few (the respondents).

These brief summaries will help you to recognise the main players in the data marketplace and their possible relevance to your marketing requirements. Table 10.2 offers some useful comparisons of how the available segmentation systems differ in linking you to the individual customer, and the ways in which the data has been acquired and held.

12. COMPARING SEGMENTATION SYSTEMS

Choosing an appropriate segmentation system will involve looking closely at how well the database is organised to give you the facts about your marketplace and compare them with your existing customer files.

Most companies will offer to analyse your customer base for a quite modest fee. For a similarly modest fee, you can also request data print-outs showing the main market segments and degree of penetration for your products or services.

Obtaining information of this kind will give you a basis for comparing different systems and their ability to effectively segment and reach your markets. You should bear in mind that overall, the postcode and neighbourhood systems are very similar in their discrimination power. However, this does vary from market to market, therefore careful selection at the beginning is well worth the effort. A ten per cent uplift in performance will pay back many times in increased profit. Table 9.2 should help to form a groundbase from which to make your decision. As a further aid you can also bear in mind the following points on the main types of consumer lists available in the marketplace.

Table 10.2 The major segmentation systems – a comparison guide.

SYSTEM	NEIGHBOURHOOD SYSTEMS	LIFESTYLE DATABASE	HOUSEHOLD SEGMENTATION
	ACORN DEFINE FiNPiN MOSAIC PiN Super Profiles	National Shoppers Survey or Behaviour Bank (by Bricoda) The Lifestyle Selector (by NDL) Facts of Living (by ICD)	ACORN Lifestyles PERSONA
LEVEL OF COVER	100%	15% - 20%	100%
LINKS TO CUSTOMER DATA VIA	Postcode	Household	Household
ALL RECORDS OR ONLY SOME	All Records	Some Records	All Records
ACTUAL ATTRIBUTES OR INFERRED (USING MODELS)	Mostly Inferred	Mostly Actual	Mostly Inferred
LINKS TO MARKET RESEARCH AND OTHER DATA	Generally Yes	Not Usually	Using a Modelling Process

12.1 Lifestyle lists

A number of companies have developed 'Lifestyle' lists. These are based on individuals' responses to lifestyle questionnaires. They contain a considerable amount of information on the respondent, including demographics, personal characteristics and product interests.

The lists have usually been compiled in conjunction with sponsor companies, who have first priority in mailing these names and addresses. Lists can also be compiled from people who respond to product offers or fill in guarantee card forms for washing machines, refrigerators and for other consumer durables. The respondents are rewarded with coupons or product samples relating to products in which they have expressed interest. In this way, sponsor companies encourage brand switching and product testing.

The names and addresses plus an agreed set of personal characteristics are then made available for wider use. Generally, these lists are quite large, with up to 6 million names and addresses. All contain detailed demographic and product interest data.

The advertiser can thus select names and addresses in one of two ways:

1. Subjectively, by combining personal attributes such as age, product usage and other factors. This selection may also use general information obtained from market research on customer characteristics.
2. By statistical analysis, 'profiling' existing customer against the lifestyle database. This relies on the user supplying a sample of customer names and addresses which are then marched to the lifestyle database. Typically, between 10% and 20% of customers can be cross-matched in this way.

If you already have a reasonable number of customer names and addresses, cross-matching with a lifestyle list can add new dimensions to your understanding of customers.

The characteristics of these customers can then be used to select more of the same from the rest of the lifestyle file. At least 25,000 customer records are needed to run a profile against a lifestyle database.

- *Strengths*: lifestyle lists are generally a satisfactory source of new prospects. The owners have a vested interest in the quality of the list and most ensure that gone-aways are deleted when detected.

  The ability to select individuals based on their personal characteristics is particularly powerful. Other large lists often infer information about individuals rather than collect the data directly.
- *Weaknesses*: lifestyle lists contain an inherent bias. They are names and addresses of people who responded to a promotional offer. This can be positive in that the respondents are pre-disposed to direct offers, but may be difficult to relate precisely to the profile of your own customers.

  Volumes may be limited even on a database of 6 million since the nature of 'lifestyle' selection criteria is very specific. For example, a file of 4 million may only yield 5000 individuals who are 25–40 years old, married with children, who have bought a new car in the last two years and live in the North-West region.

  Like any list, the lifestyle database deteriorates over time, and it is difficult to keep it up to date. It is worth checking how long the names are kept on the list and what the updating procedures are. These vary from company to company.

12.2 Compiled lists

A major source of names and addresses are compiled lists. These lists are usually very large and have been compiled by merging (and de-duplicating) one or more major sources of names and addresses.

Compiled lists include electoral rolls, shareholder databases and large combinations of miscellaneous mail order customers and subscribers. For example, ICD have merged the electoral roll, a shareholder database and a lifestyle list.

These very large lists are particularly useful if you want access to large numbers of names and addresses or a reasonable volume in a small area, such as a town. Normally, segments of very large files are created using a proprietary segmentation system. The main systems in use today are:

- ACORN and ACORN Lifestyles from CACI Ltd
- MOSAIC and Persona from CCN Marketing
- PiN and FiNPiN from Pinpoint Analysis
- Super Profiles from CDMS
- DEFINE from Infolink.

Such compiled lists normally rely on information which has been 'inferred" statistically rather than measured using customer response questionnaires. For example, some electoral roll based list owners offer segments by 'age' or 'marital status'. In both cases these are inferred.

For example, a male and female on the electoral roll, sharing a common surname and living in the same household, are assumed to be married – they may also be mother and son or brother and sister.

In the case of age, names are sometimes used to estimate the probable age of a couple. Sharon and Kevin are likely to be under 30 whilst Ethel and Arthur may be over 60. No accurate measurement of age is provided either on the electoral roll or on shareholder databases.

Using proprietary segmentation systems, such as Super Profiles or FiNPiN, market segments can be overlaid onto these large databases. This is always based on probability of some kind. For example, we may know from market research that Super Profiles Type 1 is more than twice as likely to take foreign holidays compared to the national average, while Type 25 is only half as likely. This type of information allows the user to select segments with the highest probability of using a product or service. However, they cannot provide a definitive source.

- *Strengths*: compiled lists offer large volumes for roll-out. This means that campaigns targeted at local markets around stores or cities are both comprehensive and cost effective.

  The large volume also means that only top scoring market segments need to be selected for a campaign.

- *Weaknesses*: the trade-off between database size and selectivity should be carefully watched. For example, if you are targeting dishwasher owners, the 'best' market segments may have a 30% product penetration compared to 10% on average. However, you are still reaching 70% of homes without dishwashers.

12.3 Affinity lists

These are lists of people who have behaved in some way which indicates they are suitable candidates for a product offer. In the consumer market, they tend to be subscribers to books or magazines or purchasers of particular products. For example, a holiday company may find subscribers to travel magazines a good source of new prospects. Advantages to the advertiser can include co-operative mailing arrangements and 'list exchanges' with the affinity list owners.

- *Strengths*: affinity lists can be very powerful, particularly if the product or service being promoted is closely related to the main attributes of the list.
- *Weaknesses*: the main problems with affinity lists is that they are rarely large lists (usually 10,000–30,000) and so few names and addresses are available for rental. This is even more market if the user has any regional bias. Also, it is difficult to measure the 'affinity' of the product. Most measures tend to be subjective.

12.4 Summary

Lifestyle lists offer high discrimination, but may not be able to provide adequate numbers. Large compiled lists, including the electoral roll, may be suitable if the segmentation system can select high probability groups. Here volume of names and addresses is not a barrier. Finally, if suitable affinity lists are available, they will probably offer the highest performance. However, affinity lists may be quite small.

13. INDIVIDUALLY COMMISSIONED MARKET RESEARCH

All of the options covered so far deal with quantifying your market by comparison with large groups of typical consumers. Individually commissioned research is an option that enables you to ask specific groups of people about how they react to your products or services. This is an important area to consider if you are introducing a new product or planning changes to existing products.

This information will add a detailed dimension to the marketing picture you are building with the aid of the database and will normally divide into the pre-operative

(What might happen?) and post-operative (What happened and why?) phases.

Researching what might happen will generally involve addressing very specific questions to different groups of consumers. If the product can be tasted or otherwise tried out this can also be part of the research. A variety of methods can be used, including the assembly of carefully composed consumer 'focus groups' and exposing them to the product and a variety of messages about the product to gauge their reactions.

Larger groups can be exposed to the product via questionnaire based surveys to gain a broader range of views in statistically valid numbers. While this area is generally the graveyard of pre-conceptions ('They are bound to like our product because...'), the often unexpected answers emerging from market research among potential consumers can have an important bearing on your market decisions.

Obtaining market research data in these ways and comparing it to the information in the database helps the advertiser to understand the overall behaviour of customer segments. In other words, to obtain a more complete picture of what the consumer buys, how they relax and what they feel on major issues of the day.

There are a number of professional organisations that will conduct such research on your behalf. You should bear in mind that data is normally collected under the MRS (Market Research Society) code of conduct, which means that respondents' names and addresses are not available for direct mail.

Researching what happened and why is part of the vital business of response monitoring and research to compare campaign projections with actual results. Through these processes, you can establish which market segments have contributed most responses and actual sales (the 'what happened' factor).

A continuance of the focus group and questionnaire surveys to determine post-campaign consumer attitudes is usually a wise investment in finding out 'why it happened', especially if some elements of the campaign have not performed as expected. In these ways, you can add important elements of 'decision qualifying data' to the information available to help plan your marketing.

14. DATABASE MARKETING IN THE RETAIL SECTOR

So far we have dealt with the overall picture of how a direct marketing database can work to focus in on both current and potential customers. We can now look in some detail at how database marketing can be applied in a number of areas, starting with the retail sector.

Competition and the need to expand may have some impact on this and answers provided by the database will be crucial to exponents of both the 'have and hold' and 'where can we site our next store?' viewpoints.

Retailers divide into two broad categories:

- Those that have some customers' names including addresses and transaction data such as charge-card purchasing patterns.
- Those that simply measure product sales and store turnover.

Database marketing is just as relevant to the second category as the first. Increasingly, retailers are trying to establish a database of end-user customers, using store card and other promotions (such as catalogues). However, these databases will only ever represent a minority of 10% or less of the customer base.

Therefore, if retailers are to benefit from database marketing they must find ways of 'extracting information from' and 'communicating information to' the remaining and much more elusive 90% plus of their market.

How can they achieve this? Retailers measure their customers in 'segments' rather than 'individuals', using market research to measure the behaviour of each market segment. Retailers also study stores and their catchment areas in great depth.

Much of their investment is dependent upon them choosing the best possible site, so retailers will also buy demographic data on how many people live and work around store sites and study the local competition within the store catchment area. Often the print-outs of this data can include computer mapping of store catchment areas. These will visually indicate concentrations of consumer groups and competitions around particular stores.

By combining market research on average expenditure with demographic data on the number and types of people in each market segment within the store catchment area, the retailer can calculate a local *market worth*.

The result will be a 'market model' for the locality similar to that shown in Table 10.3, helping the store management to plan where to locate the outlets and what sort of product to stock. As we can see, the total market value is £3,863,400 of which 'middle-income, young families' represent over 47%. If this store were a grocers, it would tend to sell more family-size packets of detergent or cereals because of the numbers of young families living in the catchment area and target its promotions accordingly.

15. APPLICATIONS OF DATABASE MARKETING IN RETAILING

When it comes to 'talking to the customer' few retailers collect name and address information from the majority of their purchasers. Any direct communication will therefore depend upon the retailer finding sources of names and addresses and measuring his marketplace accurately.

There are several routes deriving from the applications described below. These include loyalty clubs and data capturing responses form store promotion, both of which will yield addresses of people who have visited or at least contacted the store.

Table 10.3 Market modelling.

Market segment	Average Spend per Week	Population Store No 103	Value £000s
Affluent Singles	£35	1,850	64.7
Middle-Income, Young Families	£85	21,750	1,848.7
Middle-Income, Older Families	£60	19,000	1,140.0
Affluent Empty Nesters	£45	7,200	324.0
Retired	£30	16,200	486.0
Total Market Value			3,863.4

Contacting the local people who are not yet store customers is a specialised area in which mail can all play a part. Because retailers have so few names and addresses of their own, it is usually necessary to rent appropriate lists for mailings.

The best sources of names and addresses are those which can be matched to their existing customer segments and targeted within particular store catchment areas. Lists suited to this type of application offer national coverage based on the electoral roll, commercially enhanced to segment by geography (store catchment areas) and demography (e.g. middle-income young families), as we have already seen.

Unaddressed household distribution of store traffic builder material is a frequently used option. In this case, the database will be used to print out lists of postcodes of selected areas for distribution, aiming to concentrate on those with a high penetration of the desired types of customer.

Clearly, the retailing side of database marketing is all about knowing the locality and spending habits of the people who walk through the door, in order to persuade them to keep on shopping. These spending habits can be 'mapped' and database marketing can be applied to help to keep them shopping through:

- *Store Traffic Building*: retailers need to understand who lives and works around each of their stores, in particular, their lifestyles and purchasing behaviour. This helps them to develop promotions and offers which most appeal to the local market. Catchment area 'mapping' techniques help to target people with easy access to the store.
- *Direct Selling*: very often, there are pockets of consumers who would like to

buy the retailer's products but who find themselves too far away from their nearest store. If the retailer can identify these 'gaps' in their market, they can either opt to open another store, change their merchandising policy or introduce a direct sell catalogue.

As an example, when a major stores group launched their home furnishings catalogue, they first used market research and their charge-card customer records to identify a distinct segment of the population interest in home furnishings. Lacking store space for additional merchandise, the group then developed a catalogue operation offering quality branded home furnishings to a widely distributed market segment, generating substantial turnover.

- *Merchandise Planning*: once retailers understand the size of their stores, they have some flexibility in deciding the optimum merchandise mix. To extend the case above, the same stores group operates highly profitable (and popular) food halls where research has indicated that the floor space allocated will pay its way. They also benefit from the two-way effect of shoppers for their main clothing lines visiting the food halls, and *vice versa*!
- *Loyalty Building*: loyalty building relies on the ability of the retailer to understand the motivation and needs of their regular customers, in order to credit them with the attention and service they deserve. By developing a dialogue with regular customers, the retailer can monitor their spending patterns and study what influences them.

  Many major stores therefore offer standard and 'gold' charge or credit cards and operate regular mailing programmes offering customers privilege discounts and sale previews, together with direct purchase from seasonal catalogues. Linked staff-incentive schemes are used to maintain standards of service that encourage repeat shopping.
- *New Store Development*: only by understanding the performance of existing stores, why they are successful or not, will the retailer be able to reduce his risk when he selects another site for development.

  More and more retailers are using marketing databases, not to communicate with their customers, but to understand what makes the difference between a profitable store and one at risk. Based on this information, they are building models which predict the store turnover of new sites and identifying which stores the new site is most similar to in terms of demographic and competitor mix.
- *New Product Development*: retailers may only serve some of their customers' needs. However, the more a business understands about the aspirations and lifestyle of their customers, the more they are able to identify new products and services which will satisfy their other needs. It is much easier to sell a new product to an existing customer than it is to sell an existing product to a new customer, as the following example will illustrate.

A major high street chain identified that a high percentage of their customers were young mothers with babies and toddlers, attracted by their excellent baby products range. Store management decided that this segment was worthy of special attention and went on to develop a successful 'toddlers world' specialist retail chain.

16. DATABASE MARKETING IN THE MANUFACTURING SECTOR

The manufacturing sector is perhaps the most widely varied of all, ranging from the national and international fmcg (fast moving consumer goods) sector to makers of sectional buildings, footware, garden tools and nuts and bolts.

Priorities are similarly varied. In the fmcg sector 'brand-awareness' and 'brand share' hold sway in the fight for the loyalty of millions of shoppers. The sectional building maker will count success per hundred sales leads converted to contracts, while the garden tool and nuts and bolts makers may aim to place large volumes of their products with both large DIY chains and high street hardware stores as their prime customers.

In fact 'brand awareness' and the purchaser's confidence in the product have an important bearing on all of these manufacturers' sales. Manufactures are realising the importance of this and are developing 'life-line' channels of communication with customers to establish both before and after-sales contacts. The 1980s plethora of gimmicks and offers may well give way to a more mature 'service-based' approach for the 1990s.

Database marketing will therefore assume an increasingly important role in keeping manufacturers abreast of their markets and their customers' needs. The data will vary from facts about the 15 million families in the market for a particular fmcg brand to listings by name, title, company, value and date of last order for the customers of the garden tools, nuts and bolts and sectional buildings makers.

Each of these databases must be used as tools for developing customers' brand loyalty, monitoring customer value and researching consumer opinion and reaction to both existing and new products. In other words, to provide the manufacturer with the a broad range of customer intelligence to strengthen the positioning and sales potential of individual brands.

17. APPLICATIONS OF DATABASE MARKETING IN MANUFACTURING

17.1 Sales-force support

One of the most common applications of a marketing database is to provide supporting information to the sales-force. In fmcg the sales force may concentrate on selling in the product range to wholesalers and retailers, where in other areas the representative will sell direct to the end-user by personal calls and product demonstrations.

The fmcg database may contain information on the number and size and mix of population living, working and shopping around each of the target customers' stores.

By comparison, the sectional buildings manufacturer's sales data will include the value of each customer in terms of sales, the location of prime prospects and estimated market share of the competition.

This sort of information helps the sales-force to target their sales effort. Not only are they able to go to the retailer or distributor armed with knowledge about historical terms of supply, but also relevant information about his customer or end-user market.

17.2 Distribution planning

Manufacturers need to present a sound case to the business involved in distribution and servicing of their products. The database can absorb the facts needed to present the case and assist in arranging them as summaries of the size and value of market demand for the product in question.

Typically, the marketing database will need to deliver facts about:

- Product consumption rates by market segment
- Market share compared with competitor's market share
- Overall size of market segments
- Size of market segment within the retailer's or distributor's catchment areas
- Match between the market segments who purchase the product and the market segments who shop at the retailer's outlets or distributor's branches

17.3 Joint promotions

The manufacturer may wish to develop a direct relationship with the end-consumer, to establish product sampling and gain market share footholds for newly launched products.

In the consumer/fmcg area, a recent example of this was the food manufacturer wanting to launch a new coffee brand. Traditionally, the brand was a well-established product within the catering market. It was unknown in the consumer sector.

The manufacturer's agency rented a large consumer list, selecting areas with a high penetration of 'heavy ground coffee users'. A free pack of coffee and money-off coupon was mailed to homes of these 'trialists', achieving a response rate of over 40%. The free trial thus established a new user group overnight, plus a substantial market share within six months of launch.

Data required for an operation of this type would include:

- Market research information of product consumption identifying the key market segments
- Catchment areas of each of the retail stockists
- Prospects, names and addresses from the key market segments within the catchment areas of retail stockists
- A profile of the respondents to the first free-trial promotion plus product take-up by retail outlet.

17.4 Brand loyalty building

Building brand loyalty for established products is not easy, particularly in a highly competitive market. Brand loyalty is increased by raising the consumer's awareness of quality and providing better service.

As an example, manufacturers of baby products, particularly disposable nappies, operate in a very competitive and clearly defined market. Specialist marketing companies are available to provide manufacturers with a ready-made list of potential users, recruited via new mothers' magazines and free product pack offers to mothers-to-be and young mothers visiting ante-natal clinics and stores.

Coupon response devices offer mothers-to-be free product samples in return for their name and address and the expected birth date. The date is used to calculate the age of the baby and provides the manufacturer with clear trigger points for dispatching well-targeted baby and toddler products offers. In Sweden, this process has been taken one step further, by a manufacturer who delivers nappies direct to the mother's home.

Both of these examples demonstrate a long-term view taken by the manufacturer. They are willing to spend quite a considerable amount in the form of incentives in return for a long-term payback – the loyalty of families whose needs may extend over the infancy of more than one child.

Typically, the kind of information needed to drive this type of loyalty programme will include:

- Names and addresses of prospects segmented into key life-stages from the babies' dates of birth
- Lists of brand stockists
- Intelligence on competitive brands, e.g. special features, promotional offers and differences in target market.

17.5 Product testing

One of the most powerful applications of a marketing database is product testing, particularly where the manufacturer is investing heavily in new product development. Here the manufacturer will use market research companies to draw up test samples and quotas comprising users and non-users, employing the marketing database to hold information on:

- Data on product consumption by market segments. This helps the market research company to draw up test quotas which over-sample in areas with good market penetration.
- Names and addresses of customers, enquirers, competition respondents, etc. This provides the manufacturer with an excellent source of consumers who can be classified into market segments and then surveyed via questionnaires about their use of competitive products or their reaction to new or existing products.

17.6 Direct sell

Manufacturers may attempt to stimulate the consumer directly, while ultimately directing the consumer to the retailer for the final stage of purchase.

Typically, car manufacturers spend significant sums promoting new or updated models. Above-the-line commercials are regularly backed-up with local promotions aimed at drawing prospects into the dealership for a test drive. Many of these campaigns arc jointly funded by the manufacturer and the dealers.

Manufacturers are also establishing help or advisory lines so that the consumer can ring to find out more about the product or the location of their nearest stockist. Both of these alternatives can feed the database with a high concentration of information about the enquirer or showroom visitor, for use in planning further marketing initiatives.

18. DATABASE MARKETING IN THE FINANCIAL SERVICES SECTOR

Financial institutions broadly divide their selling activities among three principal alternatives:

- via a network of high street outlets as with the majority of banks and building societies
- via appointed representatives or intermediaries such as brokers as in the insurance sector
- direct to the customer as with institutions offering a range of personal financial services.

Selling financial services through a branch network has many of the characteristics of retail marketing. Banks and building societies are interested in who visits their branches, how far they travel and what combination of services they hope to buy.

Institutions selling through appointed intermediaries share to some extent the characteristics displayed by many manufacturers. The bond between the consumer and intermediary or broker is strong, while the broker may deal through a number of institutions to service his clients.

Institution A is therefore competing with Institutions B, C, D, and E for 'shelf space' within the broker's portfolio of service options. Not surprisingly, finance and insurance companies are becoming more aware of the importance of understanding their consumers more fully. They therefore strive to support brokers with more facts about their particular financial products and how they meet the needs of clients.

There are also an increasing number of organisations who sell exclusively direct to the consumer, with high profile names emerging in the direct selling of insurance, home finance and even full phone-in personal banking services. Their initial enquiries are generated through press and TV and fulfiled via telemarketing and direct mail. Their sales force are the telephone contact teams and the marketing database is a vital central resource for recording all outgoing and incoming communications with the customer. It is their life-line.

The main difference between financial institutions and other companies is the wealth of data they hold on customers and their transactions. Banks, building societies and insurance companies all maintain massive files containing customers' names, addresses and transaction history. However, they have had problems in creating systems which support the marketing function.

Most financial decision-support systems record the customer and their transactions *by accounts*. These are billing systems first and foremost. Account-based systems mean that a customer may appear many times on the database because they have bought several products.

The problem is that the accounts for each product tend to be held separately, so in the normal course of events, it is impossible to identify which customers have which products. This causes problems for the marketing department. If they cannot identify market segments based on 'total value of spend' or 'total product mix', the creativity of campaigns is severely limited.

Many financial institutions have therefore decided to create customer-based systems. This involves matching customers held on different account files and merging them to create one integrated record, containing all relevant transaction history.

19. APPLICATIONS OF DATABASE MARKETING IN THE FINANCIAL SERVICES SECTOR

Once financial institutions have a customer database, it is much easier for them to identify distinct market segments. There are a number of ways in which financial institutions can segment their market:

- *Using a neighbourhood classification system* to create recognisable segments by matching customer data to a national segmentation system. The ideal combination is to arrange the customer file according to both personal data (what have they bought?) compared with demographic or lifestyle codings (what might they buy?) and to use the resulting data to select neighbourhoods classified as having a high penetration index for the desired types of customers.
- *Using statistical score-cards to rank customers into best segments*: this approach is very useful if a financial institution wants to maximise sales within a distinct market. Score-card development is expensive and is usually restricted to product or services which offer a high profit margin, e.g. personal loans.

  Score-cards need refining constantly and they are only applicable to one product. They basically comprise a mathematical formula which is used to score individual customers according to their likelihood 'to buy'.
- *Using customer classification*: this approach classifies customers into distinct market segments. These segments have different behavioural and lifestyle characteristics and clearly demand different product and offers to satisfy their needs.

  The segments are created based on *customer data* such as age, sex and marital status, plus *account data* such as spend, product mix and date of last purchase. These are then combined with external data such as neighbourhood type.

  Such data will enable the financial institution to identify which customer types are delivering the most profit and which financial products to offer them. Customer classifications like the 'High £/Multi-policy' and 'Middle England' groups illustrated in Figures 10.3 and 10.4 can readily be equated to profit contribution and other 'decision aiding' data.

  Cross-selling and upselling are two of the most frequent applications of customer classification, since financial institutions probably have the best opportunities to develop relevant and timely communication with their customers.

  Customers inform their banks, building societies and insurance companies when they move. Customers are also prepared to divulge sensitive financial information as a formality. However, most financial institutions have still to harness the power of the data they hold, such is its depth, volume and complexity.

  Customer databases and customer classification represent a sound start-point, but a real marketing database which contains a more complete picture

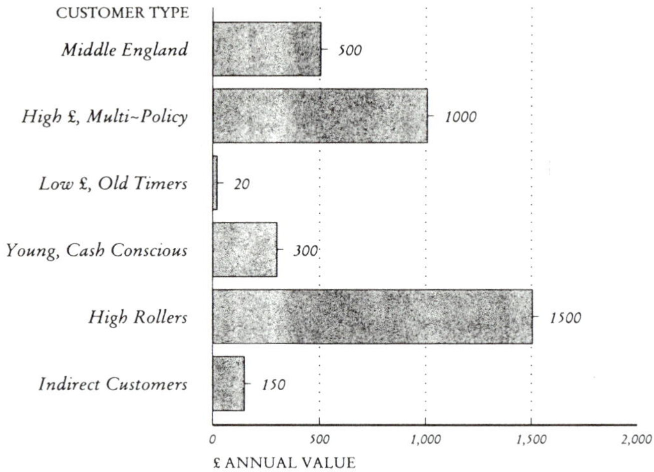

Figure 10.3 Customer classification.

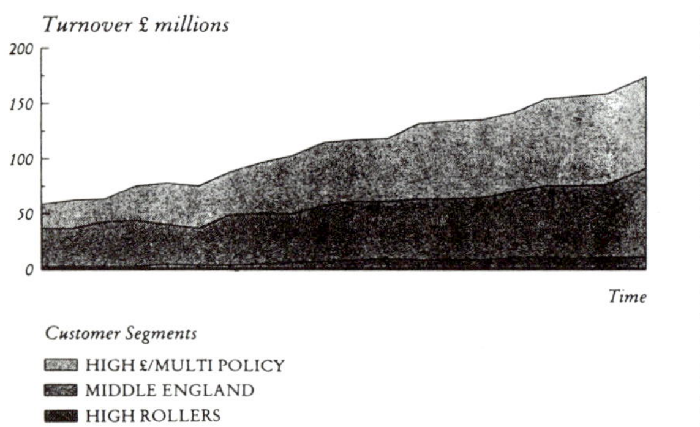

Figure 10.4 Contribution of customer segments to company results.

of the marketing process is a must. A marketing database is not just a file which contains customers' and prospects' names and addresses, it is a source of market intelligence encompassing:

- The identifiable of key market segments
- The life-time value of key market segments
- The sales potential within such segments

- Media effectiveness and reach within these segments
- Branch network expansion and new market niches
- Own and competitive market share
- Defining branch catchment areas and sales potential
- Projecting branch product mix and monitoring sales.

As an example of how this data can be applied, in 1987 a high street banking chain developed a targeting model which was used to set the bank's sales forecasts. The model took into account the underlying market potential available to each branch as well as historical performance. This helped the bank to focus attention on those aspects of marketing which are genuinely under management control.

20. WHAT TO LOOK FOR WHEN SOURCING YOUR DATA

In this chapter, we have now covered all of the major options for sourcing the data to target your future customers in the consumer sector. As the consumer database options continue to multiply in the UK and Europe, it is useful to remind ourselves that the basic list of questions that apply to your data needs will remain virtually the same. Keep this list by you as a basic thinking tool as you develop your database and investigate the various segmentation systems along the lines set out below.

20.1 Sourcing the prospect data

A Checklist

1. How many names and addresses does the database contain?
2. Can my customer files be profiled against the database:
    - By demographic codes?
    - By lifestyle codes?
    - By purchasing patterns?
3. How can my customer files be matched to the database:
    - Via Postcoding?
    - Via Electoral District breakdown?
4. How accurately can this target my key market segments?
5. What will the net total of selected addresses be?
6. What is the original source of names on the database:
    - Electoral Roll plus Census Data?

- Mail order or publishing customer universe?
- Lifestyle surveys?
- Other commercial sources (e.g. Shareholder lists)?

7. What additional data has been applied to the database to refine targeting?
8. What are the initial, set-up and running costs for the proposed use of the database?
9. How do the databases I am investigating compare with each other in the above respects?
10. Is the proposed database registered under the Data Protection Act?

21. DATABASE MARKETING IN THE BUSINESS-TO-BUSINESS SECTOR

The difference between the consumer and business sectors are reviewed below. The common ground occurs wherever the manufacturer or distributor of consumer foods must communicate with suppliers, wholesalers and (ultimately) the retail outlet.

Typically the fmcg manufacturer will wish to ensure adequate stock levels and win shelfspace in advance of media campaigns. The manufacturer's business proposition (e.g. special product launch discounts and advertising support) will need to be communicated all down the distribution chain. This involves a direct business-to-business promotion, in which the basic methods of list building and targeting are the same as for any other player in the business market.

As we have seen, consumer product manufacturer normally classify their target markets in the demographic terms, e.g. age, sex, socio-economic groups or lifestyle interests. Business markets, by contrast, classify their markets in terms of Standard Industrial Classification (SIC) codes and occupational groups. Figure 10.5 gives a useful comparison:

Another major difference is that each customer in a consumer market has a much lower net worth, as expressed in the ratio of products purchased. One consumer rarely buys more than 10 times as many products as another. Whereas, in the business sector, one business may buy 1000 times as many products as then next.

CONSUMER	*geographic, demographic, psychographic and behaviouristic*
BUSINESS	*size, location, purchasing interest, SIC code, resource level, buying criteria and buying power*

Figure 10.5 Market segmentation variables.

This means that it is vital for businesses to differentiate between high value and low value customers (or prospects). However, the power of database marketing has been slow to reach the business sector for two reasons.

1. There are far fewer businesses than consumers in the UK (1,000,000 businesses compared with 55,000,000 consumer). Consequently there is a much greater tendency for the business sales effort to be personal, a one-to-one relationship. As such, most customer facts are kept in the head of the salesman, most of time.
2. There are a number of special issues which relate to targeting and selling within business markets. A business organisation is much more complex than a consumer household. There are many different departments and management grades, each with different buying responsibilities. In other words, businesses are likely to have more than one decision-maker who will influence the buying decision.

Therefore, most marketing databases in the business-to-business sector contain detailed information about a few customers and prospects (rather than a little information about a lot of customers and prospects, as in consumer markets).

Business segmentation systems rely much more heavily on in-house data collected about the customer. Each system is heavily orientated towards the type of information needed in the sales or customer care process.

A manufacturer selling personal computers will need to understand the nature of each customer's operation, how many PCs are currently installed in each department and the likely pattern and timing of equipment replacements. A distributor of auto parts will need to know both the main lines that his trade customers are buying and their buying 'habits' to gauge what products to stock, the quantities to order and when to stock them... and when to approach key buyers to purchase more.

Both types of business are concerned to convert the depreciating value of products 'on the shelf' into appreciating money in the bank. Communicating with their key buyers and prospects at the most appropriate times is a crucial aspect of this process.

The common denominator is that both consumer and business marketing require an exact and detailed knowledge of the customer. Knowledge that is vital in both spheres as the pointer to finding and recruiting fresh customers.

Indeed, many of the database marketing techniques developed in the consumer field are now being used in the development of more and more areas of the business sector. Clearly, the differences lie in the size, source and more detailed information on individual addresses within the average business list.

11 Data integration for database marketing

Susan M Squires
Capscan Ltd

1. INTRODUCTION

Whilst it is a somewhat hackneyed statement that marketing is the process of 'selling goods and services that don't come back to customers who do', implicit in this statement is that there is, somewhere, a body of information which tells the product maker which of his products are being bought by which customers. When, how often and what is the value of purchases made are fundamental elements of marketing data which affect every aspect of the business process and every department in an organisation. How such data are organised into a base of actionable information is the focus of this paper, which examines the diverse sources of data relevant to the marketing process and how they may be integrated to provide a marketing framework for business policy, strategy and tactics.

2. THE NEED FOR DATA INTEGRATION

Database marketing is a process by which the providers of products and services create and develop a direct relationship between themselves and their customers and potential customers, not as a group, but as individuals. By using the traditional media of direct marketing (mail, telephone and the sales force), companies can advertise their products, grow market share, conduct market research, stimulate product demand, build supplier loyalty and provide a channel for customer service.

A marketing database serves both as a repository of information and as a communication tool, and as such requires a wide range of infrastructure – software systems, data and hardware – to support it. The database must provide a means of answering a set of basic marketing questions such as: Who are (or will be) my customers? Where are they? How (and how best) can they be contacted? Which products do (or will) they buy? How often do (or will) they buy? How much do they (or will they) spend on my products?

This wide range of requirements from a marketing database means that development must be an incremental process by which the functionality of the database grows in parallel with the experience of the user.

This incremental approach is not revolutionary – it is a standard approach for the majority of software systems in which new releases offer new features, wider applications and improved processing capabilities. To this end, the user must expect to glean information from diverse sources – in-house transactional and accounting data, third party data, such as competitive and market sector data, published data, and so on – gradually integrating them into a coherent whole which helps to provide marketing information, establish a channel of communication and record the results of such communications. In short, the marketing information system must eventually provide the resource which informs the policy, strategy and tactics of the business development function.

Given the diversity of information sources for fully fledged database marketing, the need for data integration is paramount. Conditioning data items so that they are in a common format and structure is probably the most simple task. Collating data from external sources – published and bureau data – which in many cases has been collected for different units and for purposes other than database marketing, is often the most challenging aspect of the process.

3. TYPES OF DATA

Four basic types of data which are likely to be found on a marketing database are considered:

- Customer data – identification and access channels
- Transaction data – information on communications and the results of these communications
- Classification data – such as geodemographic codes or credit scores
- Spatial data – locational data such as Postcodes, TV Regions, Administrative regions.

3.1 Customer data

Customer data includes that information which is used to identify the customer (or prospect) and his characteristics. The customer might be an individual or a decision making unit such as a household or a company purchasing department. It will normally include name, address, telephone number, account number and some basic demographic information such as age, marital status, family members, housing tenure, and so on.

3.2 Transaction data

Transaction data comprises the information generated through the process of communication with the customer. This might include which products were bought, when and to what value. Transactional information also includes a record of the communications (through campaigns or enquiries) with the customer and their results.

3.3 Classification data

Classification (or categorical) data relates to database segments. Individual customers are grouped in different ways – perhaps for different campaigns – by their characteristics. These segments are defined either through the grouping of characteristics (such as age or lifestage) relating to the individual – microclassification – or through the overlay of aggregate data such as geodemographic classifications using census data.

3.4 Spatial data

Spatial or locational data can range from address information or area boundary data such as TV regions to more general geographical referencing systems such as Ordnance Survey National Grid References.

Spatial data often provides the most important integrating function for database marketing for two reasons:

1. The most frequently used channel of communication is direct mail which requires an address for each customer record.
2. Most marketing data are locationally referenced in some way.

For these reasons data integration through the fusion of data items by means of a common geographic matchkey is a standard requirement for database marketing.

4. DATA INTEGRATION TECHNIQUES

Two types of data integration are considered:

- Linkage of spatial data
- Linkage of non-spatial data.

The main objective in each case is to link to a database record (e.g. an individual or household) relevant and appropriate information from other (usually external) sources. This linked information can then be used in the processing of the marketing database as though it were data 'personal' to the database record.

Both techniques require the identification of a database field (or fields) which are common to the two sets of data to be linked and which can be used as a unique matchkey to assign the correct value to the marketing database record.

4.1 Spatial data linkage

Great advances have been made in the last decade through the introduction of geographical information systems (GIS) in marketing applications. GIS is often simply seen as an information display mechanism, turning a set of incomprehensible data into a map display which shows patterns of, for example, market penetration by postcode sector. The use of overlays of broader demographic information in conjunction with these market penetration maps can often go a long way to explaining the patterns and point to tactics to expand market share.

However, the map display function in GIS is one simple application of the powerful database software and functions which lie behind it – data integration using spatial referencing is probably the most important advance made in marketing systems in recent years.

Along with the growth of this powerful software resource has been proliferation of, and easier access to, the spatial referencing systems required to support them. From a marketing point of view, the single most important spatial reference is the postcode.

The allocation of a postcode to every premise to which the Post Office delivered mail was completed in 1974. With the main function of improving the mechanism of sorting and delivering the mail, the hierarchical postcode system creates a geography for marketing analysis which is well known, flexible and easily used.

In combination with the Ordnance Survey's National Grid Reference, postcodes provide a means of handling data – particularly personal data – in small parcels of around 17 households. Databases based on postcodes and/or National Grid References can be automatically integrated with many other datasets, such as market research or census information, so that a fully interchangeable set of areas for analysis and management can be devised. For example, the sales department may change its sales territory definitions as patterns of business activity change. If sales territories are defined in terms of postcodes, then the process of change is a simple one and a fully integrated marketing, sales, finance and administrative database can be maintained.

Spatial data integration is a straightforward process when the units to be merged are small, for example individual addresses or postcodes. However, information published at a larger spatial resolution, such as 1991 Census Enumeration Districts for England and Wales which contain around 200 households, poses a challenge for the commercial users of the information.

To use successfully area aggregate data such as the 1991 Census Small Area Statistics alongside personal address based data requires an estimate of what the Census statistics would have looked like had they been collected for, say, unit postcodes.

This estimation process, called *areal interpolation*, is common in geographical analysis. It is generally required when the basic building block for data publication is larger that the data entities (such as households or individuals) being measured. In the case of the census, the building blocks for statistics publication are aggregate statistics for neighbourhoods whilst the data entities are individuals or households.

If we superimpose a boundary of any description upon groups of data entities and provide summary statistics for the area within the boundary, the detailed patterning across the continuous surface of data entities is often lost. Clearly, the larger the number of data entities contained within the boundary, the less homogeneous the area within the boundary becomes. The area aggregate data display an average picture hiding important variations and it must be assumed (not always correctly) that the data entities within this boundary conform with this average picture. For example, if 84% of the householders within a census Enumeration District (ED) own their own homes, then the same percentage of owner occupation must be presumed for the constituent postcodes of that ED.

In marketing terms, such a process allows marketing on a locality basis, where prospects are selected on a probability function relating to the likelihood of their conformance to this area average pattern. This is, of course, the case for geodemographic systems which are area classifications rather than classifications of individuals.

4.2 Non-spatial data linkage

A second type of data integration, not related to geographical linkage, is the merging of non-spatial datasets. This is generally referred to as *data fusion*. The process of data fusion is an essential component of database development, since it enables the de-duplication of information.

Exact match data fusion, where a database field (or fields) can be used to generate a unique 'matchkey' common to two datasets is used to sift duplicates from a database, or to clean out database records on some criteria. For example, matching a customer database against a current electoral roll and the Mailing Preference Service exclusion file reduces the costs of a mailing campaign by excluding individuals who are no longer at the address recorded on the customer database and excluding those who have opted not to receive mailings.

Exact match data fusion can be carried out on, for example customer account number or company registration number, but it is more likely that a combination of data items (name, address, date of birth, etc.) will be required to link database records in a reliable way.

This assumes, of course, that the individual fields used to generate the match key are in a similar format, which is not always the case. Names may have forename and initial on one dataset and initials only on another. In the case of an address, many different forms of the address can reside in different datasets.

Standardisation is often a prerequisite of data fusion and hence data linkage. This process for address information is relatively straightforward using the Royal Mail Postcode Address File (PAF). Other types of customer information lend themselves less easily to exact matching, so that a 'fuzzy' match is often the best that can be achieved, with varying degrees of confidence attached to the linkage.

Database enhancement – attaching extra information to a customer database – is a regular user of 'fuzzy' matching, where the user requires (usually) some categorical data to be available for segmentation purposes. Fuzzy matching would be required, for example, where a market research sample survey collected individual, but anonymous, consumer or household records about buying habits. The sample survey might include details of lifestage, family size, income, product preferences, and so on, and the requirement is to use this information to enhance the customer database with the likely buying preferences of customers.

In this case, the characteristics resident on both the database and the sample survey are matched on a 'best fit' basis and the buying preference information attached to the most appropriate database records.

A similar process could be carried out with the forthcoming Sample of Anonymous Records (SAR) shortly to be available from the 1991 Census of Population. The SARs contain a sample of one percent of households and 2% of the population. As the dataset name suggests, the data are anonymous, being spatially referenced only to the level of local authority, so that use for database enhancement is available only on a fuzzy match basis. Nevertheless, they are an important development for marketing analysis.

5. CONCLUSION

Data integration is an essential requirement for effective database marketing, since it provides a methodology around which to structure, clean and enhance the marketing database.

A wide variety of data sources can be pooled into a single marketing information system which drives the policy, strategy and tactics of the marketing process. With the modern techniques of data analysis and processing, spatial and non-spatial datasets can be integrated to form a coherent whole placing the best of recent developments in IT directly at the fingertips of the marketer.

12 Database marketing and a recession: how effective profiling can identify those people still spending on your products*

Jill Etheridge and Peter Furness
CACI Ltd

1. INTRODUCTION

Britain is in the midst of the longest and arguably deepest recession since the 1930s. Not only is this recession more severe than others in the post-war period, but its impact has been more widely based. Those groups who have been largely immune to other post-war recessions – those in the service sector and in the south of England – have not escaped the effects this time.

Not only the Treasury but most other economists too have been at a loss to explain events. Nearly all have forecast a recovery long before now, yet it has steadfastly failed to arrive. Slowly it is dawning on economists and businesses generally that the underlying model has changed – the realities of modern society and the policy mistakes of the 1980s have combined to undermine classical economic analysis. The result is that we are now in uncharted territory.

One problem in predicting the future course of the economy is that it is dependent upon that nebulous factor consumer confidence. This has been shattered by the high levels of consumer debt built up in the 1980s and the collapse of the housing market, not to mention the fear of unemployment. Worse, analysis undertaken by CACI in conjunction with the Henley Centre suggests that there is unlikely to be a significant rebound in confidence for a number of years. Indeed, it is our view that the consumer psyche has been scarred and possibly fundamentally altered for the foreseeable future.

Appreciating this fact is, in our opinion, now more important for businesses than attempts to assess when and where the recovery will come. As Geoffrey Mulcahy, chief executive of Kingfisher has colourfully put it:

> "The ship's gone down and they're all clinging to the wreckage waiting for the big white ocean liner called Recovery to come along, toss out the lifeboats and sweep them all to safety. But instead of floating about aimlessly waiting

---

*Editor's Note: This chapter relates to experiences in the late 1980s and early 1990s. The principles involved in the analysis would, however, apply to any future recessionary situations.

to be rescued from the shipwreck of recession, we should be learning to live with the present conditions."

And living with present conditions means re-examining the information available to you in order to understand who has been relatively unaffected by this recession – and thus who to approach in order to increase sales.

2. WHO ARE THE SURVIVORS?

Henley Centre research shows that in 1991, 54% of households had cut down their weekly expenditure in the last 12 months (Figure 12.1). They believe that this is due to four factors:

1. Unemployment.
2. Fear of Unemployment.
3. Equity loss, particularly in property, undermining confidence.
4. Concern over debt burdens built up over the 1980s.

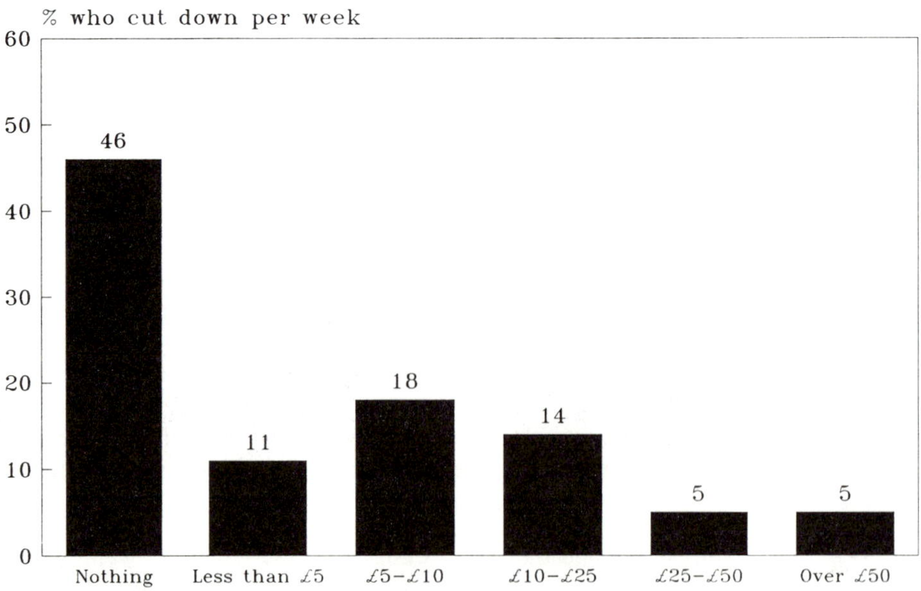

Figure 12.1 Cutting down weekly expenditure in the last 12 months (Source: The Henley Centre).

For the people affected by these conditions, and low income households which do not normally hold an attraction for most companies, much of their consumption will be restricted solely to staple items or to essential purchases such as durable replacement dictated by product failure.

Yet, for those unaffected, spending power has increased as disposable income has risen (by 7% in real terms over the last four years) and mortgage rates fallen (about £10 billion of potential spending power has been 'released' by the decline of interest rates over the last two years). Understanding who these people are, identifying them and persuading them to part with their increased affluence provides the key to increasing sales in the current climate.

The Henley Centre estimates that of the 23 million households in the UK, only 9.1 million form an attractive proposition to the marketeer. This is in comparison to their estimate of 'attractive' households in 1988 – at the height of the boom – of 14.6 million.

It is no surprise, then, that trading conditions are difficult – the number of households with reasonable discretion to spend has fallen by around 40% (Figure 12.2).

At the same time, the nature of the recession – a high proportion of house-

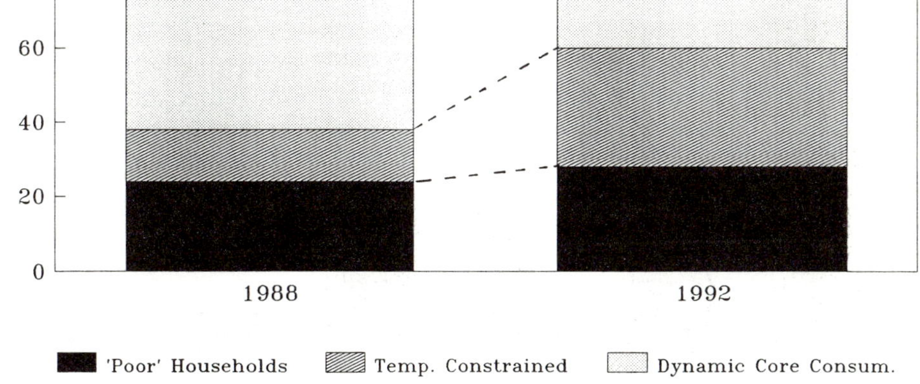

Figure 12.2 The shrunken core (Source: The Henley Centre).

holds affected, but with a core that has seen its position to improve – has accelerated the development of many markets. The large proportion who have been affected have obviously become more price conscious, boosting the discount end of the market. Those who are unaffected have retained quality expectations and have kept the premium end of markets going. It is therefore the middle ground which is being squeezed.

Looking forward to 1995, the Henley Centre does not predict much respite (Figure 12.3) – with an estimated 10.1 million households falling into the category of attractive consumer prospects. Thus business success for the foreseeable future will come from understanding who and who does not have the discretion to consume. Increased sales will come primarily from building market share based on such an understanding. A secondary source of increased sales will be in identifying niche markets and niche products where you can persuade those who have seen their financial position improve considerably over the last four years to spend more.

3. WHERE ARE THE PEOPLE WHO ARE STILL SPENDING?

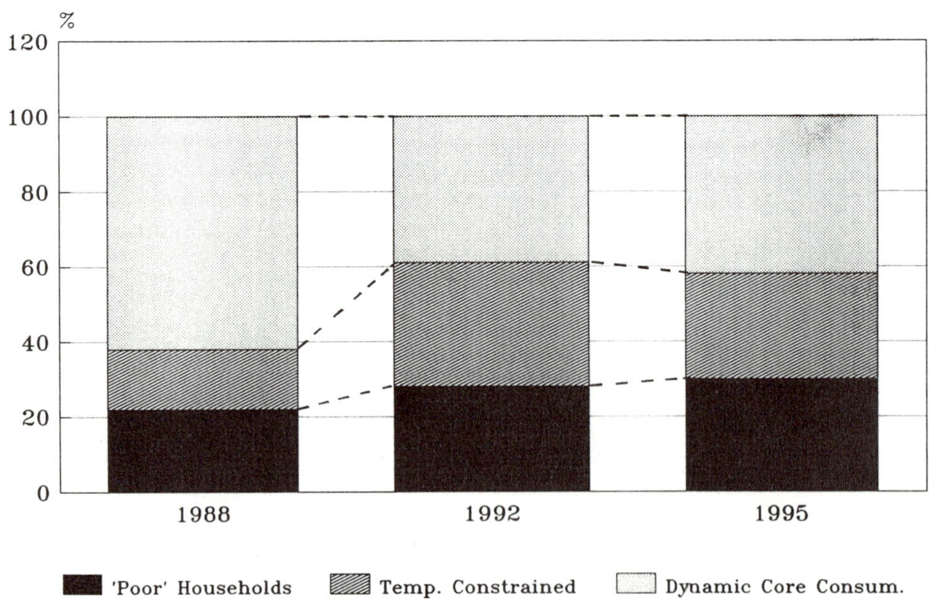

Figure 12.3 Little respite (Source: The Henley Centre).

Using the information from the Henley Centre analysis, CACI created a model of those relatively unaffected by the recession. The model was then applied across the whole country to provide information for every postcode district.

The creation of this model involved the use of CACI's many proprietary databases applied by our experienced analysts. The model itself was created in five separate segments each covering the principal elements of:

1. Low income households.
2. Households suffering equity loss.
3. Actual unemployment.
4. Fear of unemployment.
5. Householders concern about their overall level of debt.

To create each element CACI used a mixture of the following datasets:

•	ACORN	Classification of residential neighbourhoods
•	New Movers	Changes in address from the electoral roll
•	Unemployment	Current unemployment and change in unemployment
•	Income	Household Income levels
•	Social Class	Standard ABC classification
•	Age	Current age profile

All the above information is available for small areas of the country and was used either individually or in combination to define each of the five elements in the model.

Each element was defined, created and can be reported on for every postcode district in the country. All five elements were then overlayed with varying weights to create a single overall variable representing the total level of affected and unaffected in any given postcode district. This variable was then used to create maps as follows.

The first map showed the level of average income in an area. Traditionally, this has been seen as a primary driving force in making marketing decisions. As we can see in the map, incomes are traditionally concentrated in the south east with its large population numbers and high levels of wealth.

In the second map, we showed the result of CACI's analysis using the Henley Centre work. Areas which have levels of expenditure reduction combine the key factors of equity loss, fear of unemployment, debt hangover, etc.

Dramatically, the concentration in the south east and the break up of the traditional north-south split is seen. Rural areas have been less affected, but no clear pattern emerges here.

Since regional patterns are no longer clear cut, markets need to be more closely examined, with new criteria being used.

Using the information for each postcode district, CACI analysed the catchment areas of towns across the country. Using the characteristics of these catchment areas, CACI grouped each town into one of four types:

1. *Group A – Traditional Suffering*
   This group is mainly made up of city centres. Areas of low income house holds and high unemployment. These areas did not really recover from the recession in the early 1980s. They represent the traditional industrial heartland of Britain.
   Examples include Central Liverpool, Central Birmingham, Tyne Tees.
2. *Group B – Debt Hangover*
   This group of towns is made up of areas suffering from excess in the 1980s. Significant equity loss is the norm. Income tends to be above the national average, but the fear of unemployment is significantly affecting these areas.
   Typical examples are Bristol, Tunbridge Wells, Brighton, Solihull, Hatfield.
3. *Group C – Cautious but Prosperous*
   This group is dominated by standalone county towns. Towns which have missed the excessive house price rises and have maintained income levels. County towns tend to have a better mix of employers, allowing the effect of recession to be more diffuse.
   Typical examples are York, Ipswich, Cheltenham, Bath, Edinburgh.
4. *Group D – Wealthy*
   This group is made up of a small number of towns surrounded by a sea of prosperity. These areas will never suffer the full effects of any recession. It could be claimed that small shopping areas such as Covent Garden display this characteristic due to its unique flavour.
   Typical examples include Richmond (Surrey), Windsor.

There are numerous ways in which this type of information can be used in conjunction with the information on your database. However, it is worth highlighting three such areas of immediate application:

- Putting supply in the right place
- Deploying resources
- Promotion and marketing.

3.1 Network planning

To illustrate the way additional information can be used to support network planning decisions, we can focus on the macro and micro elements of these decisions.

3.1.1 Micro decision support

Retailers and network managers face constant decisions on resource allocation issues, which outlets should be refurbished, closed or supported through marketing.

Segmentation analysis allows you to focus on key areas of your business. Often it is difficult to identify patterns or concentrate resources within a large network, particularly with ever shrinking budgets. Segmentation addresses and solves these key issues.

Segmentation analysis involves creating group of similar outlets or areas based on a range of information about the outlet or area.

Breaking your network into segments obviously allows you to concentrate your resources and compare current performance. Segments can be created using internal and external information allowing you to assess the impact of a wide variety of variables across your entire network. These segments should not represent performance measures. Performance should be compared between outlets of the same type. In this way, you can move from simple accountancy performance measures to systems which reflect what is actually achievable by an outlet.

The mechanism can be created quite simply using existing internal and external datasets.

We can now apply the results of the Henley analysis as an overlay to this segmentation analysis to see which area types or outlet types will be prone to suffer or prosper in the new reality. Rapidly, you can assess where you should focus your resources. Therefore, outlets can be tailored to meet the needs of 'Traditional Suffering' or 'Cautious but Prosperous' areas.

Once we have looked at the micro decisions of the individual outlets, we can then look at overall outlet targeting considerations. Network planning can therefore be enhanced by analysis based on this new work.

3.1.2 Macro decision support

While segmentation analysis addresses key issues related to outlets, often business is faced with broad strategic decisions involving opening and closure strategies. New store opening and existing store closure both require detailed and consistent analysis.

Should you focus on York and not Birmingham, and how much difference will there be in the revenue? Does your offer best suit 'Wealthy' or 'Debt Hangover' areas?

Using the information in your database you can create models which predict the likely turnover of new outlets. By using the profile of a new store's catchment area and information from the Henley analysis, you can match the outlet offer to meet local requirements. You could tailor your offer to meet the needs of the unaffected. Often, closures are inappropriate if an effective merchandise plan can be developed to maximise the potential of your existing portfolio.

3.2 Sales management

Effective sales management is all about the effective allocation of resources. Where will your sales staff be best placed to take advantage of market demand? How are your customers being affected by the recession? How can you help them with the appropriate product for an appropriate market?

Understanding your customers and their needs is an essential function of market analysis. Understanding how the recession is impacting on these customers is now possible and essential.

Opportunities are now more difficult to spot, the traditional impressions of areas of wealth are now becoming discredited. Your sales planning has to be aware of and respond to these changes.

3.3 Marketing

Knowledge of who still has money to spend – the 'unaffected' – can be applied in the field of marketing, both to identify gaps in the market and to reach those who are still spending most efficiently. There is no point designing new products for people with no confidence to buy them, or sending offers to people who have stopped spending.

Knowing who the unaffected people are and where they live can be used in the following ways to extend markets and support brands:

3.3.1 How many unaffected people are within my target market?

By profiling segments of customers on your database, you can look at the spread of people across the country that is currently the target market for your products and services. This can be done using simple profiling techniques comparing the numbers of customers in each segment with a base (such as the GB population, or a customer related base) and the result expressed as an index, to reflect over- or under-penetration in that segment relative to the base.

For many clients this will provide all the targeting that is needed. However, some companies may prefer to use highly tuned, optimised targeting models using more sophisticated techniques. In a recession, where pressure is on to make advertising as effective as possible, such requirements are becoming more commonplace.

This is especially true where a company is dealing with very high output volumes but relatively low unit response values, where small improvements in targeting can make big absolute cost savings.

It might therefore be more suitable to use other techniques for building such prospect scoring and other targeting models – including conventional methods such as logistic regression and CHAID, and the newer methods such as neural nets. In some situations hybrid solutions are effective. The choice of methodology will depend on the nature of your business objectives and the scope and quality of the available data.

Once you have established a model for your target market, it is then possible to cross reference those specific people against the unaffected and show where you will be hardest hit..... so you can provide promotional support, or alter the offer and merchandising to appeal more to those who are more willing to spend money.

You can see what percentage of your target market is unaffected, and whether there is still scope for your products and services to be moved to new areas of the country, or to new people in your existing trade areas.

3.3.2 What methods of promotion should I use to support my outlets or products?

There are many promotional methods available to support your sales from door-to-door leafleting, direct mail to households or individuals, TV, radio, magazines and newspapers (national and local), not to mention the plethora of on-pack/ money off incentives.

As different types of people have cut back their spending to different degrees, different types of offer can be used to better effect; the Henley Centre analysis shows that, for example, half the people living in better-off retired areas or those in modern family housing have *not* had to cut expenditure in the last year, but only a third of people in the inner metropolitan areas and lower grade council estates have enjoyed that luxury. In each type of area, however, there are some who have cut expenditure and that drop has come off somebody's market sales and share. But those whose target market predominantly consists of modern family housing rather than inner metropolitan housing will be much less affected.

In the same way, profiles of readers for different types of magazine or newspaper can be analysed to see whether they are read by people who are unaffected or have cut their income substantially. This can be matched to the profile of segments of the database, to see which media best match the profile of your customers who are still likely to spend money.

4. CONCLUSION

It is apparent from this analysis of the recession and the possible applications of it, that this work has direct relevance to many business decisions. Naturally this is not the whole story, but it demonstrates how the combination of your database with external factors can be used to point you in the direction of the people with money to spend.

4
Geographic Information Systems in Marketing

13 **Putting marketing on the map**

Jonathan Plowden Roberts
Pinpoint Analysis Ltd

1. INTRODUCTION

Many of the early Geographic Information System (GIS) developments were there to meet the needs of engineers and surveyors, and because of this the concept of GIS was regarded as a big operation, i.e. GIS is a mainframe activity requiring large computing facilities, and therefore only available to large organisations.

We are all too well aware of the current economic climate, and partly because of this, carrying the right product lines for a local population or target market and recognising local characteristics is becoming increasingly more important. Indeed, 'localism' is now being seen as a means of competitive advantage.

For some years now, marketers and retailers have been making use of geodemographics classifications, such as PiN, FiNPiN, ACORN and MOSAIC, in their local planning. More and more they want to see what that means in terms of what is happening on the ground. Where are the overlaps? What is the effect of one store on another? What is my market share compared to that of the competition? Where are my customers coming from?

To do this, there is an increasing demand for maps, physical representations of the local, trading area. GISs allow marketers/retailers to handle data in a way which has previously been either difficult or impossible. With a GIS they can map catchment areas or customer locations, and overlay that with local demographics. They can create scenarios to assess the viability of opening new outlets, try out new product lines, assess shopper flows, target new customers, all from the comfort of the office.

As with many things, the more questions that are answered, the more are raised. As marketers become more sophisticated in their analysis, so they become more inquisitive and want the power to create 'what if' scenarios.

So what are the key drives behind this increased acceptance of GIS within marketing departments? I believe there are four key areas, outlined below.

1.1 The importance of the individual

The 1980s can be regarded as the decade where the individual really came to the forefront of marketers' thinking. This trend has continued into the 1990s, and can be seen not only in the great political events in Eastern Europe, with the thirst for democracy, but also in the increasing importance of local level and individual lifestyles.

The 1980s also saw an explosion of direct marketing which became more and more sophisticated in addressing individual households. Meanwhile, the privatisation of many of the public utilities became part of the change mechanism in our society: referring to individuals as customers, and not subscribers or passengers. 'Putting the customer first' and 'The customer is always right' became the message, and many management gurus preached the importance of the customer, quality, and meeting customer needs to anyone who would listen.

GISs as a part of a database marketing scenario support customer led activity by facilitating accurate targeting. By manipulating data on-screen, playing out 'what if' scenarios and plotting maps to give a physical representation of the locality, marketers are improving their knowledge of local markets.

1.2 The explosion of personal computing

Early car drivers not only had to know how to drive but also what went on under the bonnet – they needed to be able to make their car run properly and how to fix it if anything went wrong. How many of today's drivers could do the same? For the majority there is no need, it is not their problem; there is the local garage to see to that. It is the same for users of computing facilities.

One of the main reasons for the explosion of personal computing in the 1980s was the number and availability of software packages, e.g. Lotus 123, Word, Harvard Graphics, etc., which overnight put power into the hands of the ordinary office worker. They were able to start to manage their own work more effectively and increasingly to model the results of their actions. Planners could develop ever more sophisticated models using the computing facilities that were developing within the office – they were no longer dependent upon computer specialists.

GIS is yet another tool in this market which has, until recently, not been available at a low enough cost to be fully justified. However, as with all computing facilities, this is changing rapidly, and the recognition of the increased support role that these systems can make in decision making is creating new opportunities for buyers and sellers alike.

1.3 The reduction of risk

In times of expansion such as the mid to late 1980s, risk was not a major concern. There was no risk, or it was minimal because the economy was going to continue to expand, exponentially if necessary. But we all know that this didn't/doesn't happen, and in the cautious 1990s, somewhere in recession, measuring and reducing risks has become increasingly important.

Targeting the wrong audience is costly so whatever the general trading climate the need to refine targeting techniques remains high on the agenda. The costs involved in new store opening, including land purchase, construction, etc. are enormous, and getting the numbers wrong and choosing the wrong site has never carried such potentially disastrous consequences.

So all departments are looking for ways of justifying expenditure and need to have the tools to do this. A GIS which allows the 'flight simulation' of a new store, or marketing campaign proposal, therefore has a part to play in that decision making process.

1.4 The corporate drivers

Increasingly, different parts of the organisation are combining their knowledge, skills and data to become more focused on corporate goals. Marketers and retailers have developed their sophistication over the past decade. They are increasingly understanding the needs of their customers and how to reach them in more innovative ways. They understand that it is not good business practice to sell the promise of a product, if the production department cannot deliver. For example, companies are recognising the importance of not marketing to areas where they can't handle additional demands. This means thinking 'locally' and implies having the tools to do this. GIS is one such tool. Marketing departments can develop models to map areas for potential growth, and to take into account areas where there may be problems delivering service.

2. WHAT IS A GIS?

Let me briefly turn to the question of what I understand a GIS to be.

A GIS is a software tool which consists of a series of layers of data which can be integrated and analysed. The sort of information which can easily be held in each GIS layer could be:

- Census data
- Neighbourhood classifications
- Road networks
- Customer records
- Sales/transaction records
- Branch/outlet locations
- Boundary files
- etc.

The common links between these layers is a single, or a series of grid references. In this way, customers can be linked to their Census Enumeration Districts (EDs) to describe them, or to attach them to their nearest grocery supermarket, either by a straight line distance or along the road network between them.

Boundary files are also used in order to segment data. For example a TV or ILR region or store catchment has a boundary associated with it. This boundary can be used with grid references to determine which EDs fall within it, in order to define the profile of the area, or which customers or outlets, by postcode, fall within the boundary to determine, among other things, regional share.

It is a management tool for organisations, analysing and displaying information in a geographical or spatial context through the fusion of two technologies; computer mapping and relational database in one seamless package. Unlike simple computer mapping software, GIS allows two way interaction between data on the database and the map graphics. This can interrogate and update the database via the map graphics. It can be simply viewed as a window on your data.

Commonly a marketing GIS contains information from two internal databases: customer and sales. To these are added other datasets available in the public domain, such as road network and postal geography.

3. THE BENEFITS OF GIS

Computer-based GIS would seem set to take their place among those developments which will embody the information age. Indeed, they have been described by the government as "the biggest step forward in the handling of geographic information since the invention of the map."

The main benefits of their use according to the Chorley Committee of Enquiry set up by the Department of Environment in 1987 to investigate the handling of geographic information includes:

- fast and easy access to large volumes of data
- the ability to analyse spatial characteristics of data and to search for particular characteristics or features in a given area
- to link or merge one dataset with another
- to produce flexible forms of output such as maps, graphs and summary statistics tailored to meet specific needs.

4. THE BENEFITS FOR MARKETERS AND RETAILERS

The benefits for marketers and retailers are numerous, and can be best thought of in terms of providing the answers to such fundamental questions as:

- Where are my existing customers, what do they look like and where can I find more?

- What is the catchment of my store/branch/territory?
- What is the best site for a new store?
- What is the market size for my products by each area?
- How many people (and of what type) live within a 40 minute drive time of my store?
- Where do people come from to shop?
- What are the shopper flow patterns in a given store?
- How do any of the above relate to advertising?

5. HOW GIS ARE USED

This final section examines how organisations are currently exploiting GISs in several areas to answer some of the questions posed above.

5.1 Case History I – A large non fmcg retailer

This retailer uses its GIS for assessing potential store locations, monitoring the performance of existing stores and assisting in store development.

A number of tasks that had to be performed by the system to meet the distinct stages in the store location analysis were identified, including:

- Catchment area definition
- Area profiles
- Retail potential.

There are various tools that a marketing GIS can employ at all of these stages, including:

- for catchment area definition:
  - circles
  - polygons
  - drive times
  - customer penetration
- for customer profiling:
  - geodemographic type/age/gender
  - products bought
  - frequency of purchase

In assessing a store's potential and the associated market, the first stage is definition of its catchment area. For existing stores the store card penetration levels are used to define primary and secondary catchments. It is assumed that the entire population in the primary area are potential shoppers at the store. For the secondary area it is assumed that the influence of the store diminishes with distance, and a percentage weighting of the population in the secondary area is used. A program calculates the penetration of store card by postal sector and allows for the primary and secondary catchments to be flagged.

New stores present a different problem with no records available, and so drive times are employed on the best alternative. Assumptions are made in the program about the surrounding area (whether it is rural or urban, etc.), and important in this are the maximum permissible speed for the different types of road, vehicle flows and junction delays.

An alternative is to map 'shopper flows' generated from a research database which identifies the flow of people from a postal district to a centre or store.

The system is also flexible in allowing input of some subjective element to the catchment definitions; for example, the presence of competing stores would restrict the boundary, and the drive time data is overridden where appropriate. Once the catchment areas have been defined, the demographics and the potential spend are analysed.

Because the demographic profile of customers within different stores may vary, it is important that this is reflected in the product mix for each store. Using geodemographic neighbourhood classification systems, the GIS allows a sophisticated system of allocating the store product mix to match the customer profile. It also allows the profiles to be used to cross reference with any other *ad hoc* market research survey that the retailer wants to carry out. For example, if they wanted to conduct research among young couples with children, the database can be analysed to show where in each catchment high concentrations or large numbers of the selected type are found and thereby narrow the research sample size.

A further program within their GIS provides estimates of the annual spending potential within the catchment area for the products sold by the store. These estimates provide a preliminary evaluation of any new location, as well as a means to consider and monitor the performance of existing stores. The market size figures give an indication of potential sales available, and so determines the merchandise mix and the space that should be allocated in the new store. If this is done for a number of reasonable catchment scenarios, identification of the best sites can be carried out. For existing stores, such analysis would indicate market shifts over time and can help guide the merchandising mix on offer.

5.2 Case history II – A media buying specialist

This media buying specialist has only recently been formed, and they wanted to enter the market with a technological edge over their competition so as to provide them with a USP for at least their launch period. They use their GIS to assess poster sites and to plan poster campaigns for their clients not only on the basis of what is available, or what has been 'packaged' by the poster site owner, but also upon which sites will provide/deliver the required return.

An example of a typical analysis would be identification of poster sites which are available of a particular size, and will be seen by a particular target audience. This example concerns poster site identification for a telecommunication company in Bristol.

The analysis would start with an analysis of the poster sites in a specified area, e.g. a 20 minute drive time from the centre of Bristol, simply in terms of which ones fell within the boundary. Due to the nature of the client, it is necessary to identify which sites are within a specified distance from phone boxes. Obviously, not all sites will be available for the campaign, and so the next stage is to filter out those which are not available for booking.

It is also possible to identify any individual site and pull onto the screen information including the contractor, the address, postcode, size, package type, OSCAR score, etc., any characteristic which is held in the database.

Without knowing the target audience and where it can be found, all of this information would only be useful in identifying which sites were available and which were not, whereas the user wants to identify which ones he or she should book to reach the target market.

Target market location is carried out by quantifying the penetration, or total number, or both, of the target market found in each postal sector within the catchment, using geodemographic classifications or census data. This is then displayed along with the location of the phone boxes, and all of the poster sites of the required size, along with each site's availability. In this way, the user is able to identify which sites should be purchased to meet the given objective(s). They are also able to obtain statistics regarding the selected sites, which again can be used as a selection criteria, such as OSCAR score, e.g. only sites which have a score of more than 100 and less than 200.

Obviously, the selected sites may already be part of a packaged deal operated by the contractor. If this were the case, then the buyer could argue for either the package to be split or ask for a reduction in cost to recompense for the loss of accuracy and relevance.

5.3 Case history III – A large financial services organisation

This financial services organisation uses its GIS for allocation of what it calls orphans to its direct sales force.

It has long been recognised that the existing customer is the best prospect for future sales. Indeed, several surveys have shown that people buy more readily products from suppliers they know, and therefore selling to existing customers is always more cost effective than trying to sell to new clients.

Bearing this in mind, it does not seem sensible to go to all the necessary effort in signing up clients only to lose contact with them when the agent who signed them up originally leaves. Over time the number of 'orphans' can obviously grow to large numbers, and in the case of this company it was well into six figures in total.

Their solution to the problem does not begin and end with GIS, but it plays a central role in the updating and maintenance of their database. Their system allows them to access their database of 'orphans' and their database of agents.

Starting at the agent level, they identify a particular agent to whom they are going to allocate a specified number of 'orphan' clients who will then become that agent's prospect list, along with with any others that the agent may have obtained through other methods, e.g. referrals, etc.

They draw a boundary around the location of the orphans until it contains the specified/required number of records. Furthermore 'Orphans' are only shown on the screen if they are of the correct age and fall into the relevant business criteria, in terms of when they last had contact with the organisation. The boundary is drawn freehand to allow the operator to visually differentiate between two agents, and also to include clusters of orphans who may have been omitted simply through distance or drive time criteria.

Once the operator is satisfied with the boundary and the required number of orphans has been met, the system automatically writes the agent number to each of the selected orphan records on the database. As a safety procedure, an orphan once allocated an agent number cannot be allocated to another, if, for example, a second operator was allocating orphans to a neighbouring agent.

The database is updated every 24 hours and a list of orphans with name, address, telephone number, account history, product held, birthday, etc. is produced for each agent to whom orphans have been allocated in the previous 24 hours.

In this way, the client hopes to increase cross selling opportunities: at the very least not lose any more, but also once the system has allocated, all, or nearly all the orphans, including any that are created through agent departure in the meantime, it can be used for other applications.

6. THE FUTURE

The Chorley Report noted that 'information needs to be seen as a corporate resource and be more widely shared between departments and organisations' adding that 'the full potential of Geographic Information Systems will only be secured by coordinating the interests of the widely dispersed community of users."

GISs should not be regarded as a panacea, and as said earlier, such systems tend to raise as many questions as they give answers. However, I have aimed to show that in not using such systems you run the risk of asking the wrong questions and thereby not reducing the risks in decision taking.

To end on a cautionary note for anyone intending to introduce a GIS: as Machiavelli said:

> "There is nothing more difficult to plan, more doubtful of success, nor more dangerous to manage than the creation of a new system. For the initiator has the enmity of all who would profit by the preservation of the old system, and merely lukewarm defence by those who would profit by the new."

14 GIS and marketing: a tool for the 'fast lane' or 'grid lock'

John R Beaumont
School of Management, University of Bath

1. INTRODUCTION

Marketing is a function that exists in most organisations in both the public and private sectors. While there has been a tendency to link its activities only to sales (and indirectly to production), there is a growing appreciation that a business approach is necessary, viewing marketing as a corporate activity involving not only the production of products and services, but also their design, distribution and ultimate consumption. Marketing is not about products and services *per se*; the focus of attention must be on consumers (or potential consumers) and how their needs can be satisfied in the context of market dynamics and changing tastes and fashions. The consumer is 'king' in the sense that he/she should start and finish the marketing process. It is also necessary to understand (local) markets and to be able to appreciate and avoid competition.

For marketing in general, the 1950s and 1960s were characterised by 'mass' marketing, and the 1970s and 1980s were characterised increasingly by 'niche' marketing. This differentiation trend will continue through a focus on individual consumers, particularly through the growing establishment and maintenance of customer databases. Rapp and Collins (1987), for instance, have introduced the concept of 'MaxiMarketing', and there is a growing interest in so-called 'relationship marketing'. Organisations are developing concerns for service and quality with a mosaic of desired individual consumption patterns now in existence. (For an overview of marketing concepts and strategies, see Dibb *et al.*, 1991.)

The marketing maturity obviously varies by sector (particularly the basic categorisation by industrial and consumer marketing) and by organisation. The need for this external orientation, however, is increasingly a competitive necessity, as more and better competition is found in all industries. Simply stated, marketing objectives are concerned with combinations of existing and new products/services and markets, i.e.:

- existing products/services in existing markets
- existing products/services in new markets
- new products/services in existing markets
- new products/services in new markets.

Baker (1990, p. 8) suggests that:

"real marketing has four essential features:

- start with the customer;
- long-term perspective;
- full use of all the company's resources
- innovation."

Moreover, in terms of the basic argument in this paper, that information is a key strategic resource that needs to be managed for 'successful' marketing, it is interesting to note a comment by Christopher *et al.* (1980), that:

> "Good information is a facilitator of successful marketing, and indeed, seen in this light, marketing management becomes first and foremost an information processing activity."

The traditional 'four Ps' of marketing illustrate the functions responsibility for managing the marketing mix. Marketing strategies are based conventionally on the four Ps:

- Products
- Price
- Promotion
- Place.

Given the nature of the marketing function, the availability of useful and actionable information is very important, and will become even more significant for organisations in the fifth P, (data) Processing, that comprises data collection, data analysis and data presentation (see Figure 14.1). Taking the argument further, a sixth P could be People, not only as end consumers, but also, in many services, as an integral part of the production/delivery process. However, given our geographic interests, it is relevant to note that retailing, which can be thought of as the marketing of products and services, is deemed to be about 'location, location and location'.

Geographical Information Systems (GIS) were introduced in the 1960s, and developments in handling geographic data, both the theory and practice, have advanced enormously over the last 25 years. The rate of developments continues at accelerate, and in the 1990s, GIS should reach some maturity in some application areas. One application area that is highlighted frequently is marketing; this is not surprising, given the spatial dimensions of customers and competitors and of service distribution.

However, to date, it is far from clear that GIS are necessarily useful and relevant for management's decision-making in marketing.

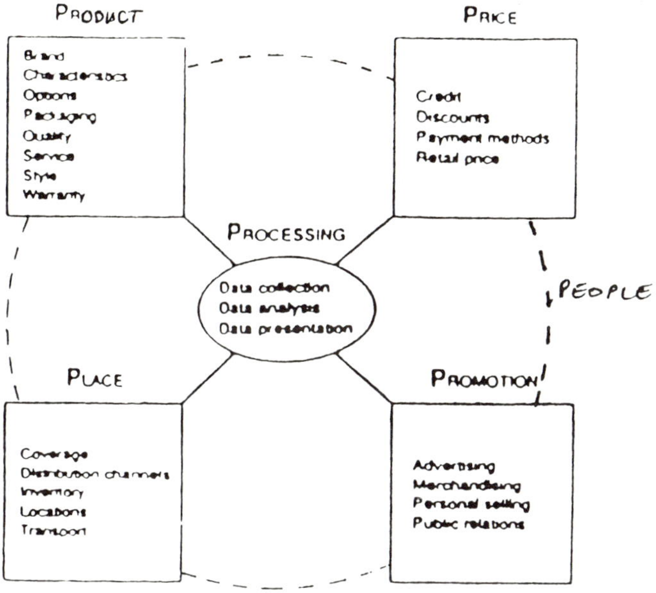

Figure 14.1 The 'four Ps' of the marketing mix.

There is no doubt, at least in my mind, that the efficient and effective exploitation of this tool, GIS, to enhance organisational performance through improved marketing is possible. However, there will need to be some fundamental reorientations, because current trajectories are unlikely to bring success and real exploitation. The starting point must be the business strategy and market opportunities, not the information systems!

The fundamental problem is demonstrated by the fact that marketeers' view GIS systems and their associated data as an administrative/business expense, rather than as a business investment. GIS, in the application area of marketing, must be positioned more at the strategic level, rather than at the operational level. It would be incorrect, unfortunately, to infer that this is a trivial task.

Moreover, today's GISs can provide some of the information required for marketing decision-making (although, currently, they are not designed to have the desired functional capabilities).

In this short paper, today's shortcomings from both a business and information systems perspective are indicated as a basis to propose an outline way forward. It is important to appreciate that the business environment of the 1990s will be very different from that of the 1980s (see, for instance, Blattburg and

Deighton's (1991) discussion of 'interactive marketing'); there will be more and better competition, customer service will be even more important, and managers will have to be agents (rather than simply managers) of change. This vision is necessary because today's GIS must satisfy tomorrow's marketing requirements. Sound information resources management (Beaumont and Sutherland, 1992) can ensure a business payoff.

In the next section, attention focuses on information resources management, particularly from the perspective of the marketing decisions which drive the need for information. Once the information requirements are specified, the necessary system design and data platform can be determined. This discussion provides a basis for considering 'where GIS is located' in relation to traditional management information systems; marketing examples are used briefly to illustrate this framework. In the final section, these two strands are brought together to indicate a personal view of a potential future outlook for 'GIS and marketing'.

2. MANAGING INFORMATION

Marketing is no longer about products and services, rather it is focussed on satisfying customers. 'Successful' organisations are those which know their customers and comprehend their needs.

As a consequence, market analysis is an information-hungry function (Beaumont, 1991; Beaumont and Clarke, 1992). For successful marketing management, a range of fundamental questions must be answered (which indicate the nature of the information requirements):

- WHO
  - should our customers be?
  - are our customers?
  - are our competitors?
- WHAT
  - new/existing products should we develop?
  - new/existing markets should we enter?
- WHERE
  - should we develop?
  - are our customers?
  - should we distribute our products?
  - are our competitors?
- WHY
  - maximise market share?
  - increase market penetration?

- improve profitability?
- increase the rate of return?

The search for answers to many of these questions requires that marketing managers are able, effectively and efficiently, to handle spatial data. (See Beaumont, 1991, for more details.)

How and why does a manager make use of the information provided by a GIS?
The capabilities of an individual's brain to receive, process, store, retrieve and apply effectively available data vary by person. Moreover, with the advances in both information and communications technologies and automatic data capture, it is increasingly more important to recognise the brain's severe limitations to handle complicated decision-making tasks and dynamic environments. Cognitive psychologists have demonstrated that more information is not necessarily helpful; indeed, in times of information 'overload', managers use less information in their decision-making than when having a near 'optimum' amount of information. There remains much-needed research to be undertaken in the field of human-computer interaction; for me, GISs can still become more 'user friendly', which will be a necessary, albeit not sufficient, condition for their greater incidence for managing information. Simply stated,

How can managers use the information from a GIS to its full potential?

The failure to fully exploit information systems is increasingly a non-technical issue. The 'information culture' of an organisation and the 'information literacy' of its managers are key determinants. There is an important educational role here, and, while case studies should be useful (noting the constraints of commercial confidentialities), there are two distinct, albeit linked, dimensions:

- the impacts of GIS on organisations and their people
- how and why organisations and their people affect the effectiveness of GIS.

In terms of managing information, it is important to appreciate that GIS applications can raise significant new management issues. As 'successful' systems often make the specification of alternative decision options and their implications much clearer, evidence is beginning to demonstrate that the resulting information can be deemed threatening (and sometimes unacceptable) to individuals. In considering the future developments of GIS, it is important not to neglect the necessary investments in human capital and the requirements to explore new ways of working.

More generally, the failure to fully exploit (marketing) information systems is increasingly a non-technical issue. The 'information literacy' of managers and the 'information culture' of their organisations are key determinants. Piercy (1990, p. 254), for instance, in his consideration of marketing information systems, suggests that

"• managers seek information to justify what has already been decided
- marketing information may be used to make sales people 'properly optimistic'
- managers may seek information as a way of delaying decisions
- marketing information may serve an 'organisational' function, for example, providing common ground or a shared frame of reference, acting as a collective memory, or functioning as a stabilising factor, or even providing reassurance."

In a linked way, the 'information culture' of marketing managers, their awareness, knowledge and experience of GIS potential (particularly as more relevant data becomes available), are important constraints. There are two opposing problems:

1. The development of user expectations that are much greater than can be delivered (at least at a reasonable cost).
2. The lack of user awareness about the effective and efficient deployment of GISs in marketing.

To make progress, there is a need for GIS vendors to provide 'business solutions', rather than overselling technological imperatives.

Parenthetically, while some researchers have started to consider decision-making in relation to the use of GIS, its real relevance to practising managers is unclear. Efforts to research decision-making are overly academic, attempting to 'program' it, seemingly not aligning academic interest in analysis with the manager's task of synthesis and understanding and reducing uncertainty.

Having outlined the different marketing decision issues, it is worth noting the fact that GIS in marketing is oriented primarily towards tactical/operational decisions, rather than strategic decisions. While benefits can and do accrue from the former application type, the real potential for GISs and marketing should be at the strategic level.

There have been claims, in recent years, of the need for and importance of the strategic deployment of GIS in market analysis, but there remains little progress in practice. The term 'strategic' is used frequently, but sometimes it is unclear what is really being proposed. Strategy is concerned with the scope of an organisation's relationship to its business environment, and the domain covers products and services, customers and competitors in the context of stated organisational goals.

With regard to current applications, in direct marketing, customer (geodemographic) profiling is used to prioritise potential customers' name and address selection (with varying degrees of name and address deduplication with existing customers). Moreover, while branch location and catchment area analyses have developed over the last five years, the type of information presented is aggregate expenditure patterns by product and service category, possibly extended in a simple way to incorporate competitive assessment. In the majority of the applications, there is no real sales forecasting, which is extremely surprising, given that the return on these capital investments is over time. Indeed, with a suitably designed GIS, it would be possible not only to include sales forecasts, but also financial modelling, capacity planning, and so on.

Even for the existing analyses, changes are appropriate. The current emphasis on the demand side, founded on geodemographic and market research data to estimate aggregate expenditure on specific goods and services for particular local catchment areas, must be extended. If we can estimate expenditure, why should we not attempt to estimate the profitability of the target customer market? It is possible to incorporate the supply-side and, from a GIS perspective, many of the costs, such as distribution, are referenced spatially. By combining revenues and costs, it becomes possible to focus on target customer profitability. Interestingly, Higby and Farah's (1991) recent survey in the US indicated that the spreadsheet software, Lotus 1-2-3, is the most frequently used by marketing managers.

All these outlined developments require more spatial analysis and decision modelling, a basic shortcoming of most GISs.

3. GIS IN MARKETING

Our visions as managers should be that the information systems can support a range of management processes and decisions. In relation to traditional computer-based information,

Where is GIS?

There is no need to reinvent the information systems literature (see, for instance Earle, 1989, for an overview.) For illustrative purposes in this discussion, it is useful to differentiate between:

- Electronic Data Processing Systems
- Management Information Systems
- Decision Support Systems.

While advances in information and communications technologies and 'corporate' databases mean distinctions between systems are being blurred, it is important to recognise they do provide different capabilities to support different tasks.

Electronic Data Processing systems are traditional transactions systems utilising computers' processing power, including point of sales systems, financial accounts management (including the use of Automatic Teller Machines), order processing and distribution. Management Information Systems provide regular (and exceptional) structured reports on different activities, such as branch and/or product sales performance and inventory management. The summary customer profiles derived from geodemographic analyses can also be useful management information.

Decision Support Systems (DSS) have received a lot of attention over the last 20 years from academics, managers and IT vendors. Spatial DSS are only one type of GIS, but for market analysis they represent the kind with the most potential, particularly if extensions into so-called Executive Information Systems also occur. DSS involve semi-structured and/or structured, simple and/or complex problems that can be explored in an interactive or recursive manner by decision takers. To allow this kind of decision-making, traditionally, four separate, albeit linked fundamental capabilities of DSSs have been recognised (see Beaumont, 1991, for more details) (Figure 14.2).

While individual systems vary in the relative emphasis given to these capabilities, the majority of GIS are orientated towards the 'database' and 'interface' capabilities – database management with automated cartography.

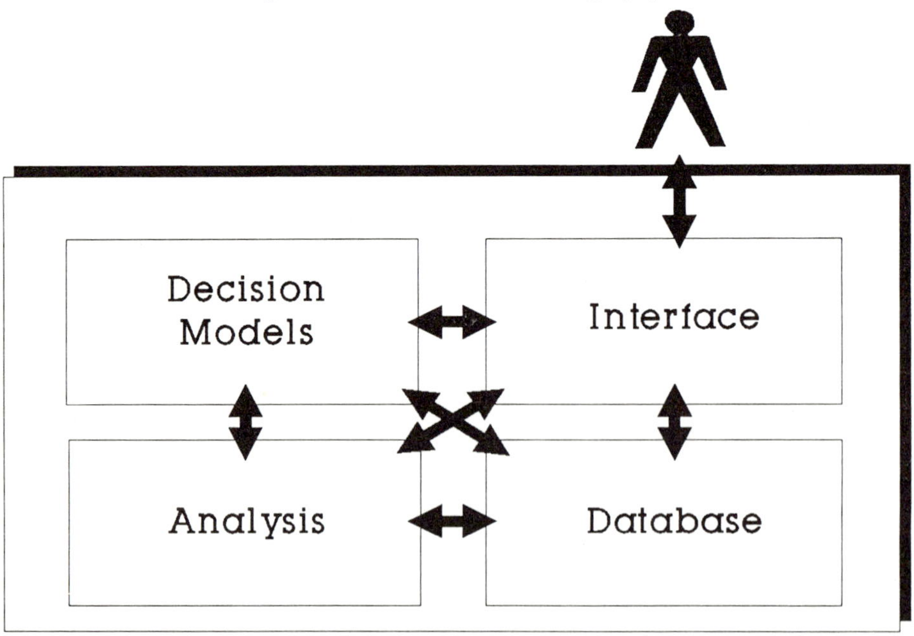

Figure 14.2 Decision Support Systems.

Unfortunately, as indicated in the preceding section, for real progress for GIS in market analysis, attention needs to be focussed on the other two capabilities: analysis; and decision models.

In terms of 'analysis', the failure to incorporate spatial analysis capabilities in GIS is staggering, given the developments over the last 30 years in spatial statistics and optimisation and simulation models. In addition, as the power of any information system increases over time with the collation of historical data, it is important not to forget spatial time series methods. Moreover, while the developments of automatic data capture, such as Electronic Point of Sale (EPoS) systems, mean that more analyses are required to avoid 'data overload', explicit attention should also be given to data accuracy and error propagation.

A statistical and mathematical analysis capability should be complemented by an explicit decision modelling capability for market analysis. The modelling facilities should include: 'what if...' options; goal-seeking routines; and margin analysis from a range of marketing decisions, such as planning and monitoring of branch networks, competitive assessment, sales force management (including key accounts), development and testing of new products, product lifecycle management, branch positioning and market segmentation, and so on. All these market analyses have an explicit spatial dimension.

At present, the majority of uses of GIS in marketing (which are marketed frequently as 'Decision Support Systems'), are of the management information system type; historical data status reporting of sales and market share. There is a requirement for a more analytic impact reporting on, say, price elasticity, advertising effectiveness and site location and merchandise mix, which should be extended from their traditional market size/share format to incorporate financial investment appraisal. For instance, in retailing given the current economic recession, managers are considering whether they should optimise their short-run activities without concern for the long-term, and the potential impact of short-term decisions on their long-term business prospects.

4. FUTURE OUTLOOK

Information technology will never, in my view, be a source of sustainable competitive advantage; it will, however, become increasingly a competitive necessity. Ultimately, the power of a GIS in marketing is dependent upon the knowledge and skills of the people who design, develop and use the tool. It is important to appreciate that progress and developments will be dependent on our people. For the marketeer,

What is the GIS pay-off?
At present, it remains largely unknown.

In terms of investment appraisal, given the speed of technological advances and improving cost effectiveness, there remains the inevitable question:

Should we wait to make the investment?
No! If you can justify the decision as a business investment now, my recommendation would be to do it! Unfortunately, however, many organisations still view GIS as an administrative cost, rather than as business investment.

Recently, I posed the following question (Beaumont, 1991):

> "In the context of spatial DSS for market analysis, are our activities and developments consistent with tomorrow's flexible networked organisations focussed on customer service and sharing information across empowered staff?"

There is the real potential for GIS in marketing. While it is possible to criticise the existing GIS capabilities, it is important to develop the systems for tomorrow's business environment, not today's! Without the necessary vision, GIS will cause potential 'grid-lock' through data overloads, rather than providing useful and actionable information.

Finally, given my discussion, my personal research would highlight:

- spatial analysis and Decision Support Systems
- GIS and organisational information management.

Moreover, as Clarke (1990) highlighted, there is a requirement to move from '"consultancy" to "technology transfer"'.

REFERENCES

Baker, M. J. (1990) 'One more time – what is marketing', in M. J. Baker (ed.), *The Marketing Book*, Gower, Aldershot, pp. 3–9.

Beaumont, J. R. (1991a) *An Introduction to Market Analysis*, CATMOG 53, Geo Books, Norwich.

Beaumont, J. R. (1991b) 'Spatial decision support systems: some comments with regard to their use in market analysis', *Environment and Planning*, **23**(3), pp. 311–318.

Beaumont, J. R. and Clarke, M. (1992) 'Strategic information management in practice for marketing', in M. J. Baker (ed.), *Perspectives on Marketing Management*, Vol 2, John Wiley, Chichester.

Beaumont, J. R. and Sutherland, E. (1992) *Information Resources Management*, Butterworth-Heinemann, Oxford.

Blattberg, R. C. and Deighton, J. (1991) 'Interactive marketing: exploiting the age of addressability', *Sloan Management Review*, **33**(1), pp. 5–14.

Clarke, M. (1990) 'Regional science and industry: from consultancy to technology transfer', *Environment and Planning B*, **17**, pp. 257–268.

Dibb, S. L., Simkin, L., Pride, W. M. and Ferrell, O. C. (1991) *Marketing: Concepts and Strategies* (European Edn), Houghton Mifflin Co, London.

Earle, M. J. (1989) *Management Strategies for Information Technology*, Prebtice Hall, Englewood Cliffs, NJ.

Higby, M. A. and Farah, B. N. (1991) 'The status of marketing information systems, decision support systems and expert systems in the marketing function of US firms', *Information and Management*, **20**(1), pp. 28–35.

Piercy, N. (1990) 'Developing marketing information systems', in M. J. Baker (ed.), *The Marketing Book*, Gower, Aldershot, pp. 250–269.

Rapp, T. (1987) *MaxiMarketing*, McGraw-Hill, New York.

15 Combining spatial market information through mathematical modelling techniques to create geographic DSSs for market planning

Paul Kelley
Head of Business Development, GMAP Ltd

1. INTRODUCTION

Few people would disagree with the observation that most producers and retailers face increasing levels of competition, and that in most markets customers' demand for products and services becomes ever more discerning, regardless of relative upmarket or downmarket positioning. This state of affairs appears equally true whether viewing our UK domestic market or established international markets, and is becoming increasingly the case in the emerging markets of Eastern Europe. One of the ways in which organisations are responding to these tough marketing challenges is to utilise geographic and demographic data to increase product and service distribution effectiveness and target more accurately the promotional and selling effort.

Consequently, the GIS industry is emerging as the key component in the marketing arsenal, providing a framework for analysis that can support both strategic and tactical marketing needs through powerful data manipulation and visual display.

The crucial issue I want to address in this chapter is this: given that there now exists an array of marketing techniques designed to woo customers, how does an organisation make the most effective use of all of its marketing weaponry? Implicit in an organisation's use of marketing techniques is the major assumption that promotional marketing activities are the front-line fulfilment of the organisation's business strategy and objectives. In a growing number of organisations it is recognised that promotional marketing techniques can be deployed more effectively if their use is integrated as part of a wider understanding of the market environment in which they operate. Crucially, this process requires cross-functional strategic planning coordination between marketing departments and their colleagues in finance, operations, property, product development, human resources, and information technology.

2. GEOGRAPHICAL ANALYSIS AND SUCCESSFUL MARKETING ARE AS ONE

At this point the obvious question to ask is: where does a geographical Decision Support System fit into this analysis? For many businesses the geographical, or spatial dimension lies at the very heart of their markets. For example, for companies involved in the car, retail and financial services markets, geographical analysis is crucial to their understanding of distribution, customer demand and competition. At the most basic level, given that customers are out there somewhere and that businesses wish to reach them somehow, it would seem obvious that the geography of who is where and how consumers and providers interact is information that is likely to be useful. Yet, surprisingly, the potential use and power of geographical analysis has only very recently started to be applied beyond traditional 'map-on-the-wall' uses such as marking out sales territories and possibly identifying towns and cities with population levels of, say, above 100,000. And yet many businesses need to address crucial marketing questions which have a strong geographical element. For example, the issues facing the major players in the banking and building society market. These range from the high-level strategic to the need for local market initiatives and typically include:

- the need to re-appraise the number, location and function of branches
- consideration of alternative means of distribution – everyone is watching the First Direct branchless banking operation launched by Midland Bank with close interest
- the need to understand customer transaction and product acquisition patterns in relation to where people live, work and shop
- the desire to cross-sell additional products to existing customers
- the desire to attract and service a wider customer base.

Promotional marketing activities such as advertising, local marketing campaigns and direct mail campaigns need to be implemented and measured in the wider context of major geographic and demographic marketing issues that go before, such as:

- How is distribution organised?
- Where are products and services located?
- How do customers behave?
- Where are competitors located?

To illustrate the point in a car marketing context, manufacturer and dealer local target marketing efforts will be more successful where the manufacturer has good dealer market representation in relation to competition, and where particular models are promoted in line with the consumer characteristics being targeted. In this deceptively simple statement lies the crux of what good geographical intelligence can deliver. Geographical analysis and modelling techniques now exist to provide detailed insights to the crucial questions of who and where are the target customers, where the competition is located, where opportunities exist and therefore where your own activities should be concentrated.

3. COMBINING DISPARATE DATASETS TO CREATE INTELLIGENCE

The development of geographical referencing, as an increasingly important analytical tool for direct marketers and strategic planners alike, is closely linked to the rapid growth and accessibility of computing power (in the form of the ubiquitous PC) and the explosion in data capture through technological advances such as EPOS. Put simply, the environment now exists whereby data on customer types and market behaviour, households, population levels and competitors can be gathered together, manipulated and displayed via a computer terminal.

However, there is a further danger here, and that is for a geographical IT application to do no more than automate manual systems: the map on the wall becomes the map on the monitor. Whilst the storage, retrieval and display capabilities of computers bring convenience benefits, our objective at GMAP is to develop geographical systems that take and transform data beyond information and into intelligence, by employing mathematical modelling techniques that *combine* disparate datasets for supply and demand and identify the customer and revenue flows that lie between. The capability to understand and examine these *interactions* between consumers and suppliers is of crucial importance for all types of business, because the small area market intelligence that can be generated adds further to the efficiency and precision that is increasingly at the core of successful competitive strategies.

4. GEOGRAPHICAL DECISION SUPPORT SYSTEMS: DEVELOPMENT AND OUTPUTS

So, how is a Geographical DSS developed and what outputs are typical? Firstly, it is essential in my view to recognise that each and every application must vary to reflect differing market and individual business characteristics. Distribution arrangements vary in type and location, customer profiles and buying patterns vary for differing product types, and so on. All of which means that for a system to be meaningful and effective it must be specified to meet each client's particular objectives and unique market characteristics. However, the components of a typical system will use spatial interaction modelling techniques to include the following demand and supply outputs.

4.1 Demand

- Client's own sales data. One of the most valuable of data sources is each client's own information. Data used will typically include revenue data broken down into product groups, for each outlet or distribution point. Computerised data capture methods for payments and stock control are increasingly making organisations *data-rich but information-poor*. One of the benefits to be derived from developing a customised geographic decision support system is the increased usability of the client's existing data.
- Customer data captured either routinely, as in the financial services markets, or gathered through customer surveys, is used (where available) to help mathematically model customer and revenue flow *interactions* between home, work and product outlet points.
- Market research sources are used to identify market sizes and further support customer type and buying behaviour patterns. This information is modelled down to small area level (i.e. postal sectors, or even Enumeration Districts where appropriate)and cross-checked against observed client data.
- Census-derived data is used to establish small area population and household levels, broken down by age, sex and socio-economic groupings. The 1991 census produces around one billion items of statistical information gathered from 23 million households, and provides a potentially very rich source of information for planning and target marketing purposes. This presents the challenge to identify and to combine relevant data and make it usable for decision-making, an area in which spatial modelling and geographical display techniques are ideally suited.
- In addition to census-derived data, lifestyle databases have grown in importance in recent years through companies such as NDL being able to offer a database of several million consumers, giving details of lifestyle and consumer preferences linked to income levels.

4.2 Supply

Again, the clients' own data is valuable to identify both own and competitor's presence in the market-place. Infrastructure characteristics for all outlet locations and other relevant supply channels (such as ATMs for banks and building societies) are identified and weighted according to relative market strengths such as brand, product range, regional presence, and so forth.

Supplementary information is used to complete the supply side and thus build up a comprehensive market picture. Sources such as Yellow Pages and business sector-specific directories are also used to cross-reference and 'clean' the data.

Once all the data is assembled, mathematical models are written to reproduce expenditure patterns for each product group between all competitors and by each area of demand (both residence-based and work-based, as appropriate).

This process produces two major output categories:

1. What is? information showing the current market position for the client and all categories of competitor.
2. What if? analysis, enabling the user to examine the impacts of a wide range of scenarios, to support both planned changes and sensitivity testing (for example, to a competitor opening a new outlet).

5. USING LOCAL INFORMATION TO IMPROVE OVERALL RESULTS

Information created by developing a customised Geographic DSS can be viewed by mapping, tabulation and business graphics routines, and is typically examined through a series of client-specific *performance indicators*, examples of which include the following:

5.1 Residential indicators (e.g. by postal sector)

- Total expenditure
- Expenditure per head
- Market penetration
- Census data
  - population change
  - percentage population, age, sex, socio-economic groupings
  - economic groupings
  - actual population, as above
  - population densities, etc

5.2 All major and minor trading location indicators (i.e. shopping centre, retail park, secondary centre, out-of-town traders, etc.)

- observed and modelled sales for each trading location (i.e. number of outlets, by type
- sales/catchment populations – per capita revenues
- distances travelled
- modelled market shares.

By analysing local differences in market share and levels of competition, it becomes possible for marketing initiatives to be targeted in small areas where, for instance, market share and competition are relatively low, yet the customer type in certain postal sectors matches the target profile. In reality, we have found market shares vary hugely when viewed at the small area level. National shares of, say, 7% for a financial product vary between less than 1% to over 40% by small area.

Overall performance can be increased in two ways. Firstly, by identifying underperforming locations which offer the greatest potential, resources can be concentrated in the short-term to increase local market penetration. Secondly, in the longer term, distribution and outlet channels can be planned to shape the client's supply chain to meet consumer demand and competitor supply more effectively.

The power and accuracy of custom-built geographical decision support systems have been proven in recent years in markets as diverse as motor retailing, high street and out-of-town retailing for clothes, mixed goods, DIY, furniture, etc., financial services (banks and building societies), healthcare provision, pub and leisure markets, and utilities and public sector applications

Geographical analysis and modelling techniques originally researched and developed over a 20 year period at the University of Leeds' School of Geography are now being applied increasingly in overseas markets, in particular in the USA and Europe. Recent development work for a leading UK-based car manufacturer has included work in Italy, and is extending into other European countries. Whilst national geographies and data sources clearly differ, the same techniques operating successfully in the UK are proving themselves equally valuable in markets abroad.

5
Some Proprietary GIS Sources

16 Postcode geography: current situation and future developments

Dan Rickman
Independent Consultant

1. THE POSTCODE SYSTEM

Postcodes, in the format which is familiar today, were introduced in the 1960s by the Post Office. The main motivation is to assist sorting and delivery of mail in the UK. The postcode system is based around a four tier structure:

- Postcode *Area*
- Postcode *District*
- Postcode *Sector*
- *Unit* Postcode.

Postcodes are split into two parts; the outward code (the first half) and the inward code (the second half). For example, in the postcode MK42 9WA, MK42 is the outward part and 9WA is the inward part. MK (i.e. Milton Keynes) is the Postcode *Area*, MK42 (the outward part in full) identifies the *district*, MK42 9 determines the postcode *sector*. The outward code determines where the mail is sent for further sorting, the inward code is used for the detailed sorting by delivery staff.

The final part of the postcode which determines the unit postcode is made up of two letters, excluding the letters C, I, K, M, O, V and certain letter combinations. This allows up to 400 unit postcodes per sector, with approximately 9000 sectors in current use in the UK.

Larger users' postcodes are defined for business users with sufficient volumes of mail. These differ from other unit postcodes in that they will refer to one address or part of a building. There are 1.6 million small user postcodes in use, covering nearly 25 million addresses, and approximately 170,000 large user postcodes.

Each postcode should contain no more than 100 addresses. In practice, this varies considerably.

The Royal Mail produce and market the Postcode Address File (PAF). This is based on a mainframe database system which contains comprehensive and regularly updated information relating to postal addresses and postcodes. It is based on the following data sets stored by Royal Mail:

- localities file
- thoroughfare file
- thoroughfare description file
- building names file
- sub-building names file
- organisations file
- address file
- Mailsort file.

A variety of products based on this data are offered by the Royal Mail.

2. POSTCODE GEOGRAPHY

Postcodes were initially allocated Ordnance Survey National Grid co-ordinates in the 1970s and early 1980s to provide data for the Department of Transport Regional Highway Traffic Model. Travellers provided postcode information about start and destination of their journeys, and this was used to relate this information to the National Grid. This data has been maintained by the Office of Population Census and Surveys (OPCS) in England, Wales and Northern Ireland and the General Register Office (Scotland) – GRO(S) – in Scotland.

OPCS produce the Central Postcode Directory (CPD) which provides a 100m resolution OS grid reference for every unit postcode in England and Wales. This is updated at least bi-annually (on the basis of the latest PAF) and includes the following data:

- postcode
- year and month of introduction and termination if applicable
- OSGR (or Irish grid reference in Northern Ireland)
- NHS area code
- electoral ward code
- postcode user type (small or large)
- grid reference accuracy indicator
- country code
- ward code.

It is marketed to the private sector by the Royal Mail as the Postzon file.

The grid reference is taken from the first delivery point in the unit postcode. The grid reference is then either read from the appropriate large scale Ordnance Survey map to 100 m resolution, or is input from existing information (with a confidence estimate reflected in the grid reference accuracy indicator).

The situation in Scotland is different. GRO(S) maintain their part of the CPD to a 10 m resolution for each unit postcode. They have produced digitised unit postcode boundaries. These unit postcode boundaries have been designed as building blocks for Census Enumeration Districts in Scotland. GRO(S) are offering this data as a product, as described in the 1991 AGI Yearbook. The different approaches and the use of geography in the census is more fully discussed in *The Geography of the 1991 Census* (HMSO).

The accuracy of the information in CPD/Postzon has been widely discussed. A consultancy report in 1987 estimated that the accuracy for grid references was 72%. However, it must be stressed that this is some years out of date now, and even subsequent analyses have not been able to fully take into account the significant efforts by the Royal Mail and OPCS to improve the quality of the data. It is certainly advisable for potential users of this data to evaluate the accuracy of appropriate subsets within the context of the required use, and to estimate any additional effort to make necessary corrections.

3. SOURCES OF POSTCODE GEOGRAPHY RELATED DATA

There are a large number of resellers of postcode related data. For a comprehensive list see *Postcodes: The New Geography* (Raper, Rhind and Shepherd, 1992). Complementary data sets include:

- Enumeration District (ED) boundaries. These will be available from two suppliers – ED-Line from MVA Systematica in consortium with Taywood Data Graphics and the Ordnance Survey; and ED91 from Graphical Data Capture
- ward and other administrative boundaries from Ordnance Survey
- digital postcode sector boundaries – these are available from a variety of suppliers in a number of different formats. These include the Geoplan product produced in conjunction with the Royal Mail, and files input from Postzon by CACI, GeoMatrix and Bartholomews
- paper map products, including maps at varying scales from Bartholomews and Geographers A to Z
- digital postal area boundaries for Europe from the Automobile Association
- retail property data from Chas E Goad
- availability of postcoded data from British Telecom through directories and PhoneBase on CS.

There are also a number of suppliers of software to handle and manipulate address and postcode related data. These are listed by Raper, Rhind and Shepherd (1992).

4. SURVEY OF POSTCODE APPLICATIONS

Any review of postcode data applications has to be incomplete as the scope for utilising postcode based information will include:

- any applications which contain address or address range based data;
- applications where postcodes can be used as a method of linking external data sets. For example, this will include any surveys including population samples as people will almost always know their own postcode and almost never know their OS grid reference!

There is a wide variety of organisations which are either current or potential users of postcode data. These include:

- Central Government
- Local Government
- Health Authorities
- Retail companies
- Direct Marketing data companies
- Lifestyles data providers
- Distribution companies
- Armed Forces
- Police Forces
- Utilities
- Environmental Agencies
- Academic institutions
- Emergency Services
- Financial Services Sector
- Cable TV companies
- Consultancy/Service Bureaux
- Market Research Bureaux
- Estate Agents/Advertising Companies/Bailiffs, etc.

The companies making most use of postcode related data for geographical analysis include the retail companies and market analysis companies.

Marketing applications depend upon customer segmentation, which can include demographic, geodemographic, lifestyles and psychographics related data. The key characteristic is that it is indicative of relevant need, preferences and consumption patterns. The segmentation must also be:

- measurable, i.e. using variables which can relatively easily be identified and measured

- economically viable
- accessible either geographically or through cost-effective media.

Commercial organisations have used cluster analysis to analyse the key lifestyle measures amongst the 9000 census variables. Examples are CACI, which takes 79 variables into account, and CDMS, which uses 55 variables. Using this type of profiling provides a method of collecting information for customer surveys. By adding locational information they can correlate information on income, age, sex, household size and occupation to provide a better understanding of the current and potential customer base.

GIS can be used to integrate this data with other data sources to provide analyses by ED, postcode sector or other appropriate geographical breakdown down to unit postcode. A wide range of consumer related databases are available for integration with these systems.

There is an increasing amount of detailed data becoming available to support market analyses. For example, NDL Direct Marketing have information based on 10 million lifestyle questionnaires completed over approximately the past five years. They suggest that they have on average up to 1000 forms for every postcode sector in the UK. If so, this may require integration at unit postcode level, where possible, to make most effective use of this data. This, together with the production of Small Area Statistics (SAS) from the 1991 census, which will be broken down to Part Postcode Unit (PPU), will allow far more detailed analysis of data to be undertaken.

There are many misleading ways of presenting population based information. Martin and Bracken give some interesting examples and discussions of the issues, including some detailed algorithms and procedures for analysing socio-economic data using postcodes and EDs.

Apart from retail marketing, applications have been described in community healthcare, analysing local house price applications, town planning, local economic analysis and education research. Raper, Rhind and Shepherd (1992) include detailed descriptions of these applications and references.

5. PROGRESS TO DATE WITH GIS IN THE ROYAL MAIL

The key stages have been:

- feasibility study for postcode
- cost/benefit analysis
- pilot study
- review of strategic scope for use of GIS in Royal Mail, in particular for deliveries and collections (this is currently in progress).

The key results of the studies so far (which we can include in this paper) have indicated that:

- the postcode is becoming a building block for the design and operation of key business activities in the Royal Mail, such as deliveries (which involves over 60,000 staff in the UK) and collections (i.e. collecting mail from post boxes and large users). The use of postcodes is particularly important in the Royal Mail's substantial programme to automate letter sorting;
- to achieve this, the unit postcode must have some 'geographic integrity', in the sense that it represents a sensible area that can be navigated around, and that the postcodes can be related to geographically sensible postman's walks
- while there are direct benefits for postcodes, the key benefit areas are within the operational areas of the Royal Mail, whereas the main costs of GIS implementation (systems and data capture) will be borne by postcodes staff
- therefore a strategic and coordinated approach is required to achieve sufficient business benefits for Royal Mail to justify an investment in GIS
- as a national organisation, the 'cost per seat' of a GIS implementation is a key limiting factor. The prevalence of PCs in regional offices and the cheaper licence costs for PC-based GIS solutions make it difficult to cost justify a UNIX-based solution which would require major hardware purchases and greater licence fees. However, the market for PC-based GIS solutions is very limited, especially if raster and vector mapping is required. The GIS solution will also have to handle Northern Ireland National Grid coordinates, as well as the UK National Grid
- the 1:10000 map scale is the only possible cost effective option for GB coverage
- there is a significant amount of data to be captured. To optimise the data capture process a more sophisticated set up is required. This can also be used for complex analysis by the Address Management Centre and one-off data handling jobs (such as generation of bespoke boundaries)
- there are several ways to represent unit postcodes. It can be argued that postcodes are point, line and/or area entities and the representation will impact on the potential for use in internal and external application areas
- a pilot was carried out during 1992, which looked at:
  - data capture costs using a range of options for data capture, i.e. capturing unit postcodes as points, line and areas
  - use of external datasets in data capture, such as digitised sector boundaries, Postzon and GRO(S) data
  - assessment of practicalities of working with Ordnance Survey in developing Address-Point data
- on the basis of the pilot, a scoping study has now been initiated which will identify the main benefit areas and prepare a plan which will ensure that these

benefits are realised within a realistic timescale

- once this has been completed, authority to proceed with a divisional rollout of GIS will be sought from senior management within the Royal Mail.

6. GENERAL LESSONS LEARNT IN DEVELOPING GIS AT THE ROYAL MAIL

This section is, of necessity, a general discussion with particular reference to the requirements definition stage based on experience at the Royal Mail and other large organisations investigating the potential use of GIS.

As experience of implementing IT has grown several common factors emerged as the prime causes of project failure, and these included some clear estimates of the 'cost of poor quality' in systems development. The primary aim of a 'quality' IT system is essentially one that meets the needs of users. As systems development moves through the project lifecycle, errors are created which will prevent user requirements being properly met. It has been estimated that the cost of errors multiplies tenfold as projects progress from requirements through to development and implementation. It is clearly essential that appropriate attention is paid to user requirements both to ensure that the systems produced are similar to those expected and to avoid costly errors.

The growth of the use of (especially PC-based) packages software has helped encourage an environment in which the problems of bespoke software development are frequently overlooked. Despite the flexibility of packages and their relatively low cost when compared to more traditional approaches, it should be remembered that:

- requirements analysis is still an essential component as successful projects must be requirements not technology-led. It is, nevertheless, feasible and often desirable to use packages on a prototyping basis as discussed below
- there will always be a degree of customisation required to meet organisational needs
- packages are limited in scope (almost by definition). Sometimes it is easier and faster to use a 3GL approach to problem solving rather than try and develop highly complex macro-based functions. For example, it is not uncommon to see complex spreadsheet macros which have been developed where a simple program could do this job faster
- specifically the GIS market is still relatively immature, and the functionality of GIS packages is still a significant restriction. Care should be taken that using a GIS package is actually better than a bespoke development. There are examples where selection of a GIS package has generated the vendor's production of significant bespoke additions to the functionality of the product

with the main cost borne by the user.

The key problem with requirements analysis is that it is a vital stage of a project and it is hard to get right. This is because:

- requirements definition is a complex 'multi-disciplinary' process which requires staff who can understand user requirements and translate them correctly into a systems-oriented requirements document
- requirements often change in large organisations. This is due to organisational changes and shifting business conditions and requirements
- a common sense approach is required. While methodologies can be useful they can be misapplied especially for interactive systems, e.g. one such system recently described to the author which had been developed using well established analysis techniques had several hundred menu choices, which meant that it took the user several minutes to find a given menu choice
- it is easy to miss out those aspects of the requirement which the users require as too obvious to explain to a systems developer.

To minimise these problems, it is very useful to break complex application areas into sets of more straightforward areas. This is increasingly becoming possible with the widespread acceptance of multi-tasking and the multi-user operating systems which can support distributed, client-server based computing models. This allows a strategic view to be taken for data, while building applications which are straightforward and share data and functions with standardised components such as relational and/or free-text databases, word processors and spreadsheets.

The use of methodologies can be effective, if appropriately used. Structured methods such as SSADM have been applied effectively (up to the logical design level) for GIS developments and the CCTA and Local Government Management Board (LGMB) are currently sponsoring work to examine the use of SSADM for GIS in more detail (this is scheduled to be available in 1994). Formal methods such as Z and VDM have not been used for commercial GIS development to date (as far as the author is aware).

The specific problems for GIS are related to the two universal 'laws' of geography (Raper, Rhind and Shepherd, 1992):

- most things influence most other things in some way (hence the wide applicability and multi-functional nature of GIS data)
- nearby things are usually more similar than things which are far apart (hence the benefit of spatial analysis).

These factors arguably are at the root of what gives GIS a special flavour as an application area and why a strategic view of requirements is required to ensure that needs are properly addressed. The next section examines the strategic issues in more detail.

6.1 Strategic analysis

There are many approaches to the development of information systems and information technology strategies. There are two aspects of strategy development which often affect the potential use of GIS, irrespective of the way in which the strategy has been developed:

- Information Management, in particular geographic information management, is not addressed in strategy development
- GIS is covered inadequately (or not at all) as a strategic IT technique within application areas.

The reasons for this include:

- lack of awareness of GIS
- many organisations process geographic information using paper-based systems with no IT component. These can be overlooked in an IT-led strategy process
- GIS is a 'horizontal' technique which can cover many 'vertical' application areas such as operations, marketing and asset management
- as a rule of thumb, data collection for 'conventional' IT constitutes up to 30–40% of project costs and therefore the strategic considerations focus on the IT systems rather than the data. For GIS, data capture costs can typically be as high as 70–80% of overall project costs. The strategic significance of this is not always appreciated.

The absence of GIS within a strategic framework presents some significant problems, which include:

- coordinating the introduction of new technology, identifying who should be responsible and how new procedures are defined
- establishing data 'ownership' across departments and with the data collecting organisations, where applicable
- making it difficult to see whether a GIS is appropriate for the geographic information processing requirement, or whether another technology such as Document Image Processing would be more appropriate, how GISs should relate to other IS/IT and how to prioritise GIS within overall IT expenditure
- ensuring that potentially significant business problems which GIS could help address which involve more than one section of a department may be missed.

For example, rather than providing a Drawing Office GIS, looking at a joint system with the users of the Drawing Office data
- ensuring awareness of GIS at senior level and, in particular, identifying the best opportunities for introducing GIS within an organisation.

Ensuring that the issue of GISs is addressed at a strategic level involves reviewing the following issues:

- Undertaking a geographic information audit, looking at current users of paper-based geographic information. This includes a wide variety of information. As an indication of the breadth of geographically related information, the following is a non-exhaustive list of some types of geographic information which should be considered:
  - paper maps, especially those overlaid with organisation-specific data
  - address related information
  - information about location of assets (fixed and mobile)
  - distribution networks;
  - geodemographic data
  - information about catchment area constraints, e.g. land use, planning constraints;
- reviewing the information needs of other departments, which may not currently be met due to the constraints of a paper-based system.This requires looking at potentially significantly different ways of working
- reviewing existing IT systems which may contain geographical data (as a rule, when geographic coordinates are stored as numbers they tend to have a significant error rate)
- reviewing existing IT systems which could be enhanced/replaced by the use of GIS.

The introduction of a GIS on a strategic basis involves three key strands of activity which will develop in parallel as GIS is increasingly used:

1. Identifying geographic data and establishing data standards for exchange.
2. Creating an internal (and frequently an external) market for this data.
3. Developing GIS systems which can be integrated with other IT systems using appropriate Open Systems standards.

There are various tools and techniques for strategic analysis which can be utilised for this process, including methodologies such as PRISM. These methodologies are based on a business and not technology led approach, and aim to produce:

- a Business Problem Definition Report

- a Feasibility Study for each application area identified.

The issues in applying strategic methodologies to GIS are to ensure:

- awareness of the broad potential and scope of GIS within an organisation
- a realistic assessment of costs. For example, many projects are not started because a solution based on large scale Ordnance Survey maps is considered too large, where it may be feasible to meet 80% of requirements by using smaller map scales
- awareness of the technology and how it is likely to change over a strategic time frame.

7. SUMMARY

This chapter summarises where we are and how we intend to proceed. The Royal Mail recognises the wider significance of the project for all users of postcode related data and the growing postcode geography market. It is for these reasons that the Royal Mail has participated in an industry-wide collaboration led by the LGMB to develop of an address standard. BS7666 part 3, which includes a definition of an address for mailing purposes (the Postcode Address File), has now been introduced as a British standard.

The Royal Mail are happy to receive input from interested parties regarding the development of postcode geography products and requirements for enhancement of the currently available product set*.

REFERENCES

Martin, D. and Bracken, I (eds.) *New ways of Representing Socio-Economic Data*, University of Wales, Dept. of City and Regional Planning.

Raper, Rhind and Shepherd (1992) *Postcodes: The New Geography*, Longman Technical and Scientific, London.

---

*Editor's Note: Any enquiries should be sent to Mr Stuart Pretty at Royal Mail, Address Management Centre, 3/4 St George's Business Centre, St George's Square, Portsmouth PO1 3AX. The author would like to thank the Royal Mail for their assistance with this chapter. (Progress to date describes the position in mid-1993.)

17 Maps – the base tool for GIS

Mark L Edgerley
Ordnance Survey

1. INTRODUCTION

Much analytical thinking within a business requires information about 'who' will undertake 'what' task. Another vital element is often 'where', the geographical position of much data and its relationship to other deciding factors can be sourced through an overview of the area being studied. Ordnance Survey can provide that overview through its various Map Products.

The Concise Oxford Dictionary defines a map as:

> "representation usually on plane surface of (part of) earth's surface, showing physical and political features etc....."

It therefore follows that within a Geographic Information System (GIS) undertaking that same analytical task, a fundamental ingredient must still be mapping; now, however, a digital map is required rather than the traditional sheet of paper.

2. GIS, DIGITAL MAPPING AND ORDNANCE SURVEY.

Digital mapping simply is:

> "The representation of cartographic images (maps) in an alphanumeric form such that they can be held in and manipulated by computers."

Ordnance Survey has a history of over 200 years producing maps. We are now a government agency with a staff of around 2300. From a headquarters in Southampton providing support for almost a 100 survey teams based all over England, Scotland and Wales, we have a surveyor based very near most geographic changes. Our task is to survey change shortly after it occurs – in urban areas we would define this as normally within six months.

Some 20 years ago we started to invest heavily in the skills and technology required to produce our graphic products by means of – then very new – digital techniques. It became clear that this in-house tool had a potential for supply outside our organisation. Initially, our customers were limited to our traditional public utilities and local government markets. As our product range has expanded and the availability of the hard/software has increased, our markets have widened to take in the complete spectrum of industry, commerce, communication and transport.

When we refer to our products, we often quote a map scale; this would normally be the scale of the graphic (paper) map produced from the data in-house. Map scale is often thought to be irrelevant in the digital era: of course, you have a lot of functionality within a GIS to adjust the map scale, but the scale gives a number of clues about whether a digital map is fit for your purpose.

The smaller the map scale, the larger its descriptive representative faction, the greater the geographic area within each map unit. Therefore, a 1:250,000 map file would contain basic information such as roads, railways, urban settlements, rivers, some boundaries and names associated, for an area of 50×50 km. A 1:1250 map would cover a fairly small, 500×500 m area of geography, but would detail buildings down to the size of a domestic garage, and include details of house names and numbers as well as a greater range of local government and parliamentary boundaries. Clearly, the absolute accuracy of the map information is related to its source scale.

Ordnance Survey continues its work to develop capture methods that may lead to a single master archive map that would be all things to all users. Until that dream is fulfilled, there will be incidents of features such as major roads appearing on some but not all of our maps of a particular area. For example, it is very quick and easy to add a motorway in to our 1:250,000 data where it will be used to produce our motoring atlas range; the very detailed survey for the 1:1250 map cannot be completed until completion of the road build, which is often only days before the road is opened for public use.

3. DIGITAL MAPPING IN A COMMERCIAL GIS.

The choice of the most appropriate digital mapping for applied GIS in marketing, retailing and distribution depends to a large extent upon the activities the user wishes to pursue. Ordnance Survey has data products suitable for many different applications. In each case, the GIS concept allows the user to integrate other database information with the map base, superimposing on the map view, for example, a scatter of predefined symbols or perhaps colour banding defining areas where a set of criteria or given phenomena are evident. The interpretation of the resulting analysis is then made more effective by reference to the underlying geography represented by the mapping.

An example would perhaps be when planning a site for a distribution centre. For instance, access to the motorway network would be important in this case, but the siting of a superstore near a motorway without careful consideration of the relative constituency of shoppers would be reckless. In the first example, the motorway is a benefit; in the second it might be a physical barrier encouraging shoppers to visit a rival.

To establish which digital mapping product(s) are most appropriate for particular applications, let us consider a range of commercial business functions.

3.1 Management of premises and facilities

Almost all business operates from offices, shops, factories or similar fixed premises. Whether a company employs a sub-contractor to manage these resources or uses its own staff, a good knowledge of the geography of the premises is vital to ensure that the best return is gained from this large investment in business infrastructure.

Ordnance Survey Land_Line map data – of urban areas sourced at a scale of 1:1250 and of rural areas at 1:2500 – can be introduced into the most sophisticated GIS systems, or into simpler CAD-based technology. It can offer immediate benefit; the maps already show every building, most fences, every road and are kept up to date.

Land_Line data is already available for every urban area, together with a significant number of rural areas. Full national cover is scheduled to be available by April 1995.

Since these are the same digital maps which are increasingly used by local government planners when dealing with development proposals, the whole business of property and infrastructure management is made easier. Details of site layout, the provision and location of utility services, relationships to neighbouring properties, scope and location of land available for development, and all the other myriad of property management issues can be integrated with the mapping to provide a comprehensive geographic database.

Overlaying service alignments identifying emergency infrastructure, planning maintenance schedules, modelling development proposals – these and similar tasks become much simpler using a map-based GIS. The ability to work through alternative options without losing the basic information must be seen as a bonus.

3.2 Supplier/customer locations

Every efficient business should want to know about the geographical distribution of suppliers, agents or customers. This information is essential to planning the logistics of the company, and maximising the return on investments in procuring raw materials, in meeting the expectations of intermediaries, and in satisfying the needs of customers' profitability.

Perhaps it is a question of siting a distribution centre, or establishing optimum territories for sales staff. It could be that the products dealt with have a limited life-cycle so transportation and storage delays are critical. By using smaller scale mapping in digital form, these analyses become much easier. It is no longer a question of simply sticking pins in a wall map. Using a map-based GIS, supplier and customer databases can be linked to the mapping so that the analysis of these business aspects by geographic area becomes a matter of routine.

By choosing a range of data sets from differing map sources, comparisons can be made quickly and efficiently. First perhaps over a wide area – national and regional (e.g. show all customers of a given category in the south east of England). Then having identified a specific aspect by zooming in to a larger scale map, a more detailed inspection of relationships within local environment can be analysed (e.g. identify all customers within a given radius of a nominated depot highlighting delivery day).

Each business will have its own applications and needs for information, but again, OS has a range of digital mapping products which can enhance the GIS analysis of these issues. OS small scale data at 1:625,000 includes the principle road networks and major urban centres and destinations. It is available nationally in five data subsets. Ideal for national and regional distribution and location modelling. It can form an excellent 'index map' for our other more detailed products, enabling the user to quickly select the relevant area of the country for further investigation on a more detailed OS data product.

1:250,000 national data is derived from the mapping used to produce our Routemaster and Atlas printed products. The digital data contains, in three subsets, all settlements from major conurbations to small hamlets, all roads from motorways to country lanes between villages, and a good selection of roads within the urban areas themselves. Other features include railways, airports, tolls and serve gradients as well as a wide range of landscape information.

The geometric structure of both these data products make them ideal for modelling business activities at a regional level, including the benefit of polygon building and network analysis. Applications already include route planning, calculating shortest route by distance or time, graphical map output, distribution and fleet control and statistical analysis for social, environmental and marketing needs on a user-defined basis.

For many lay users, however, the Ordnance Survey map is the 1:50,000 scale Landranger, the modern version of the equally famous One Inch Map. The Landranger is unquestionably the most widely used of all OS products within commerce and industry, offering significant areas of geography within each map while providing a wealth of detail about the landscape and built environment.

OS continues its preparatory work to produce a full vector dataset based on the 1:50,000; we are, however, able to offer the map series as a full colour raster product. This competitively priced product forms an excellent backdrop image for GIS systems. The quality checks on the data ensures that after scanning any scale or rotational distortion is removed, also major features are edge matched. A national data set of the height information from this map series is available as either a vector contour set or Digital Terrain Model.

OS was pleased to announce recently the production of a dataset derived from our 1:10,000 map series. This map series gives a detailed overview of the nation, the specification enabling the identification of all but the smallest property. This is again only currently available as a raster image, this time as a high resolution mono image at a resolution of 400 dpi. The height information from this series can be made available as a separate data set in the form of a vector set of contours or the data to produce a Digital Terrain Model.

Height data is widely used in the communications industry for radio wave propagation analyse. Its use within businesses managing the environment is growing. The European Commission requirement to undertake environmental impact studies as part of large development planning cycle has encouraged the take up of this type of data.

3.3 Logistics, distribution and route finding

Perhaps the most problematic aspect of business in today's world is simply moving about. Whether it is getting goods to the market place, transporting raw materials or simply making progress through the traffic to that important business meeting, traffic and travel are a headache, a major cost for many commercial and industrial operations.

All the datasets already mentioned have a part to play in the navigation of the nation. OS does have one specialist product for this market, developed from our Land_Line product, OSCAR (Ordnance Survey Centre Alignments of Roads) which is in effect an imaginary centre line drawn down the centre of every motorable road carriageway. The data is currently available for all major urban areas in GB, and as complete coverage of South Wales, the South West and the South and East of England. Full national coverage will be available by the end of 1993. The vector, link and node data has attributes added carrying details of D Tp road classification, road names and length of links. Once the national dataset is available, OS will concentrate on an exciting upgrade programme to widen both the range of attributes and the form of the data supplied. Using the functionality of your own GIS, it is thus possible to link in attributes derived from your own database information.

Use of OSCAR within command and control as well as traffic modelling modules of GIS is increasing. The availability of ground-based and satellite positioning systems at affordable prices opens the opportunities to remotely monitor 'at risk' moving objects. Applications known to us at the moment range from temperature monitors of perishable goods, location of security vehicles, control of emergency vehicles, even the location of people through the carrying of a small transponder.

3.4 Local and address level location

For many commercial applications in retailing and marketing, the ability to determine customer locations to either local (e.g. postcode) or even individual address level is highly desirable. OS also has a range of products for these applications.

OS has collaborated with others to make available the ED_Line family of products. These digital boundary sets, based on the 1991 Census Enumeration Districts (ED), form a bridge between census data and the location. Using ED_Line census data for social, economic or demographic purposes, information can be modelled down to very small areas within the community, normally approximately 160 households, a powerful tool for target marketing.

Boundary_Line is available currently for England and Wales. This definitive local, national and European electoral and administrative boundary data is offered as fully maintained information, enabling links to be made to a range of real world datasets.

We have just launched Address_Point. The product will be released in stages over the next three years, and will form a register of every postal address in Great Britain. Giving each address a national grid reference will enable the easy link between any address-based database and the map, therefore enabling links to non addressed data – a true 'bridge' for any GIS user. Initially the data will include postal number, road name, postal town, postcode, national grid reference and a unique OS Address Point reference. We will work with Royal Mail to ensure a very high level of completeness and accuracy; production of the product will result in improvements to Royal Mail's own Postal Address File. Plans are already in-hand to upgrade the product to contain other address related information. This national reference product will introduce new standards into the market place, and our network of local offices across the country will ensure that the products are both complete and current.

We have an increasing range of gazetteer products containing details of all the names on our printed map series. Currently, the 1:50,000 gazetteer is available to compliment our raster product of this map series. Development of the business case for a national gazetteer of the names on our 1:10,000 series is in hand.

3.5 Specialist marketing, distribution and retailing applications

At the end of 1991, OS announced its willingness to collaborate with specialist users of digital data to make available new map-based products. We have many years of experience working with the publishing trade on the production of maps and atlases, and we wanted to take that expertise into the GIS market place. A limited number of products have already been announced, and work on many more is at a very advanced stage. We are still actively seeking partners with ideas that, perhaps by linking to OS, could reach a wider and more profitable market.

We wish to exploit the benefits of our data products to the full.

OS is also able to tailor its products for the specific one-off market. By using the various GIS packages available to us, our expert staff can change, adapt and add to our standard data the information you require. By combining products we can deliver your specification map information. Recently, we have produced Land_Line data with building height information added, height information tailored for specialist flood potential assessment, contoured Land_Line data and 'clipped' datasets, where some of the information has been removed from the standard data to facilitate its use where the full set was not applicable for the task in hand.

4. DELIVERY OF ORDNANCE SURVEY DIGITAL DATA.

Each data product is available on a range of magnetic media, $^1/_2$" tape, cartridges and floppy disc. Most data is transferred to users as a system independent character file (ASCII or EBCDIC) data transfer format. OS currently offers National Transfer Format (NTF) version 1.1 as standard; we shall be upgrading all our products to the British Standard, NTF v2.0, from November 1993 onwards. A limited range of products are offered as a value added service in Digital eXchange Format (DXF) especially for CAD-based applications.

While there are already hundreds of users of Ordnance Survey data products in a very wide variety of systems, potential users should always check with their software supplier regarding the feasibility of using OS digital map data of a particular type in their system, and on the translation processes necessary to enable that system to 'read' the OS data. Users must remember that the ability to pursue a particular GIS application is as much a matter of whether the chosen software and system has the necessary functionality to perform the required data manipulations and analyses as it is a question of choosing the correct digital map for the purpose.

5. CONCLUSION

Ordnance Survey has more than two centuries of experience in meeting the changing needs of those who require good geographic information. OS has been involved in digital mapping since its infancy, and has gained a worldwide reputation in recognition of its experiences in this area. With a growing nationally based portfolio of digital mapping products for GIS, OS is ideally placed to fulfil the needs of those in commerce and industry who are learning of the benefits of GIS and who wish to take advantage of them in the pursuit of commercial efficiency and profitability.

Our policy of constant product enhancement will ensure that OS continues to make 'plans' for your GIS.

(Editors Note: Obtaining OS digital data: details of terms and conditions of supply as well as the data is readily available from: Ordnance Survey Digital Sales Romsey Road Maybush Southampton SO9 4DH. Customer Information Line: Southampton (0703) 792773

There is a team of marketing and account executives available to offer specialist advise and information on the full range of OS products. Call the information line for the contact point for person most appropriate to your industry and location.)

18 Mapping out your business with AA data

Christopher Greenwood
Kingswood Ltd

1. INTRODUCTION

This paper fall into three parts, covering the historical development of the Automobile Association's (AA) digital database, describes the main features in the data and their benefits to GIS users, and finally, outlines some of the uses to which the data is put.

2. DIGITAL MAPPING FROM AA

The AA is the largest motoring organisation in the UK with over 7.5 million members. It is also in the *Guinness Book of Records* for the largest single print run for its publication of the AA Members' Handbook.

The AA has four digital databases at present. Firstly, the Great Britain database used to publish all the AA Road Atlases, Members' Handbooks and other specialist maps; secondly, a digital database of Europe stretching from Eire to the East of the Black countries in Western Europe; and finally, a database of Central London stretching from Hammersmith to Docklands.

The AA is in the process of digitising its conurbation mapping. The conurbation mapping shows town centres in significantly more detail than the main GB data, but not every street is shown. Road names are given in the database rather than the road numbers in the national mapping.

2.1 History

An important landmark in the History of AA publishing was a copyright agreement reached in 1950s by Mr Cann-Evans, the then Chief cartographer of the AA, and the Ordnance Survey to give a licence to publish maps of the UK for a one off payment of £10,000. The agreement continued for some years until 1987, when it was found that a licence did not cover the use that the AA had identified their members required for larger scale data. Continuation of the agreement would have entailed the AA paying a per copy royalty fee to Ordnance Survey rather than an extension of the one-off fee from the previous agreement.

The AA then decided to create its own database. Satellite photography was digitised at a base data scale of 1:100,000. The work took a period of 12 months, using up to 77 people full-time to generate the first mapping coverage at a scale of 1:500,000 used in the members' handbook. The full coverage at 1:200,000 detail took a further 18 months.

The satellite pictures were augmented by data from aerial photography, ground checking using the AA Patrol and also from the AA's own archives.

Because the data is also used for large volume paper publications, it has enormous public exposure and comment. The data is revised continuously during the year by the AA Cartographic Research Department. The following year's atlases are prepared for publication during the preceding July and August, at which point digital updates of the data are available. Great care is taken to correctly define at what point during the coming year new roads will be opened, and to ensure that they are correctly mapped. The correctness of these predictions is looked at very competitively in the map publishing business.

The European database base mapping is derived from the ONC (Operations Navigation and Charts) mapping. Further detail has been added from out of copyright material, and through association with the other European Touring Clubs and Mapping Agencies. Preparation of the database has taken over two years at a cost of over £500,000; it has been updated twice during the course of the work.

The data has also benefited from the AA European Routes database. This information has been used to give printed details for holiday makers or business travellers. AA members are encouraged to comment on the routes; one particular member regularly produces 24 page travelogues of road changes, road numbering and signposting details; this information is used by the AA to improve the quality of the mapping.

This data will be used for the preparation of the AA's forthcoming series of European Digital Maps. The digital mapping is one of the first commercially available databases that gives the whole of Europe as a continuous sheet of mapping on a since projection. Currently, the data is on an orthogonal axis with a kilometre grid. The database will also be converted to spherical coordinates in the near future.

The main European data is on the same projection as the European Postal Polygons mapping, and can be overlayed onto it. The base mapping for the polygons is at a smaller scale than the main database, and owing to generalisation there are some cases where boundaries are 'in the surf'.

3. TECHNICAL FEATURES

With the exception of the postal area, the databases have been designed primarily for use by AA for publishing. One of the benefits of both the Great Britain mapping and the European mapping is that the feature codes for the data are designed to allow maps at different scales to be published from them. Feature codes, like library codes, identify what a particular line segment or point within the database represents. For example, a single carriage B-road needed to compete the detail on a 1:200,000 publication of the mapping has a feature code 32.51. By selecting sets of feature codes relevant to smaller scales, complete maps can be built up which are cartographically attractive; an important advantage to the GIS community, where the line between a cluttered map and one that is too sketchy to convey useful information is often thin.

Since the road data is coded according to road type, for example dual or single carriageway, and by using the town sprawl information, a measurement of urban congestion can be gained. A frequent use of the data is in drive time analysis. A number of GIS products allow the user to determine, for example, how far from a particular site a proposed retail development or a warehouse a driver can be expected to travel in a given time. The data can then provide the basis for sophisticated modelling of the expected catchment area.

The AA use a simple ASCII format known as 'Map Data'. This has been readily translated into leading GIS software formats. The base data for the Great Britain database is 90 MBytes and for European data 144 MBytes.

3.1 Raster data

The data has also been successfully used in its raster format by a number of GIS systems. The AA have been able to supply data at a number of different scales directly from their Scitex Raster Editing Workstation. Although this is a very cost-effective way of getting high quality map images on screen, it has the drawbacks of not having the 'intelligence' of road numbers or names attached to the data, and is less flexible in the way in which it can be used, for example, in zooming in and out.

In addition, the cartographic editing of the map data can, for example, separate out a river and a road that run close and parallel to each other and that would otherwise fall on top of each other during printing. This is done when the raster image is created. The vector data from which the raster image is made is therefore free from this distortion.

3.2 Compatibility with other data

A key requirement for any spatial database is that other data has to fit with it. Comparisons of the Great Britain database with large scale Ordnance Survey mapping, the Royal Mail Postal Boundary files which are digitised from larger scale Ordnance Survey mapping and the Royal Mail PAF database with 100 m precision have all been successful. The data has the advantage of coming from a single survey and offering a 'seamless' mapping.

3.3 Data availability

The data can be provided in a number of different ways, either by type of object (e.g. primary road), by area (e.g. county, region or country) or by scale; for example, the difference between the 4" to the mile atlas and the 1:500,000 Members' Handbook. The data license is normally purchased at a one-off price, and annual updates are available. The data is competitively priced.

4. USES OF THE DATA

4.1 The Great Britain database

This is the most widely used of the AA datasets to date. It has been used for retail planning, in the financial sector, by international oil companies, as a backdrop for telecommunication coverage analysis and for environmental and conservation mapping. The database is at an appropriate scale for use within a GIS system for both national and regional studies.

Typical uses of the data by oil companies involve the prediction of change in market share by altering pricing policy, investment in forecourt facilities and design, and the opening and closing of petrol stations by the company or its competitors. The Great Britain database has been suitable for these studies as it has an appropriate level of detail to allow the developments to be placed in their context, and the road system can be used for network analysis to predict traffic flows.

Environmental and conservation groups have been using the data to provide background mapping to mark pollution problem areas, sites of special scientific interest and as base mapping for coastal erosion studies. They have used the mapping both on-screen and also as a base mapping for their own paper maps for specialist groups.

The AA also use their own data internally. The mapping interface for their RoadWatch database, which was designed to grid reference traffic-related incidents, uses the handbook level data. This positional information is then used to determine the roads affected, and also which radio station areas need to be informed of the situation.

4.2 Global positioning

Global Positioning Systems (GPS) at consumer prices are becoming available, and will undoubtedly continue to fall dramatically in price over the next decade, assuming that the satellites are not taken out of service by the United States. Typical accuracies for non differential detectors (i.e. where there is no base station) are of the order of 100 m. This is of the same order as the mapping database accuracy. Trials with GPS and other tracking data have shown the data to have a suitable coverage for background mapping. Software systems that can use the data with a GPS signal often have the ability to snap the tracking symbol of the vehicle to the road database. The pitfall here is to ensure that the symbol does not take the wrong turning at a level crossing.

4.3 The European database

The first use of the European Database was for a holiday company to generate routes to and between their travel destinations in Europe, and to help locate their destinations on travel maps. They were able to use the road network to calculate the best routes for their clients. The data is also being used by a national telecommunications company to help examine the opportunities for business development in Europe.

The European Polygons have an important role to play in European mapping for strategic planning. An example of this is an oil company with a known and large customer base over Europe. They were able to use the postcode information in their addresses to determine the approximate location of their major customers. In this type of study, the exact position of the customer is probably of lesser importance. In a strategic study – for example the planning of different distribution scenarios – the forecast of future demand will often be subject to greater uncertainty than the geographical location accuracy offered by the first digit or digits of a postcode.

5. CONCLUSION

The AA digital data sets offer comprehensive small scale mapping of Great Britain and Europe. The data sets, though originally geared towards the uses of the motorist, have been well structured and are suitable for general use, and are both reliable and current. The data is competitively priced and available in a number of different GIS formats.

6
Case Studies

19 Making a business case for IT in sales and marketing: a hypothetical case study

Geof Leigh
Managing Director, Bayleigh Business Services Ltd

1. INTRODUCTION

Before discussing the potential impact of automation in sales and marketing, it is worthwhile asking ourselves why we are interested in improving this function, and, indeed, why it is so important to us (Figure 19.1).

It is important because it is a very costly function. Sales and marketing is one of the most expensive functions in most organisations. The cost of sales and marketing often makes up 15% to 35% of the total corporate cost. It can cost about £140 for a salesman to make a call, and typically £450 to close a call. Even modest advertising costs hundreds of pounds, and may run into thousands. Market research exercises cost thousands, often hundreds of thousands of pounds.

1.1 Why is sales and marketing such an expensive operation?

One of the reasons is that sales people don't spend very much of their time with customers. Statistics show, when we actually look at how salesmen work, they are only spending at best 25% of their time face-to-face with customers (Figure 19.2). They spend the remainder of their time on the telephone, attending meetings, travelling, waiting, and on administration and paperwork. This also has an impact on why marketing is often expensive. Often our best researchers are our sales force, but we don't always use them properly to gather data, or perhaps we haven't got the systems to process the data even if we did bother to collect it. Instead, we spend thousands of pounds on specialised market research exercises.

- it is expensive
- increased competition
- shorter product life cycles
- high turnover of staff
- customers becoming more sophisticated

Figure 19.1 Why automate sales and marketing?

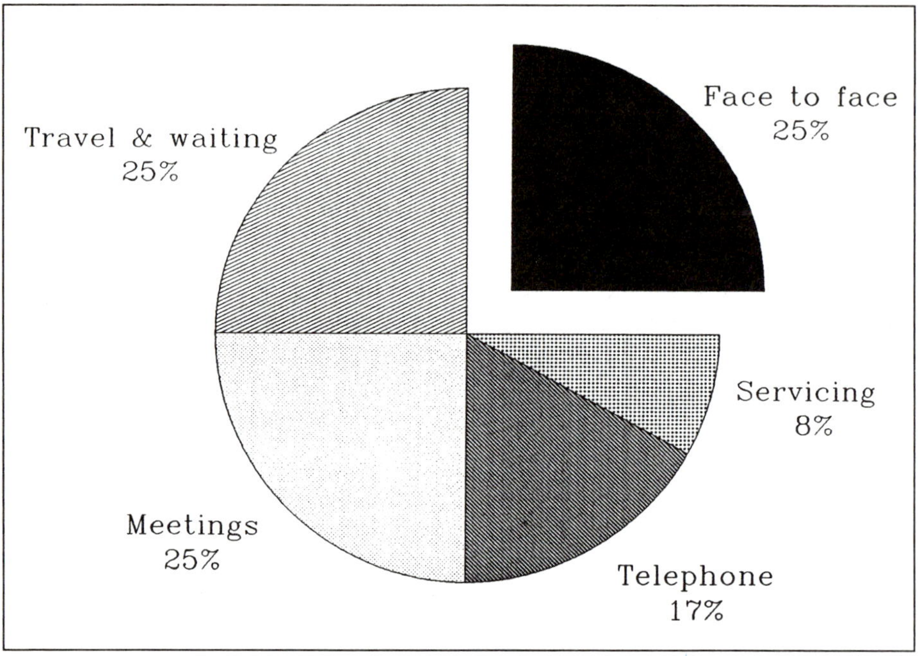

Figure 19.2 Sales persons' time (Source: McGraw Hill Research).

1.2 Increasing competition

Another reason why automation is important is increasing competition. Many companies in the UK are facing increasing competition from the US, Japan and Europe, and the single European market in particular has caused a lot of UK companies to look in that direction.

1.3 Shorter product lifecycles

Modern technology generally is resulting in shorter product lifecycles. Readers are probably aware that the lifecycle for PCs is getting much shorter, but it is getting shorter for many other products as well. It is important, therefore, to make sure that we can get in front of the right customers at the right time, recover the cost of developing our products, and generate surpluses to make profits, before we move on to the next generation of products.

1.4 High staff turnover

Another problem that we face is high turnover of staff, particularly in sales and marketing. It is important, therefore, that we do everything we can to retain the staff that we have, and to enable new staff to become as productive as quickly as possible.

1.5 Sophisticated customers

The last reason why automation is important, and this is probably the most important reason, is the customers themselves. Most would agree that customers are getting more sophisticated, meaning that they are demanding the highest quality service and products that meet their expectations in terms of both price and performance. More customers take their business elsewhere because of poor service rather than price (Figure 19.3).

2. EXPECTED BENEFITS

By way of an introduction to making a business case, I would like to set out some of the benefits we can expect to get from IT (Figure 19.4). I do not go into this in

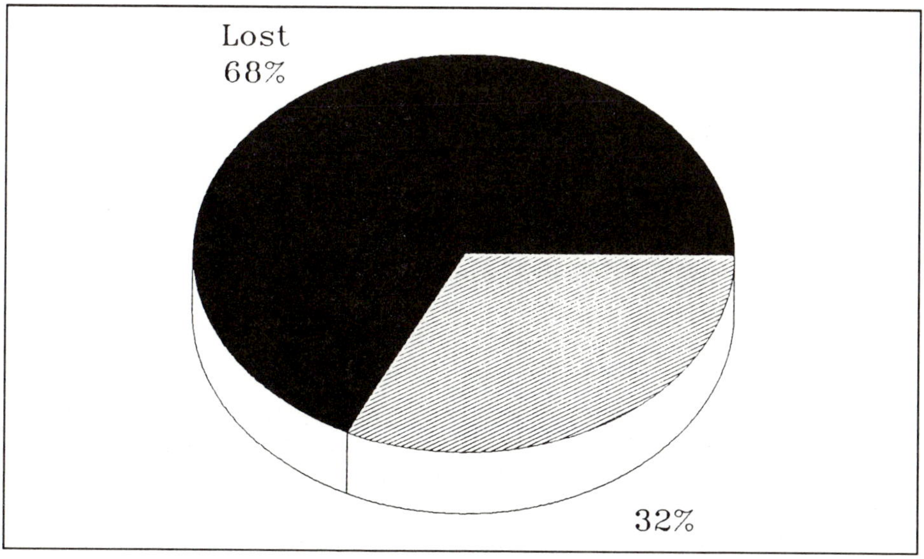

Figure 19.3 68% of customers are lost through poor service *not* because of price.

improving things we already do:
more time for selling
better use of information collected

better management
concise information to take the guesswork
out of decisions

Figure 19.4 Expected benefits from IT in sales and marketing

too much detail, but mean to set out just enough to set the backcloth for presenting the business case.

2.1 Improve what we already do

The first set of benefits comes from using IT to improve what we already do. Salespeople spend a great deal of their time doing things other than face-to-face selling. If IT can be used to reduce the amount of non productive time, more time spent in front of the customer is going to lead to an increase in orders. In marketing, a great deal of time is often spent sifting data, analysing results and carrying out endless routine calculations. Automation of these tasks will give marketing staff more time to think and be creative, and will probably make their jobs a lot more interesting along the way.

2.2 Better management

The next set of benefits are derived from better management. Sales managers and marketing managers are usually very busy people. They don't have the time to collate information to help them make decisions. Consequently, in many organisations decision making is intuitive, managing 'by the seat of the pants'. The use of IT can help present up-to-date, concise and accurate information to help managers manage, rather than plan by guesswork, or make the decisions too late.

3. THE BUSINESS CASE

Now we can start to look at making the business case. In doing so we first look at how information technology can have an impact on a company in different ways. Two examples will be used to do this: the first is improvements resulting from greater efficiency; the second is results from improved effectiveness. What is meant by greater efficiency is, for example, being able to make more calls in any given period of time; effectiveness is being able to get more output from a call. With improved efficiency we shall have more time to do the real job. For example, for a sales person this could mean spending less time at meetings or travelling and having less paperwork, leaving more time to make more calls. On the other hand, improvements through greater effectiveness mean that we can do the job better, perhaps because better quality information is available. So again, in the case of salespeople, this may mean that, armed with better background information when making calls, they stand more chance of getting an order, because the time in front of the prospect is far more productive.

3.1 A hypothetical company

To give some idea about how to present a business case, we shall now look at a hypothetical company. You may disagree with some of the facts and figures, but this is only being used as an example – you're not expected to go away with a ready made case for your company. Hopefully, you will gain some ideas which may help you think through how to start putting a case together for your own organisation. Many readers are likely to feel quite enthusiastic about the use of IT. However, just because you are full of interesting ideas, your financial director is unlikely to part with thousands of pounds without some hard facts and figures. The examples given here could form part of a business case, built around the salesforce in a hypothetical company. While the examples are based around research carried out in the USA, and thus you may feel that in the UK we could expect different results, the principles involved are equally valid.

This company has 100 salespeople who make a lot of calls, six calls a day. They generate £75,000,000 turnover, and cost about £10 million as a sales and marketing operation. So we have a 100 salespeople making six calls per day, about 30 calls per week, and based on a typical business year of 44 weeks, that means they are making 132,000 calls. A fairly simple calculation shows that the average revenue per call is £568. It is costing about £10 million to get these 132,000 calls, so another simple piece of arithmetic shows that for every £568 in revenue it is costing us £75 per call (Figure 19.5).

3.2 Improve efficiency

Let us say that we can improve our methods; make one more call, per person per week; perhaps because the salespeople no longer have to spend half an hour at the end of each day preparing their call sheets. This means that the calls have gone up from 30 to 31, and we can now actually measure the impact. Let us assume that we get the same revenue per call, for every additional call. That will give us an

- 100 salespeople - £75 million turnover - running cost £10 million - 6 calls per day 30 calls per week 44 weeks per year 132,000 calls per year

Figure 19.5 Hypothetical Ltd.

increase of £2,500,000 over sales which I stated previously were £75,000,000. Many of you are perhaps thinking that my figures, and my assumptions are a bit too general, or naive. Perhaps, but the point I am making is that from a fairly modest increase in efficiency we can often create a significant improvement in productivity. This is an example of an improvement in efficiency.

3.3 Improve effectiveness

Let us now look at effectiveness. If we can give the salesperson better tools to do the selling, and those tools can equally be used to gather information that can help marketing, then we may not just increase the number of sales calls, but we may get much more value out of each call. Let us say that as the salespeople make their calls, they have a full history on that customer – they know all about outstanding proposals, all about previous problems, all about the history of products that the customer has bought. They know about their contacts, so that when the meeting starts, the salesman can ask polite meaningful questions about the contact, and perhaps his family. The customer will then think, "This sales guy is really great, he only sees me once a year, and he has managed to remember my wife's birthday". With the same set of tools a salesman can have an effective mechanism for passing back useful information gathered during that visit. It may be suggestions that the customer has for providing a better product service; it may be a snippet about what the competition are doing; it may be that the salesperson wants to record some major planned event as part of the customer's business plan, so that the company's resources can be in there ready to help at the right time. Periodically, the information gathered can be passed to marketing, to be analysed and help improve products, customer service, etc. This is an example of an improvement in effectiveness.

Let us now look at an example of improved effectiveness through improved targeting. As before, this is rather a crude and simplistic example, but it will hopefully give you some idea about how you can set about measuring the impact of effectiveness in your organisation. Let us say that 25% of calls made are generating 75% of our revenue. You find that these high value calls are generating £1705 per call, while the remaining 75% of calls are only generating 25% of our revenue, i.e. £189 per call. Many companies will be familiar with this sort of division. What it means is that for every call we can switch from a low value to a high value; by improving targeting, we can get an additional gain of £1516. As before, you may argue about the detail and the figures, but let us say if we increase just 1% of low value calls to high value calls, we would get an approximately £500,000 increase in revenue. If we increased it by as much as 4% we would get a £2 million increase. As in the previous example, the important point here is that a fairly small increase in performance can often produce a dramatic increase in profitability.

3.4 Staff turnover

One of the problems mentioned earlier is that many companies face a high turnover of staff. In the next example we look at the turnover of sales and marketing staff, and how long it takes a new salesperson to get up to speed. A good average is probably six months – for some highly technical products it could be as much as a year. Some companies will even argue that it takes 18 months for highly complex, high value products. In our example company they find that it takes an average of seven months for a new salesperson to reach quota. They have a turnover of 12% of the sales staff each year. Remember that we have a 100 salesmen, so they lose 12 people every year. Also, they expect to have a growth in income of 8% each year. So again, simple arithmetic shows that they need 20 new salespeople every year. If, by giving each new salesperson the right tools, using IT, so that from day one they can have all the information they need about their accounts with a full history of each customer, we might reduce this learning curve from seven months to six months. Again we can measure the gain; for a one month improvement we gain £1,250,000:

20 new sales people per year.
Reduce learning curve by 1 month.
Gain 20 man months' extra income
Total income £75 million for 100 sales staff.
Equals £62,500 per man month.
Gain £62,500 × 20 = £1,250,000.

3.5 Costs of IT

Installing IT in marketing can be expensive. A comprehensive system for a single salesperson or marketing person to include computer hardware, software, installation, training and ongoing support can typically be around £7500. In the case of our hypothetical company, if we wanted to give each of the 100 salespeople a system, this would cost us £750,000. Most would agree that if you walked into your financial director and asked for the best part of £1 million you would be expected to have a pretty strong business case. Your business case will almost certainly need to be more sophisticated than the simple examples shown here, but hopefully they have given some idea about how to prepare such a case, and how to measure the potential impact of improvements in efficiency and effectiveness.

3.6 Business case summary

If we were to use the figures from my examples, and restrict the impact to that from just these three potential benefits:

- increasing the number of calls per week
- increasing the effectiveness of the salesperson at each call through improved targeting
- reducing the learning curve for new staff

we would get £1,250,000 in additional revenue, that is contribution margin not turnover. A summary of the components of the business case is shown in Figure 19.6.

This would mean we would be paying for this installation in less than eight months. Two other factors that we need to take into account are the time and effort it takes to make the decision and implement the system, and the learning curve during that implementation.

If we take these figures and apply a typical learning curve to it, you can see that this defers the payback time by only a few months (Figure 19.7).

Area of Improvement	*Benefit (£s)*
Increase number of calls	2,500,000
Improve target marketing	500,000
New staff up to speed quicker	1,250,000
Average margin	28%
Increased margin	1,200,000
	Cost (£s)
Cost per system	7,500
Cost for 100 people	750,000

Figure 19.6 Hypothetical Ltd business case summary.

- 100 Sales people
- £75m turnover
- Running cost £10m
- 6 calls per day
  30 calls per week
  44 weeks per year
  132,000 calls per year

Figure 19.7 Hypothetical Ltd pay back period.

As said repeatedly, some of the figures and assumptions used in the hypothetical company are crude, simplistic and perhaps naive. The final part of this chapter gives some information about what companies have actually achieved in using IT to improve their sales and marketing. Professor Hubbert Hennessey of Ashridge Management College has spent the last seven years looking at the experiences of organisations that have implemented this sort of technology. His findings show that these companies have 15–20% more viable prospects. Wrangler Jeans found out that by using information technology when placing orders they reduced their stock out by 430% in the first year of their systems, from systems which cost them less than $1 million, and which generated $13 million in additional revenue. Hewlett Packard automated their salesforce; they did a detailed time and motion study beforehand, and found that they were only spending 26% of their time with customers. Through the use of technology they increased that to 40%, or a 54% increase in productivity. Rank Xerox have installed an internally developed system. They credit it with a 10–20% gain in salesforce productivity, and that it trimmed $3,000,000 off their 1987 sales and marketing budget. In the UK, Allied Dunbar are indicating that their salesmen, who are using PC-based systems, are generating four times as much revenue as salesmen not using IT. Heinz indicated improved forecasting, less travel, better communications, better management and better productivity. Sun Life of Canada reported a 30–45% increase in premiums.

The *Harvard Business Review* ('Automation to Boost Sales and Marketing', January–February 1989) shows that from a survey of companies which have installed computers in sales and marketing, they have experienced increases in sales ranging from 10–30%. Salesforce productivity seemed to increase by as much as 30%, with staff attrition decreasing by 40%.

A parting thought:

> "Unlike many other assets which depreciate with time, a sales and marketing system increases in value as its information content grows in volume and quality."

20 Sun Alliance International's ADaM system

John B Gimson
Sun Alliance International

1. INTRODUCTION

The seed that led to the development of the ADaM system had been sown in the late 1980s, as the potential of improved portability of personal computers was emerging. It coincided with the need within the company, as in other companies, to explore the options of converting manual, paper-based systems used by the sales force to the 'electronic age'.

Market conditions also brought pressures to bear. The 'freedom of services' legislation from Brussels and the various Financial Services Acts, coupled with considerable investment capital, led to over-supply in the market. As growth goals were pursued, rate cutting took place, which led to a period of the highest levels of losses ever known in the UK general insurance market.

Claims of unprecedented size and number came from all quarters – subsidence in the UK, with earthquake, typhoons and floods elsewhere; auto accidents, arson, and theft rates soared; malpractice and negligence actions against professions thought to be safe and responsible – and the insidious growth of claims for gradually developing diseases, pollution, etc. The recession didn't help either.

The highest priorities were the restoration of profit and improvements in operational effectiveness at the lowest cost.

2. SUN ALLIANCE INTERNATIONAL

In addition to various corporate services, the Sun Alliance Group has four main insurance operating companies – covering Life & Pensions, Overseas, UK Domestic (i.e. home and motor, etc.) and International. Group wide, we have representation in over 50 countries

The role of the international company is the provision of a general (non-life but including marine) insurance service for commerce and industry. We operate from ten regional centres in addition to our strong presence in the London market. Sun Alliance International is the largest insurer of UK-based commercial risks.

Being part of a Group which was established in 1710, it is not difficult to appreciate that throughout those 280 or so years, the organisation has seen considerable change. Rather than react to it, we consider the need to manage change –

whether it be social, economic, political, environmental or technical – to be a business reality, if success is ultimately to be achieved.

With a clear vision for the future, we have formulated a strategy for achieving our business objectives – and central to this is the provision of the highest quality of service to our customers. In business terms, this means matching the risk management solutions to insurance needs (i.e. the protection of your assets and earnings plus the financial effects of your liabilities).

However, the key to success in our industry is the ability to offer our brokers (those professional intermediaries from whom we get the bulk of our income) and some direct corporate clients the combined benefits of one of the foremost risk management teams of any major insurer worldwide; a highly proficient claims service (the ultimate test of any insurer) and regular day-to-day customer service of the highest quality – all supported by unquestionable financial security.

In providing this range and quality of service, we strive to support our staff with good quality training and development programmes – and systems designed to optimise their effectiveness. An example of this is the ADaM sales administration system.

3. SYSTEMS WITHIN SUN ALLIANCE

Like banks and other large financial organisations, 'computer' means mainframe – where there is an overwhelming need to track and record the millions of transactions related to our customers, their policies, their (or our) premiums, their claims, our statistics, etc. It is hard to imagine that situation changing.

Personal computers, as their very name implies, were introduced by dedicated enthusiasts for whatever personal computing application was relevant – mainly spreadsheets and database work – but later moving into word processing, desktop publishing and graphics work, usually on a stand-alone basis. Subsequent developments led to expert systems, specialist applications and networks.

The one area of the business which remained furthest from this emerging technology was the sales force (for obvious reasons), although electronic and direct marketing strategies were being successfully developed and introduced.

4. AIMS OF THE ADaM PROJECT

ADaM is our mnemonic for Agency Development and Management – agency being the age old term for the intermediary through whom the bulk of our business is placed. Our sales force therefore is focussed on building relationships and the selling and servicing of business through such intermediaries, and we have relatively little direct contact with the policyholder.

The pressures referred to earlier led to the formulation of key strategies to sharpen the focus of our sales force onto those market segments of most importance – and to recognise the increasingly vital need for a better flow or exchange of information throughout the company, both about our agents and customers as well as our competitors.

Also, we needed to contain our expenses, some of which would be achieved through closing some of our smaller rural centres, concentrating our technical staff on the 10 regional centres and seven other major locations in the UK.

Thus, late in 1991, the seed planted in the late 1980s took on a major impetus – and we started our quest for a suitable system to provide sales and sales management support to a small number of sales staff who no longer had an office from which to work. These two-dozen people were to become OTRs ('on the road') sales executives.

5. SELECTION OF THE PRODUCT AND SUPPLIER

Like all large companies (and probably smaller ones too), we get our share of 'offers you can't refuse' and invitations to exhibitions and demonstrations of all sorts. Somewhere in this electronic haystack was our needle! The first step was to set a broad specification of the system we were looking for.

5.1 Customisation

Firstly, we had to have a system that could be customised to the way we operate – and not having a new way of working (as well as thinking) imposed by a system.

5.2 Database structure

From a technical point of view, we needed a relational database, large enough for a large number of records, and a lot of information in each record. The system had to satisfactorily interface with our existing mainframe, the source of the core information about our intermediaries as well as data for performance reports.

5.3 Sharing information throughout the company

We needed to have one common database, with the ability to slice up the segments for each user, each constantly updating it, and sharing it with other users. Initially we planned to have about 50 users – some 26 sales staff and about the same number of managers, and about half a dozen in Head Office. We expected to bring the whole sales force onto the system in time.

5.4 Cost

Cost was also a critical issue. We knew we were going to have to spend some money, but if we were seeking savings from office closures we could not let it all go on a new system!

5.5 Delivery

In addition, the new system had to be delivered in a very short (as far as system developments go) timescale. We were working on plans to close some 20 or so offices within the next 6/7 months and had to have proper support for those sales staff from day one.

5.6 Criteria of the supplier

The final point was the 'X' factor the aspect which is hardest to define. Being in the business of selling mainly intangible services, through highly professional intermediaries, we both know and value the importance of good relationships. Our potential supplier had to not only have the ability to deliver a suitable system to the required specification, on time and within the budget, but had to be able to work with us comfortably.

5.7 Supplier decision

We fairly quickly found half a dozen or so systems which could provide the functionality we were looking for, and many more that couldn't, even though we were told that the next version was just round the corner. We had several demonstrations, both in our offices and further afield, and finally chose ISS (Integrated Sales Systems Ltd.) as the supplier.

In our early discussions with ISS we found them to be anxious to hear about our requirements; clearly telling us what could or could not be provided; were sufficiently flexible and adaptable as the specification changed; and generally came very close to becoming part of the family. It may have had something to do with the fact that they were a new company, keen to have a major corporate as a customer – but it wasn't a motive we were going to take exception to!

6. DEVELOPMENT PHASE

Just before we signed a formal contract for the supply of the system, we asked ISS to provide a prototype of ADaM, i.e. what we could expect to see in a customised version of their core Oxygen product. We needed to know that the system we were asking our sales force to use, was, in essence, an electronic version of the paper system they were familiar with.

After the contract was finalised, we had just over three months to get the pilot version in place, and two more months for the full working system to be ready.

While the core Oxygen product had much in its structure that fitted our requirements, we needed to spend a considerable amount of time on the preparation of a detailed specification. Once the key points were crystalised, we sought the views of potential users.

While the software development was taking place, we simultaneously investigated the way in which our mainframe applications teams could organise regular downloading of data, as well as other aspects of the interface.

We also had to address the issues of hardware, both for the central database (including the LAN for the Head Office users) and for the equipment to be used by the sales people.

7. THE ADaM SYSTEM ITSELF

ADaM is the Sun Alliance International version of ISS's Oxygen system. If you were to look at both systems you would see undoubted similarities in screen layout, system structure, user interface, etc. You would also see the amount of customisation to our way of thinking and working and some unique features.

7.1 Distributed database

Probably the most fundamental aspect of the system is the nature of the distributed database. In practice, this means that the information put into the system by the sales executive – about his activity or the customer – is held on his or her PC until a comms session takes place. This information, or changes to the database, is then passed to the central database server. In turn, it goes to the database held locally by the salesman's manager.

In essence, we have a copy of the same data in four places – the salesman's database; that of his first line manager (the Area Sales Manager); the Regional Marketing and Sales Manager above him; and finally onto the central database in our Head Office.

7.2 The structure of ADaM embraces

7.2.1 Agency Records

The Agency entity holds the core records of our customer base, with space for all the information you would ideally like to have about them. Basic information about name, address, etc. held on our mainframe computer is downloaded into ADaM, and regularly refreshed as the mainframe records change. Part of the Agency entity comprises a series of 'profile' screens, designed especially to hold the valuable marketing and management information about the customer and his or her business activities relevant to us. These profile screens also provide a snapshot of agency performance (i.e. our trading position with the agent). This data is also fed in regularly from the mainframe.

7.2.2 *Contacts*

As part of the Agency records,there is provision for Contact details – the people in the Agency with whom we are in regular contact. By the way, be aware of the provisions of the Data Protection Act when it comes to holding information of a 'personal nature'!

7.2.3 *Events*

In the same way that Contacts are tagged on to the Agency record, we have Events Records tagged on to each Contact. Events are simply the history of calling activity by the sales executive.

7.2.4 *Task Management*

ADaM (like Oxygen) incorporates a Task mechanism – which is the means by which the sales executives' workload is controlled and planned. From our point of view a Task is something to be done – which when carried out and logged becomes an Event.

The Task mechanism allows all users to set tasks for themselves, as well as others, and the system itself can create tasks automatically where, for example, one call requires a follow up at a later date – and logging the first will generate a new task.

7.2.5 *Mail*

A Mail messaging system exists within ADaM – similar to most of the electronic mailing systems available. The one key difference is that mail messages, like any other data, can be written at any time, and they are stored on the PC until a comms session is carried out. A little bit like writing a letter and posting it later.

7.2.6 *User Reports*

ADaM also incorporates a suite of User Reports – pre-structured to provide almost all the day-to-day reporting a user or his manager might need. In practice, Reports are 'requested', generated by the system and delivered to screen or printer as specified.

Reports are usually menu-based, allowing the user to specify the scope of his enquiry – covering such things as productivity levels; performance analysis of the 'Top 20' or similar; summaries of activity on sales campaigns generally or on specific products, etc. You think of it, and we can get a report on it!

7.2.7 The Organise facility

Probably the most significant feature of the system is the in-built Organiser – a mechanism which is available as part of the Agency, Contact, Task, Event and Mail entities within ADaM. While each of these parts of the system provide a Summary screen where a list of records can be viewed, the Organiser allows users to very quickly select and sort information held in the database to an almost infinite degree. For example, which customers with premium income above or below a set level are in a certain postcode; which of my Contacts plays golf or cricket, etc.; which agencies fall within set occupation groups; etc.

The Organiser will also provides sets of pre-defined outputs and special selections, e.g. a basic mail merge, name, address and telephone lists, etc.

7.3 Communications

The ADaM system also includes the Comms software to support the regular transfer of data to and from the central database – not just a file transfer operation, but updating individual records in the database.

8. EQUIPPING THE 'ON-THE-ROAD' SALES EXECUTIVE

To equip our sales staff with the means to work without the facilities of a modern office, we needed to provide:

- A 386 Notebook Computer (Mono), complete with the ADaM system and database
- A compact modem (for data communications)
- A BT business telephone line (for both voice and data comms)
- An Answerphone with remote message retrieval facilities
- The means to dial in to our Mainframe computer for general enquiry services, Email and other MI systems.

By planning a pilot phase, we were able to get users' views on both the hardware and the software. We regarded this as an essential step in the process, particularly important when introducing any new system and a new way of working – and a useful opportunity to check the current experience of our potential users of personal computers. We soon discovered that one of the first four 'guinea pigs' had never before used a keyboard, let alone anything more complicated.

The pilot working was not intended to 'see if it works' – we were well past that stage. We were committed to the introduction of OTR working, supported by the ADaM system – and the pilot was the prudent step before the major roll-out to the first phase of users in June 1992.

While it provided us with the opportunity to test the robustness of the software, we also experimented with different hardware.

For the pilot phase we had four salesmen, two managers, three users in HO, two different notebook PCs, two different modems – but the most important ingredient was a huge amount of goodwill, enthusiasm, energy and support from all involved. We held a two-day briefing workshop from which we gained valuable insight into the hopes and expectations of potential ADaM users, as well as their concerns and fears.

We also had valuable help from BT – not unsurprising in view of the expected use of the telephone – but particularly the information contained in a small booklet *A guide to working from home*. While we had some experience of some staff working from home (e.g. surveyors, claims inspectors and engineers), the concept of switching to a non-office method of working, supported by new technology was a new challenge. This booklet, part of a suite of information from BT, provided useful information about many practical and social issues associated with such a change.

While we encountered a fair number of technical problems, no major obstacles prevented us from moving towards our planned roll-out.

9. PHASE 1 RELEASE – JUNE 1992

In the planning stage, we recognised that the first line sales manager had a pivotal role, and focused our efforts on the 14 involved. Jointly with our central training unit, we held a three day workshop, with the time roughly divided between the aspects of managing the change (and the people affected) and the 'hands on' training for the new system. Again, we found a wide range of PC experience – from never having touched one through to the enthusiast.

For the OTRs, we held two separate two-day workshops, focused mainly on the ADaM system, but encompassing some of the other working practices which would have to be modified. Bringing all users together provided a useful opportunity to issue the kit – having separately organised the installation of carphones, new phone lines and the combined telephone and answerphone. Also, where possible, we paired up the more remote users so that at worst, some level of self-help or moral support was available. They and we were aware of the pioneering role these people were about to embark on.

10. IMPLEMENTATION – AND THE FIRST SIX MONTHS

Again, as in the pilot phase, we encountered our fair share of problems – of almost every description. Some were minor ('I need another power point, my wife has to unplug the modem when she wants to mow the lawn') through to major technical problems when carrying out longer than average comms sessions from the West country.

We soon discovered that however good the ADaM system was, we started listing the enhancements that would be built into release 2. We had a few equipment failures. We learnt a lot from our implementation plan, the key points being:

1. Involve both business managers and IT specialists. In our view it is crucial to have a joint approach to changes of this nature – involving both the systems/technical people with the business managers – in our case Marketing and Sales management.
2. Changing the culture. Recognise that there will be a change to the business culture, which will require not just changes in working knowledge and skills, but also in attitudes.
3. Benefits to users. There is a need to ensure that all affected by the changes, and the potential users of the new systems and technology, can see the benefits for them in making the change.
4. Minimise the risk of 'big brother'. Where possible, dispel any feeling that the new system will incorporate a 'big brother' element. For example, all the information in the ADaM database available to managers about an individual's customer base and his activity, is also available to that individual. The only 'closed' areas at the centre relate to systems usage, security and similar reports.
5. Pilot testing. It is important to have a pilot exercise prior to the first phase of implementation. Many small lessons are learnt; much is gained by engendering a positive outlook on what in many respects is a 'voyage of discovery'. It also enables the views of others less close to the development work to come forward.
6. Training. It is essential to provide good quality and timely training.

11. RELEASE 2 AND PHASE 2

As mentioned earlier, while ADaM's development was stimulated to support the introduction of OTR working, it was part of our longer term plan to extend it to the whole of the sales force when the opportunity (and finance) was available. I mentioned, too, the recognition we gave to future enhancements as we gained more experience of using the system and wanted even more functionality than that originally planned. Quite simply, continuous improvement and evolution.

We introduced release 2 of the system at the end of January 1993 – when we took the opportunity to bring together all 26 on-the-road sales executives to both review and share experiences to date, as well as provide training for the up-dated system.

Phase 2 is concerned with extending the current user base significantly this year – within the next six months. This will mean that all managers will be on the system, and more than half our sales force of around 140. While all these next group of users will be office-based, we intend them to have the same portability of a Notebook PC – using a modem for comms sessions via our internal telephone network. We are also investigating the support that 'work-grouping' might provide where we have many users on one site.

Our current plan is to extend ADaM to the whole sales force during 1994.

12. BENEFITS OF THE ADaM SYSTEM

1. Enables improved customer service. ADaM is enabling us to re-engineer some of the business processes involved in developing our relationships with our Agents. The system provides the means to capture and store details of our trading activity, just as we did with our manual system – but we now have the ability to analyse and share the information, previously an impossibility in any practical sense.
2. Better information. The system provides all users with more and better information about their activity and productivity levels – as well as a powerful aid to work planning and the setting of priorities.
3. Improved communications. The technology supporting ADaM and OTR working also provides quicker and more reliable communications between the marketing and sales staff and with the other parts of the organisation.
4. More reliable information interchange. The database itself, and how it interfaces with our mainframe, provides significant potential for more reliable and cost-effective data transfer, and the generation of routine management information reports without unnecessary duplication of effort.
5. Monitoring competitors. The database also helps us monitor competitor activity – information which is gleaned in the day-to-day calling routine can be logged and analysed far more efficiently and systematically than before.
6. Performance management and reporting. Overall performance management is strengthened by monitoring the collective sales activity and efforts, over time, against business results – with the ability to analyse, sort and examine from a wide range of perspectives. We are also investigating whether there are any performance differences between ADaM users and sales staff without ADaM.
7. Cost-effectiveness. While we have yet to face the expense associated with extending ADaM to the next groups of users, we have achieved economies from phase 1, while maintaining, if not improving, the quality of service provided by the sales force.

13. CONCLUSION

As stated earlier, we are firmly committed to maintaining the highest standards of service, and intend to support this objective by developing and exploiting the potential of emerging technologies, and managing the changes involved.

Inevitably, we have had to face up to some problems – both related to the new technology and the ability of our staff to adjust to working with it – but these have been quite small in relation to the overall benefits the ADaM system provides. Indeed, the challenges to which we are now having to respond are from sales managers and members of the sales force who are anxious to become ADaM users!

14. UPDATE – JUNE 1994

ADaM marches on! Main developments since this paper was originally presented include:

- *System releases*
  Version 2.1 was introduced in the last quarter of 1993; a new release (2.2) is under development and should be introduced in September 1994. Both revisions improve system operation and the amount of marketing information held.
- *Users*
  As planned, the whole of the sales force are now using the ADaM system. The total number of designated users increased to around 170 – with many others with experience of the system. In addition to practical training sessions for new users, an extended range of support measures was introduced.
- *Notebook PCs*
  New users were equipped with Toshiba 486sx machines.
- *Communications*
  Higher specification modems are being introduced to improve the speed and reliability of comms sessions.

The systems – and the breadth and quality of information it contains – have been of significant value in planning and implementing current strategic initiatives. The range of benefits outlined in section 12 continue to be achieved.

21 IT and direct mail operations

R Britton
Teaching Company Associate, Innovations plc and
Department of Mathematics and Statistics, Brunel University
W H Foster
Department of Mathematics and Statistics, Brunel University

PART 1: INNOVATIONS AND DIRECT MAIL

1. NATURE AND OBJECTIVES OF THE COMPANY

The Innovations Group is a unique multi channel distributor of innovative merchandise. Best known for the Innovations Report – a home shopping catalogue containing hundreds of innovative products designed to make life easier, the company also produces several other mail order catalogues including Home Free (value for money goods and no postage charge), StockingFillas (Christmas gift ideas and stocking fillers) and catalogues for the Science and Natural History Museums and the British Heart Foundation. Syndications of these catalogues for insertion into credit card (etc.) statements are produced for various clients; this was indeed the foundation on which the company grew. Products are also offered via other direct response media (including off the page press advertising and off the screen TV advertising) and via retail outlets.

Innovations is a wholly owned subsidiary of the Kleeneze Group, whose stated aim is to be the foremost home shopping organisation in the UK. Innovations (Mail Order) Limited (IMOL) is a division of the Innovations Group, responsible for all mail order aspects of the Company's activities.

1.1 Innovations and database marketing

Innovations has accumulated a database of several million UK individuals. These are customers who have responded to one or more of the offers presented by the company.

When a customer orders from one of the Innovations offers, their name and address details are captured – along with details of the transaction. These details are required for fulfilment of the order, but are also passed to the central marketing database. This database is one of the company's core assets; it is extensively used for marketing purposes and the success of the company is heavily linked to its effective use.

2. DATABASE MARKETING AND INFORMATION TECHNOLOGY

We have seen that database marketing is about collecting and using information on customers, especially accurate data on the response of customers to previous direct mail offers. The key is effective use of quality data, and as such it is an ideal implementation for information technology. Large volumes of data are required to be captured, stored, manipulated and updated .

The best source of future custom is from those already shown to have an interest – existing customers are the best prospects for future purchases. Collecting and using information on customers helps in identifying target markets, selecting products, effective inducements using special offers and in every other aspect of the marketing mix.

There are many areas in direct marketing in which information must be collected, stored and communicated:

- Information on each transactions must be captured for any order to be fulfilled.
- For the order to be delivered a correct name and postal address is needed.
- Product despatch instructions to the warehouse or external supplier requires capture and communication of the product requirements, including details of sizes, colours, etc. (where applicable).
- Values, dates, etc. are naturally required, not just by the accountants, but also for confirming charges to credit cards and many other purposes.
- By law, customers must be given the opportunity to 'opt out' of receiving subsequent mailings; this data must be captured and efficiently actioned, for both commercial and legal reasons.

So that this information be used subsequently for commercial benefit, it must be converted into a meaningful and readily accessible form for the marketeers and decision makers. A computerised marketing database is the natural solution. A list of customers and their transactions is not sufficient – customers' details must be included with all their transaction history (including purchases, returns, refunds and cancellations). Also appended must be details of all communications sent to the customer and any other use of the customer's details (i.e. rentals to third party list users). All other information known about the customer (e.g. where a customers has opted out of receiving mailings), lifestyle and demographic information (e.g. date of birth, occupation, etc.) either known or inferred must also be saved. All of this information is of use for both strategic and operational decisions.

2.1 The Innovations marketing database

The Innovations marketing database uses relational database management

(RDBMS) techniques to store and manipulate information relating to previous customers. These customers have placed over several million orders and each order has resulted in over three mailing pieces on average; all of this information is stored within the Innovations marketing database.

The structure of the marketing database is shown in much simplified form in Figure 21.1 and Table 21.1. This database forms the central store of customer information within the company; data integrity and security are vital.

The marketing database is put to a multitude of uses:

- Customers are selected from the marketing database for direct mail campaigns.

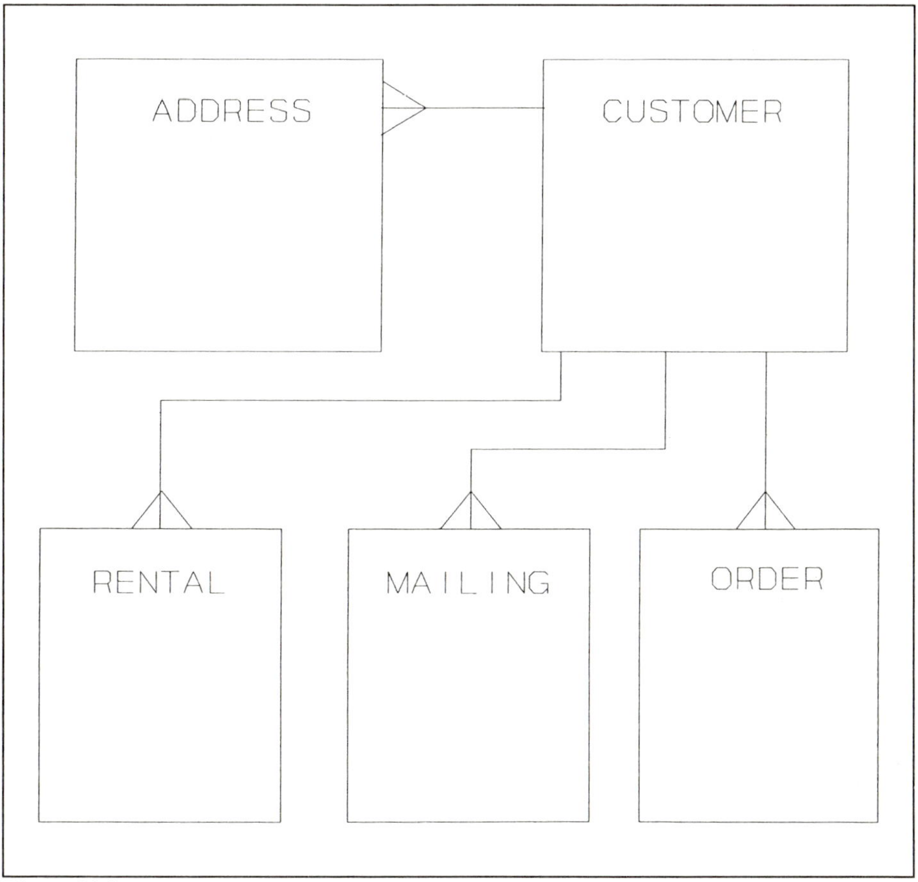

Figure 21.1.

Table 21.1 Elements of the marketing database.

Entity	Related To ...	Description and Attributes
ADDRESS	CUSTOMER on unique address identifier. (There can be many customers at one address)	Information unique to the household (eg. full postal address). Derived information about the household (eg. total transaction value)
CUSTOMER	ADDRESS on unique address identifier; RENTAL, MAILING and ORDER on unique customer identifier. (Each customer may have been selected many times for RENTAL or MAILING and may have made many ORDERS)	Information relating to each individual who has a relationship with the company. This includes title, forenames and surname, status indicators (eg. opt outs, deceased flags) and personal information (eg. date of birth).
RENTAL	CUSTOMER on unique customer identifier. (Each customer may have been rented many times) .	Information relating to rentals of customer details to third parties
MAILING	CUSTOMER on unique customer identifier. (Each customer may have been mailed many times)	Information relating to communications sent to the customer by the company.
ORDER	CUSTOMER on unique customer identifier. (Each customer may have ordered many times)	Information relating to transactions made by the customer. Includes brand, value, date, type of transaction (eg purchase, return, refund, etc.)

- Analysis of the database gives management and marketing information for pre-campaign planning and budgeting, customer targeting and post-campaign analysis.
- Incremental income is generated by renting customer names and addresses to third parties for their own communications.

2.2 Direct mail and the marketing database

The largest profit base of the IMOL operation is direct mail. Direct mail is an aspect of direct marketing involving the presentation of offers direct to the customer (via the post). This process involves IT in many areas, and to better understand how IT is used in a commercial DM operation, the rest of this article presents a case study which, though fairly specific, displays many of the generic processes involved in making a DM operation work.

PART 2: CASE STUDY
INFORMATION TECHNOLOGY IN DIRECT MAIL

The Innovations Report is the flagship of the Innovations brand. It is the best established and most widely known of the mail order catalogues produced by Innovations. It contains hundreds of products designed to make life easier. Most of the products offered are new and innovative and generally unavailable elsewhere. Because of this, and the high margins required by direct mail operations, most of the products are premium priced.

Three factors are important in determining the profitability of a mail shot:

1. Product pricing.
2. Yield rates (e.g. monetary yield per 1000 customers).
3. Overheads.

Small changes in yield rates typically give large changes in profit margins (given constant overheads) due to large mailing volumes.

Following from this there are two important aims:

- Increase yield rates.
- Minimize the variation of the yield rate.

Increasing the yield rate is an obvious aim, but once a satisfactory rate is achieved it should be stabilised as much as possible enabling a sound planning platform on which to build the business. Both of these aims are achieved through better targeting and treatment of customers.

This case study examines how:

- Individuals are selected for receiving the Innovations Report via direct mail
- Subsequent orders are fulfilled
- The information is captured and subsequently used.

The emphasis is on the use of IT and, in particular, the marketing database in these processes.

1. OVERVIEW OF THE PROCESS

Figure 21.2 gives an overview of the processes involved in the direct mail operation. This pictorial description examines the system in terms of entities and flows. The flows can be divided into *primary* tasks (which must occur for the system to exist) and *secondary* tasks which whilst essential to the long term survival of the system are not prerequisite.

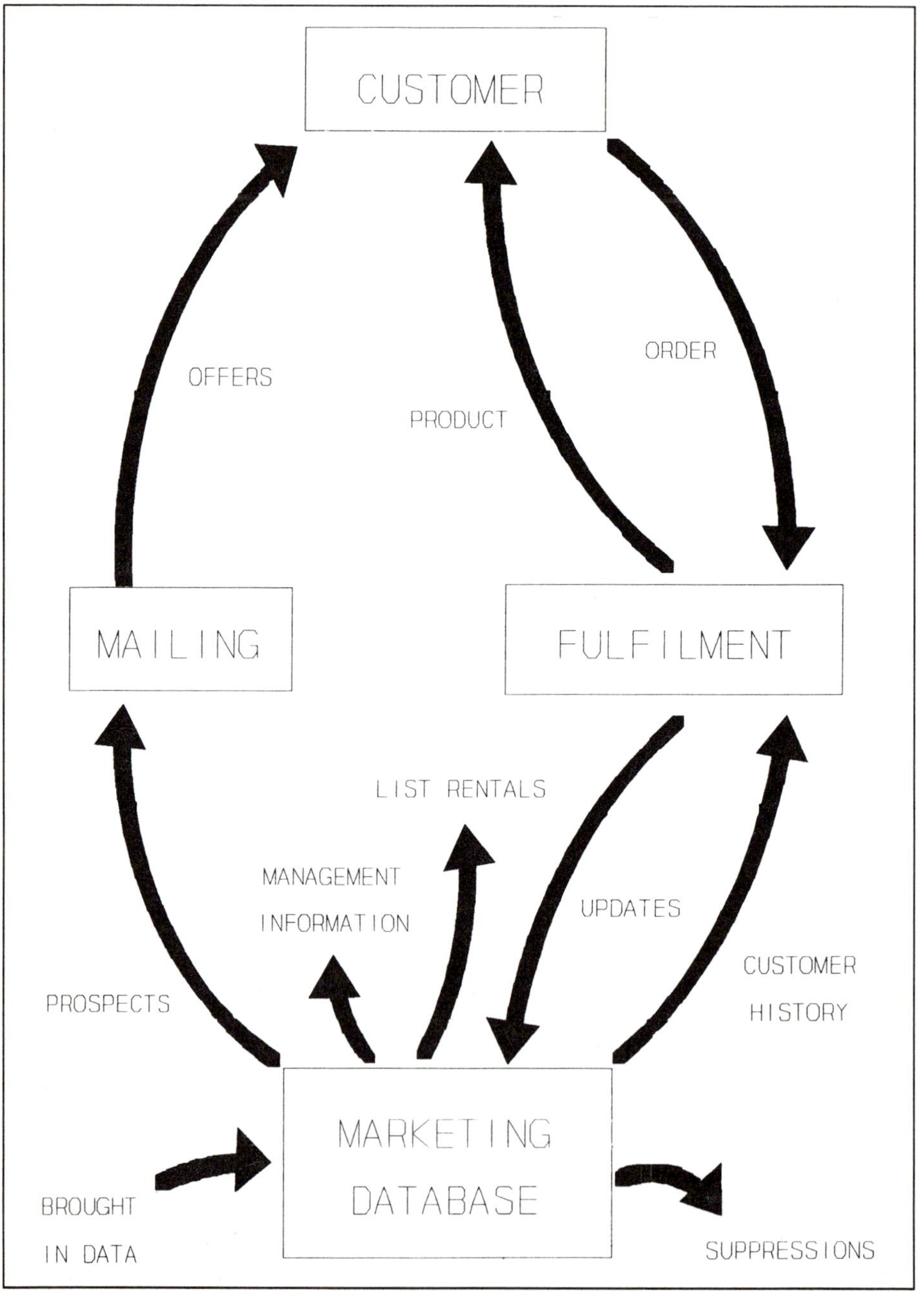

Figure 21.2 Overview of the mail order operation.

2. THE ENTITIES INVOLVED

The four entities identified are the *marketing database*, the *mailing*, *customer* and *fulfilment*. Of these, the marketing database has already been described.

2.1 The customer

The *customer* is the individual who places the order. This will normally be the recipient of the mailing, but may be the target's spouse or a family member, a friend to whom the catalogue was passed or someone entirely unconnected with the original target.

2.2 The mailing

The *mailing* is the selection and communication of the offer. This process covers such diverse aspects as product selection, catalogue design and production, personalisation, enclosing and delivery of the mailing piece. This case study must restrict the coverage of this aspect and concentrates on the processes involved in getting the right offer to the right customer.

2.3 Fulfilment of the order

Fulfilment of the customer's requirements requires order taking and processing, timely despatch of the product to the correct address, dealing with enquiries, complaints, refunds, cancels, etc.

3. PRIMARY DATA FLOWS

Without the primary tasks, there could be no mail order operation. They are prerequisites of the system. Figure 21.3 displays the relationships of the primary tasks, which form a loop connecting the four entities described above.

The mailing cannot happen without *prospects* for the mailing being identified from the marketing database. The customer will not *order* unless the right *offer* is presented. There will be *no prospects* to select unless *transaction details* have previously been passed to the marketing database.

3.1 Selecting the prospects

Selecting the best prospects for any particular offer involves analysing the relationship which each customer has with the company and the brand and assessing the propensity of the customer to buy from that offer. Accurate targeting of the

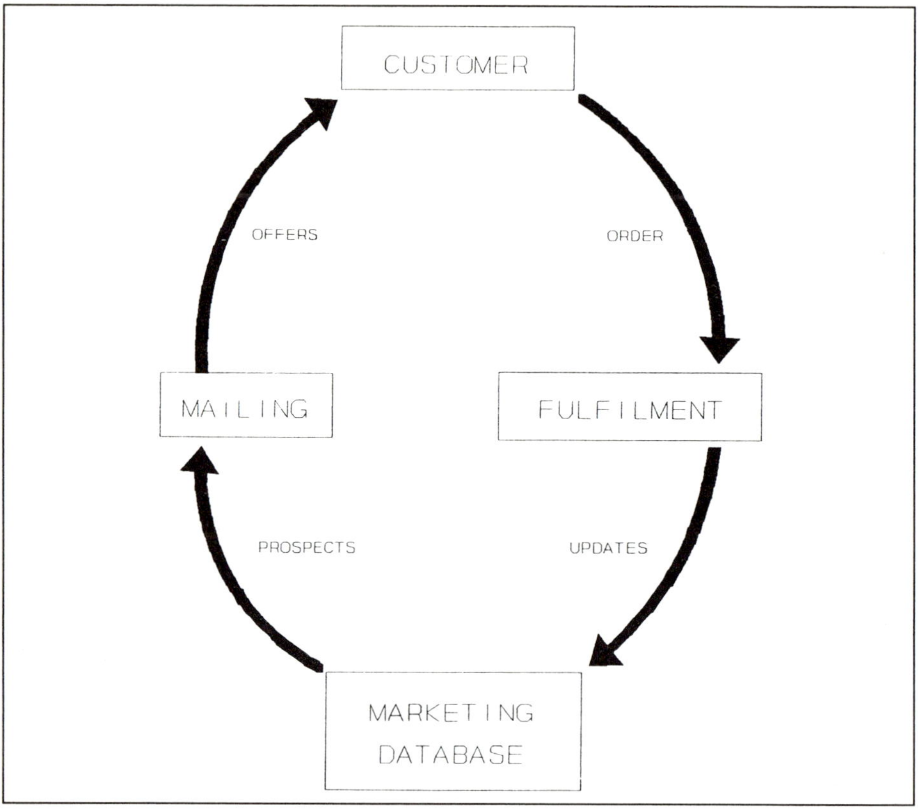

Figure 21.3 Primary aspects of the mail order operation.

best prospects is a vital element of any successful mail order operation, and potentially has the largest influence on profitability. The high (and sunk) promotional costs associated with mail order lead to high financial gearing – influencing response rates to an offer by just a few points can turn a significant loss into a substantial profit.

IT plays a major role in targeting for mail order offers. The marketing database must permit the efficient analysis of customer relationships across the whole database, considering factors such as:

- recency of latest purchase
- value of purchases
- brand and product affinity

- lifestyle and demographic information.

Statistical techniques such as linear regression are widely used tools, as are analysis packages such as CHAID (Chi-Squared Automatic Interaction Detector). Both are used in the identification of the best prospects for each mailing.

All analysis and targeting must occur within tight time frames - not only to maintain commercial schedules, but to maximise the recency and applicability of the data being used. With up to 1 million customers being selected at a time, performance of the marketing database is of paramount importance. Additionally, and once again, the quality of the data being analysed is also vital.

3.2 Presentation of the offer

The output of the targeting process are the prospects to whom the mailing will be sent. The presentation of the *offer* to the selected prospects is the next ingredient.

There are many aspects here which could be discussed, from the design of the envelope to the day of the week on which the mailing is released. All of these affect response to the mailing, but none perhaps quite as much as personalisation of the mailing piece.

Without the power of computers and the application of IT such personalisation would be impossible as it involves knowing the purchase history of each customer.

3.3 Processing the order

Assuming that the right offer is presented at the right time to the right individual, an *order* will follow. The customer can place an order by post, 'phone or fax and the order will then be processed. It is envisaged that there will be a place for computerised interfaces for order taking in the not too distant future.

The fulfilment operation, though driven by the customer, is supported at every stage by IT:

- Details of the customer and the transaction are entered into the fulfilment system.
- The Postcode Address File (PAF) is used to enhance and verify postal addresses.
- Credit card details are taken if appropriate and verified.

The customer receives a confirmation of the order (with details) within 48 hours. This confirmation is system generated. This also provides an additional selling opportunity as catalogues are enclosed with the advice note.

3.4 Updating the marketing database

The marketing database is updated on a regular basis with all transaction details for the preceding period. For data integrity and processing efficiency the marketing database is separated from the fulfilment operation and batch updating is used (as opposed to on-line updating). Magnetic media are used for this transfer. The update includes all details of purchases, refunds, opt-outs, etc. which have been processed by the fulfilment operation.

Accepting this data onto the marketing database involves:

- Creating new records for first time buyers.
- Identifying repeat purchasers and appending or amending their relationship history.

The last activity brings up the subject of deduplication, i.e. whether or not this is the same person at the same address. This is a sensitive area of customer care and much attention and effort has been expended in deduplication. Again, IT has a prominent role to play in the deduplication process, but identifying matches between incoming and existing records also highlights the inherent weaknesses of logic-based processing, especially when using incomplete or missing data. However, recent strides in this area have been made by the application of genetic and neural technologies.

4. SECONDARY DATA FLOWS

The secondary data flows are important to the profitability and long term survival of the mail order operation. Figure 21.4 identifies the secondary data flows.

4.1 Suppressing customers from future mailings

Suppressions are indicators of eligibility for mailing. They come from a variety of sources. Mailing pieces may be returned by the Post Office as undeliverable (i.e. bad address details), goneaway (i.e. home movers) or refused (the 'junk mail' image still lingers over the mail order business). Deaths of customers may be notified by a relative or solicitor.

Opt-outs, where customers have indicated that they do not wish to receive follow up mailings, may come directly from the individual, via the transaction process or via the Mailing Preference Service (MPS), who maintain a database of individuals requesting that unsolicited mail not be sent. Where not a legal or industry requirement, it makes good business sense to act quickly and efficiently on these suppressions to exclude them from future mailings.

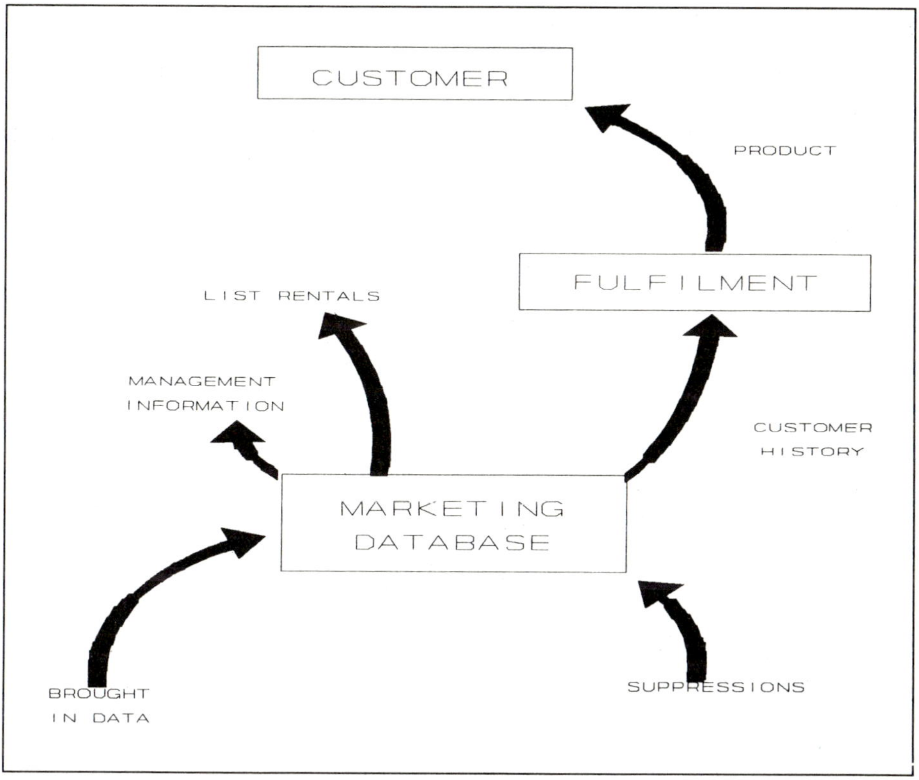

Figure 21.4 Secondary data flows in the mail order operation

4.2 Delivering the product

When a customer places an order or requests a replacement he or she must naturally receive the goods. This must be the right products, delivered to the right address and in an acceptable time period. Products ordered via mail order must be delivered within 28 days; Innovations normally delivers within 10.

The majority of Innovations products are delivered to the customer direct from the supplier. This direct despatch operation minimises the physical stock holding of the operation. The supplier is provided with a despatch label (with product and delivery details) and is required to ensure delivery. Many different suppliers are involved in this process, and IT performs an important role in maintaining and controlling the direct despatch system.

4.3 Accessing customer (relationship) histories

To ensure data integrity and to maximise processing efficiency, the database is separated from the fulfilment operation. However, to provide quality service to customers, customer (relationship) history information must be made available to the fulfilment operation on-line and in real time. This covers details of all previous transactions made by the customer (including what bought, when, delivered to whom, whether refunded and why). This enhances the ability of operators effectively to meet customer requirements.

4.4 Providing management information

The marketing database must be capable of providing marketing and management information to aid decision making. This requires interrogation of the database to provide analysis and information on which to base or support strategic, marketing or operational decisions. This will include pre-campaign budgeting and planning, post-campaign analysis of profitability, ad-hoc demands (e.g. rate of repeat purchase)

4.5 Supporting prospect targeting

As well as the functionality required for management information reporting, the marketing database must also support the targeting processes already described for prospect targeting. In addition to the ability to support effective targeting via statistical packages and such like, the system must also be able to report on the success of the targeting decisions made.

4.6 List rentals to third party clients

Fast and accurate interrogation of the database is necessary for processing list rentals for third party client mailings. Innovations works with many clients who rent customer details from the marketing database for distribution of their own mailing pieces.

Key aspects of this service are the fast counting of customers on the marketing database who meet the client's requirements, and the fast output of the selected customers for delivery to the client.

The requirements for customer selection are usually far simpler than for targeting to Innovations' own catalogues; for example, a random sample of customers buying within the last 12 months. However, quick and efficient cross-tabulation of the marketing database to provide counts of eligible customers meeting the client's requirement is an essential element of the list rental system. Once customer selections have been confirmed (and this might include excluding previously rented customers), fast transferral and despatch of the names and addresses to the client concludes the deal.

4.7 Accepting brought in customer data

The marketing database must be capable of accepting customer data from external sources. These fall into two categories – rented names and acquired names. Rented names are provided by third party vendors for once only use. The information normally consists of name and address only. They will form part of a mailing campaign, and to avoid customers receiving more than one mailing piece the marketing database must be capable of deduplicating the incoming names against prospects already chosen for the mailing.

Acquired names are normally the result of company acquisition. The data comprise at least name and address, but will often include relationship history (i.e. transactions, mailings and rentals received by each customer). The marketing database must be capable of incorporating this information for subsequent use. Concepts such as brand must be incorporated within this functionality.

5. SUMMARY

The above case study highlights the crucial role that the control of data quality and flow holds in direct mail operations. The successful operator in this area will need to handle customers sensitively and to further refine the targeting of these customers. Both of these activities are reliant on good communications between all aspects of the operations. For example, the ongoing and constant analysis of buying patterns of customers on the database will lead to marketing decisions on the segmentation and better matching of both customers and products.

22 Applications of marketing information systems in the recruitment of undergraduate students

Mark Gabbott
University of Stirling
Ewan Sutherland
University of Wales

1. INTRODUCTION

A series of significant changes has occurred in the structure of the UK market place for higher education; an increasing number of institutions call themselves universities and each tries to expand while competing for a declining number of potential students. The government has added further complications to this by using student numbers to drive higher education finances, first encouraging institutions to increase their intake then restraining and redirecting the expansion. Such changes and uncertainties emphasise the need for universities to understand the market places in which they find their students, if they are to maintain both market share and the quality of their applicants. A centralised national application system simplifies the processing of applications but does little to help universities accurately predict the total number of applications and students they will receive, yet such predictions must be central to institutional planning. This chapter describes a technique by which admissions can be better understood and be more accurately predicted from applications; allowing better planning, we also hope that it lays the foundations for a more systematic approach to communication with potential students.

The three key issues concerning higher education in the UK over the last few years have been:

- population
- competition
- funding.

The first concerns the well-documented 'demographic time bomb' (see, for example, European Commission, 1989). It was anticipated that a significant drop in the birth rate during the mid-1970s would result in a substantial drop in the number of 17–18 year olds by 1993, with a corresponding increase in the proportion of people aged over 45. Other things being equal, this would mean that university recruitment should have been adversely affected. While the reduction in this pool of potential applicants is not disputed, schools have been surprisingly effective in maintaining the number of school leavers with minimum university entrance qualifications. So much so, that they have been criticised for failing to maintain traditional standards. Universities have also used alternative routes to higher education which had been devised to tackle the problem of developing new groups of applicants, primarily 'mature' applicants often from special 'access' courses. The number of 17–18 year olds is due to start to climbing again in the late 1990s and it would appear that higher education has been fortunate in weathering this demographic trough.

Competition is a complex issue, especially with the removal of the binary divide between universities and polytechnics that has joined together two competing sets of offerings. While universities and polytechnics have traditionally considered themselves to be in separate markets, distinctions had already narrowed in many areas such as admission standards, degree awards, subject range and perceived status. The emergence of their own centralised admission system, the Polytechnic Central Admissions System (PCAS) emphasised the similarity between higher education offerings. The adoption of the title 'university' by polytechnics seems to have rapidly altered customer perceptions. As a result of increasing and changing competition institutions need to analyse and keep under review their market position and their differentiated product offerings if they are to survive.

Until recently, the funding of higher education in the UK was channelled through the Universities Funding Council (UFC) and the Polytechnics and Colleges Funding Council (PCFC). Over the last few years a number of changes have been made to the way in which the central government grant is allocated, the most significant of which is the closer relationship between funding and student recruitment. In one sense 'money follows students', making it imperative for universities to recruit in order to secure funding and thereby grow. Three new Higher Education Funding Councils (HEFCs) have taken over with the division being geographic for England, Scotland and Wales, rather than sectoral as it is for the research councils. It is already clear that this is giving rise to much greater scrutiny of the funding of individual universities. A major and unexpected change was made in the funding of arts and humanities courses at the end of 1992, effectively capping growth in that area.

One combined effect of these changes is to put substantial pressure on university recruitment, which has highlighted a number of deficiencies in the management of recruitment. First, in an effort to engage in some sort of forecasting, conversion calculations have been made on total applications, i.e. a target number of offers is set in the knowledge that an approximate proportion will convert to admissions regardless of course. Second, that admission standards or offers of places are raised or lowered in order to secure the target number of admissions which has a direct effect upon the quality of students admitted.

The problem is that because the UCCA system was based upon future expectations, admissions selectors had to judge the conversion from applicant to admission using instinct rather than analysis. Planning on this basis can be either remarkably accurate or disastrous depending upon A Level and Higher Grade examination pass rates and the profile of subsequent offers and acceptances. The final outcome of the process is far from certain and subject to little control by universities.

2. MARKETING HIGHER EDUCATION

There has been considerable debate among academics concerning the appropriate application of marketing techniques in higher education (see Maclean, 1985; Green, 1990; Rickard and Walters, 1984). Stone and Thompson (1987) highlight the major problem associated with the idea of students as customers, which is the implicit acceptance of demand-led education. Traditionally educationalists have seen marketing as a simple promotional activity designed to maximise the profit of a company through selling as many products as possible. It is not surprising therefore that educationalists were not drawn to marketing. Despite conceptual differences there are also a number of practical problems, notably defining the product. From the point of view of a university the product has been seen as the course, consequently colleges and universities have been offering a wider variety of course formats, full-time, part-time, distance learning, combined studies, modular degrees, etc. From the point of view of the student-as-customer, the value is probably much wider than mere qualification, comprising skills, competences, career prospects, social status, contacts, intellectual stimulation, an escape from home, an avoidance of 'real' work, an interesting social life and so on. The outcome of the debate is clear that higher education marketing must embody non-commercial or non-market considerations. It must cope with multiple aims and objectives in terms of quantity and quality and a 'product' which has many different and often conflicting definitions.

This anti-commercial argument has been used in the past to distance the management of higher education from other organisations which more clearly operate in markets. As a result universities have, to a degree, 'thrown the baby out with the bath water'. However, many commercial marketing techniques can be applied without necessarily compromising the clear differences between the market and non-market culture.

Kotler warns that organisations operating in a 'seller's market' tend to avoid or ignore marketing until too late:

> "Organisations typically become aware of marketing when their market under goes a change. When buyers, members, funds, or other resources needed by the organisation get scarce or harder to attract." (Kotler, 1982, p 8).

It is in these circumstances that the higher education sector now finds itself. The central problem is the pressure on maintaining the recruitment of students faced with a declining pool of 17-18 year olds, enormously increased competition and numbers-based funding.

Changes in the market have placed renewed emphasis upon the marketing of higher education, i.e. the adoption of modern marketing techniques in order to provide solutions to organisational problems. These techniques include the opportunities provided by rapidly advancing information technology of which, perhaps, the most interesting has been the facility to analyse markets in much greater depth and to provide detailed market information for use in strategic planning.

One of the buzzwords of current thinking in marketing is 'de-massification', the phenomenon of markets being broken down into ever smaller segments (Rapp and Collins, 1987). The idea being that mass or undifferentiated marketing is not the most efficient mechanism for communicating with the growing number of identifiable market segments. Communications in this environment need to be tailored and targeted to the individual or group in order that specific needs and desires can be addressed. Success in implementing this type of marketing requires four key abilities:

- to identify various classes of actual or potential consumers
- to define their distinctive needs and desires
- to communicate with the target group
- to convert target group members.

The effective use of the data already held by institutions can help achieve these objectives and offer new opportunities for growth.

3. APPLICATIONS OF MARKET ANALYSIS

The first stage of any market analysis is to establish the characteristics of existing customers, the applicants. Traditionally the applicant group has been important in two respects. First, in terms of the gross number of applications received which is seen as an indicator of expected admissions based upon historical conversion rates. The second reason for the importance of this group is in determining the overall pattern of applications to different departments to ensure that admission targets were met. However, without detailed information about the applicants subtle changes can be missed in the applicant cohort which can have disproportionate effects on admissions.

Once the characteristics of the applicant group are understood the next stage in defining target markets is the identification of the admitted group as a subset of the applicant group. By concentrating analysis on this group two outcomes can be achieved. First, if we can identify the characteristics of the likely 'entrant' this will allow identification of potential entrants from the applicant population. This could provide the basis for simple administrative screening of applicants to highlight the best prospects. The second outcome is the provision of a basis for targeting literature and other marketing communications to 'convertible prospects' on the basis of geographical area, school type or other characteristics. This is in keeping with the practice of customer 'cloning', whereby characteristics of a customer group are sought from a wider population.

The high level of rejections of applications by universities is worrying. On one level they cost money to process and so are clearly wasteful. They also represent wasted efforts by applicants who have either failed to understand the admission criteria or whose schools have not indicated that their forecast of results is well short of the minimum standard for the particular course. The problem of schools misleading pupils or not counselling them properly could now be addressed by writing to individual headmasters drawing their attention to the problem. Universities must also seek ways to position courses so that admission criteria are more clearly understood by applicants.

If a university is to increase its intake an obvious place to look is at applicants it would normally reject. An analysis of this group gives a sense of the elasticity of demand, how far it might be necessary to reduce the admission standard to achieve the new target. In many cases it is possible to obtain the final destination of those rejected, both by university and course code that indicates their preferences.

This discussion has been from an institutional perspective but there is no reason why such an analysis could not be pursued by a department using the population of applications for a given course or a group of related courses. Departments or faculties can identify their own target market in the same way as an institution. Generalised university communications could be 'bundled' with specific course or faculty information to schools which have a history of providing entrants.

4. THE UCCA SYSTEM

The key to the analysis of existing and potential markets for university education has been the Universities Central Council on Admissions (UCCA). This system was established in 1961 by the UK universities to manage the problem of growing complexity in applications, arising primarily from the increasing number of applications to universities. Over the years most universities have abandoned separate admission schemes in favour of UCCA, with the result that the system is now largely transparent; each university able to see what other universities are offering to their applicants. In the mid-1980s PCAS was introduced to perform a similar role for applications to courses leading to degrees, Higher National Diplomas and Diplomas in Higher Education in the polytechnics and colleges. In 1991 a common form was used for UCCA and PCAS applications with separate sections for applications to universities and polytechnics which are shown only to universities and polytechnics respectively. In 1993, PCAS and UCCA merged to form the Universities and Colleges Admissions Service (UCAS) with applications for new and old universities fully integrated.

All potential applicants, including those from overseas, completed a standard application form, which they had to submit to UCCA by 15th December of the year prior to admission or 15th October if it included Oxford or Cambridge Universities. (Late applications, i.e. those received between 15th December and 26th May were still processed, but these were clearly marked 'Late' and in the case of very popular courses were likely to be rejected.)

An applicant could make up to five choices of course and university, for example:

- Aberdeen Geography
- Aberystwyth Geography
- Oxford Earth Sciences
- Salford Environmental Sciences
- Stirling Environmental Science.

The UCCA Form was scanned and laser printed copies (A3 size) were sent to the relevant universities. Certain details were keyed into the UCCA computer system which were made available to universities on magnetic tape, via file transfer over the Joint Academic Network (JANET) or through a computer terminal. This information included the following:

- surname, first name(s) and initials
- title
- correspondence address, including postcode
- area of permanent residence
- sex
- marital status
- date of birth
- school ID number

- country of birth
- nationality
- residential category
- disability
- examinations to be taken
- choices of universities/colleges and courses
- date of application
- occupational background (parental occupation)
- ethnic origin (not forwarded to institutions).

Universities processed the forms, ensuring that applicants met the general entrance requirements, were likely to meet specific course entry requirements and often called applicants for interview. They then made a decision on whether to make an offer to the applicant which could be unconditional, conditional or the application could be rejected. Conditions usually referred to examination performance, for example, five subjects at B grade in Higher examinations and might include a specific requirement, such as a B grade in geography. Offers were notified to UCCA which informed applicants at once if the news was good, or after other decisions were made if it was not in order to save postage. The applicant could wait until all offers were received and then respond with a firm or insurance acceptance, or the offer could be declined. One 'firm' and one 'insurance' offer could be held at the same time, if conditional offers had been made by the institution or one 'firm' if an unconditional offer had been made.

Once the examination results were announced in August, the final decisions were confirmed. If students had firmly accepted an offer and they achieved that offer, then they were automatically accepted. If they fell just short of the offer, the university might condone the failure and make a revised offer. Where a university had places which remained unfilled after the processing of the examination results it was possible to go into 'clearing' to fill these places. This involved adverts and tables appearing in Sunday newspapers and a great deal of telephoning around by applicants in search of places. A side-effect of clearing is that it attracted a certain stigma to the courses and institutions involved.

The introduction of UCAS has substantially changed this process and the data available. It constrains the choice available to applicants through the number of slots on the form and forces old and new universities into more direct competition. By allowing institutions to see applications made to rivals across the now vanishing binary divide it is making competition more transparent. UCAS is currently examining the use of Document Image Processing (DIP) to improve the system of applications and to reduce or eliminate the need for handling of paper-based records.

5. ANALYSIS

The application process was recorded in such a way as to allow an almost complete analysis of the applicant pool by any institution which was part of the UCCA system. Periodically information relevant to each applicant was made available to all the universities which appear on the applicant's form. This information was the individual university's portion of the main UCCA database.

The initial personal details were usually static and would rarely change during the admission period. The offer by the university to each applicant was sent electronically to UCCA, where it was batch processed overnight with offers from other universities. The updated information on all applicants to a particular university was then sent back. This process was on-going and incorporated the applicants' responses to each university's offer. At this point each university had access to details concerning the applicant and the 'transaction', i.e. offers, conditions and replies, which could be used to build profiles of applicants for any particular period and details of the transaction, i.e. course applied for, offer and reply. Additionally, data could be obtained from UCCA describing the applicants for any recent year of admissions.

One key feature of the application process was missing, which has a significant effect upon the direct marketing potential of the data, this was the details of the school or college from which the applicant comes. UCCA prepared an annual schools tape which contained detailed information about all schools known to UCCA. The information, such as size of school, fifth and sixth year class size, head teacher, type of school, address and post code, was the result of an annual questionnaire issued by UCCA. Individual universities could obtain a world version or a UK version. Information on the schools tape was linked to each applicant's details by a school identifier code which was entered on the UCCA form.

For the purpose of this analysis data were extracted from a portion of the database which contained applicant information for a single target university for the years from 1986 to 1992. From this portion of the main UCCA database the names and addresses of the applicants were removed, but not their postcodes. Individual applicants were linked to their school's data using the school code numbers. It was also important to know which applicants had been admitted. Student registration numbers at the target university were linked to the original UCCA/USR (Universities Statistical Return) number in a look-up table. By sorting and merging the main data file and the look-up table it was possible to identify which applicants had been admitted.

Each year's applications, from 1986–87 until 1991–92, were compiled in separate files and then substantially recoded in order to convert alphanumeric characters into numeric variables and to provide named categories for the selected variables. A number of other manipulations were carried out such as inserting missing postcodes from the up-dated schools file, coding geographic areas for mapping purposes and the truncation of post codes to give postal areas as well as full codes. The data were analysed using SPSS-X. POSTZON was used to convert post codes into map references using a FORTRAN program, maps were plotted from this using GIMMS. All performed on a Hewlett-Packard 9000 minicomputer running under Unix.

While the data set is extremely useful and was available in a readily analysable format there are a number of limitations that need to be identified. First, the data set consists only of applicants to the target university, a badly skewed sub-set of all UCCA applications. Second, only students who have applied through UCCA are included, it does not include exchange students or other forms of direct entry. Third, there are variations in the quality of the source data, for example, some applicants claim that Barnsley and Merton are English counties and that Selkirkshire is a county in Scotland.

In the processing of the data, some of the fields were overwritten. For example, a conditional offer would be changed into an unconditional offer at confirmation. Equally, a course code will be overwritten if the applicant or the university changes the course being applied for. Sometimes an offer was changed, with the original offer lost.

6. RESULTS

The result will be presented in three parts:

- the applicant group in terms of age and sex profile as well as school type
- details of the transaction based upon the same variables
- characteristics of the group of entrants.

Analysis is rudimentary since the derivation of the main data files has been the overriding objective, however, as the quality of the data increases so the facilities for more complex analysis increases. The authors would like to state that the data at this stage is insufficiently robust to undertake any more than simple frequency counts.

6.1 Applicants

The sex and age profile of applicants to the target university is broadly in line with the changes experienced by the higher education sector as a whole (see Figure 22.1). An increasing proportion of higher education applicants is women and an increasing proportion of applications is now being received from the older age groups. The change over the last five years can be seen in Tables 22.1 and

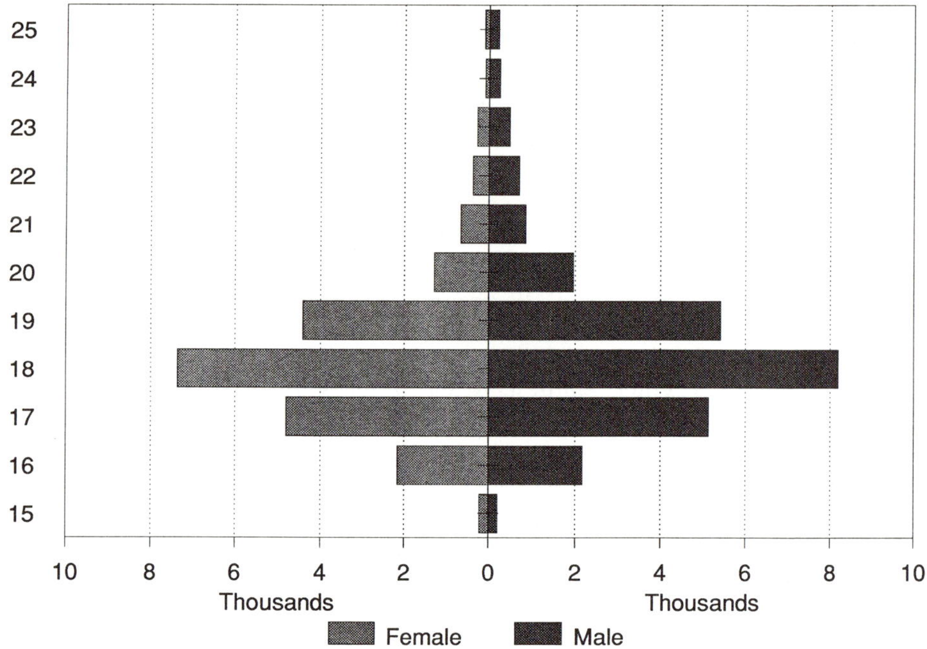

Figure 22.1 The age-sex profile of applicants.

Table 22.1 Age of applicants at date of application (percentage of total applications).

Age	1987	1988	1989	1990	1991
> 21	4.5	5.0	5.4	6.1	6.7
21	2.5	1.0	2.2	2.6	2.6
20	4.8	2.3	3.8	3.6	4.5
19	11.8	9.0	10.4	11.1	11.1
18	35.6	39.9	37.1	37.0	36.9
17	34.6	40.2	36.4	34.9	34.9

Table 22.2 Sex of applicants (percentage of total applications).

	1987	1988	1989	1990	1991
Male	52	53	54	55	53
Female	48	47	46	45	47

22.2. In itself this is not a remarkable result and it would be expected that the profile would be broadly in line with that of other higher education institutions.

National statistics for applicants in terms of the classification of school types are not published using the UCCA criteria and therefore it is difficult to provide any conclusive evidence that the profile of the particular institution is different from other institutions. By far the dominant applicant group is the comprehensive school sector but the profile is skewed (see Table 22.3). More significant is the contribution from the grammar school sector and further education colleges from which the university receives a large proportion of its total applications. The growth areas are represented by the tertiary colleges and the grammar school applications, though underlying trends would also point to the further education sector.

It is possible to analyse the applicant group by postal area (e.g. AB for Aberdeen or G for Glasgow). This analysis is more meaningful in terms of marketing activity if it is done for the school rather than individual applicant; post codes of both are available but in terms of providing information to future applicants, the school post code is the more important. In terms of overall applications, Table 22.4 shows the postal areas from which the university gained the most applications. This table is a ranking of the top eleven postal areas in 1987 and 1991. The two main features to note in this case are the dominance of the Glasgow, Belfast and Edinburgh areas alongside the changing pattern of English applications.

6.2 Transactions

While the applicant group is clearly important in terms of size, the transaction provides another level of detail. By looking at the patterns of offers it is possible to arrive at some assessment of the extent to which applicants meet university entrance criteria. Figures 22.2, 22.3 and 22.4 break down the offer (unconditional, conditional and reject) in terms of age, sex and school type.

Table 22.3 Percentage of applicants by school type (percentage of all applications).

	1987	1988	1989	1990	1991
Comprehensive	43.8	40.7	39.8	38.9	40.9
Grammar	11.3	13.4	13.1	12.0	12.2
Independent	3.7	4.2	4.3	4.1	3.7
Other secondary	0.5	0.5	0.5	0.5	0.6
Higher education	0.7	0.7	1.0	0.9	0.8
Further education	9.7	10.4	11.0	12.1	10.5
Sixth Centre	0.5	0.6	0.6	0.6	0.7
Sixth College	6.7	8.3	8.2	8.2	8.3
Tertiary	1.9	2.6	2.7	2.9	3.2
Technical College	0.8	0.9	1.1	1.7	1.0
Other	2.6	1.9	2.0	2.4	3.0

Table 22.4 Rankings of postal areas by number of applications.

1987	1991
Glasgow	Belfast (2)
Belfast	Glasgow (1)
Edinburgh	Edinburgh (3)
Motherwell	Motherwell (4)
Falkirk	Kirkcaldy (-)
Kilmarnock	Aberdeen (8)
Paisley	Falkirk (5)
Aberdeen	Newcastle (10)
Kircaldy	Perth (-)
Newcastle	Birmingham (-)
Exeter	Kilmarnock (6)

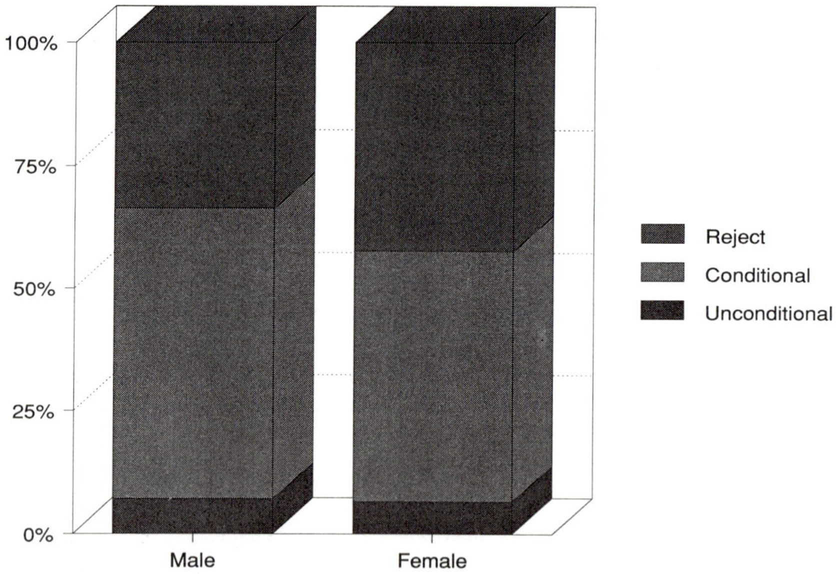

Figure 22.2 Offers and rejections by sex.

Women applicants are on the whole more successful in meeting the entrance requirements and in having sufficiently good Higher Grades or Advanced Levels or prospects of them to make some sort of offer worthwhile. The age profile suggests that the older age group, i.e. over 21 years of age, are polarised into those to whom the university is prepared to make an unconditional offer and those to whom it is not, there are many fewer applicants in this age group who are made conditional offers. In general the older the applicant the higher the rate of rejection.

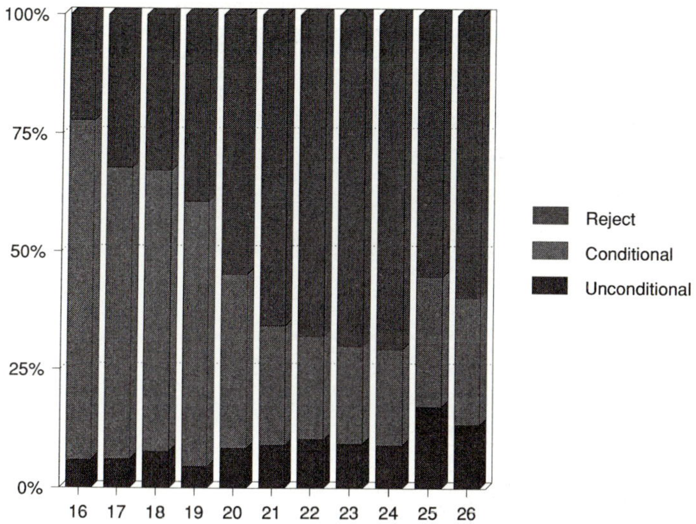

Figure 22.3 Offers and rejections by age of applicants.

The final variable by which to consider the offers is the school type, here there are marked differences in the patterns of offers to applicants from different types of schools. As could be predicted the grammar schools are the most successful in terms of unconditional offer. The most unsuccessful are those applicants from higher education colleges. This profile can be compared to conditional offers where the applicants from the comprehensive schools form the dominant group with the least proportion of conditional offers being made to applicants from grammar schools. Finally the rejected group, where the greatest proportion come from higher and further education colleges, suggesting that while applications from this category are growing, information about the entrance requirements is lacking or there is some discrepancy between the expectations of the applicants and the requirements of the selected university. The highest numbers of applications are received from comprehensive schools, a group which would appear to provide the best quality applications with the highest number of unconditional offers and the lowest rejection rate. Clearly there may be explanations in terms of age and examination completion rates though further analysis would have to be undertaken.

6.3 Entrants

The analysis of entrants used the information available from within the selected university to identify those applicants who had applied through UCCA and who

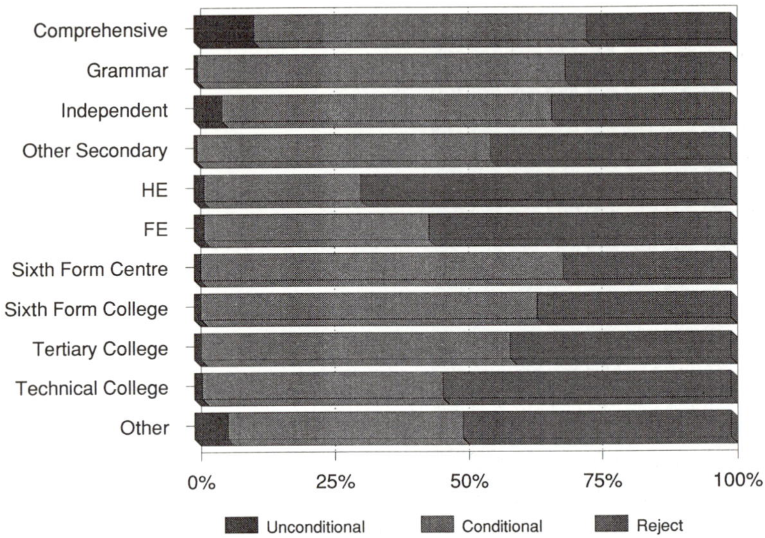

Figure 22.4 Offers and rejections by school type.

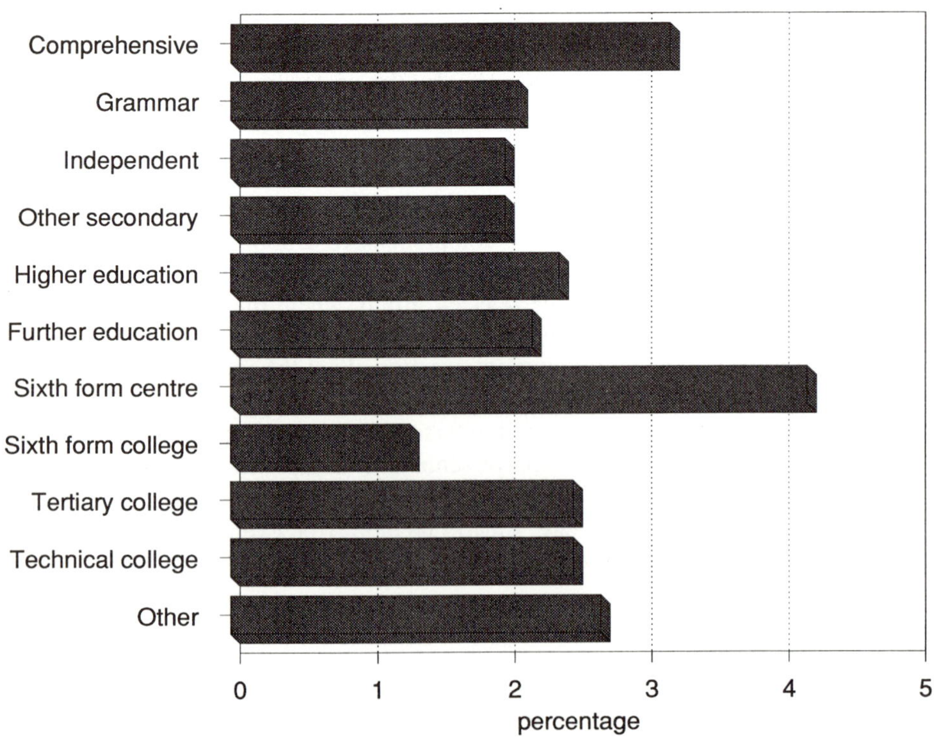

Figure 22. 5 Percentages of successful applications by school type.

had been given a registration number. This analysis allowed the offers to be assessed in more detail, for instance by identifying the proportion of successful applications by school type (see Figure 22.5).

In 1991 there were almost 1400 applications for admission to a single business subject which eventually resulted in twenty-nine students sitting in a lecture theatre (see Figure 22.6). A large number of applicants had little if any hope of attaining the admission standard (BBBB at Higher Grade or BBB at A Level) and were rejected. Similarly, because applicants can nominate up to five institutions at no more cost than one it must be assumed that a large number of applicants had little real interest in the target institution since they did not accept the offer.

Because the application system is shared, details of the offers by other institutions are available on a pooled basis, allowing competing universities and courses to be identified. Using multidimensional cross-tabulation it is possible to establish the responses applicants made to the different offers. For instance, of the students who declined an unconditional offer in the selected course it was possible to establish that many subsequently accepted an unconditional offer from another university or an unconditional offer from the same university but for a different course. Some applicants preferred a conditional offer from another institution to an unconditional offer from the target university which has implications for the nature of competition in certain subject areas. A similar story can be seen in

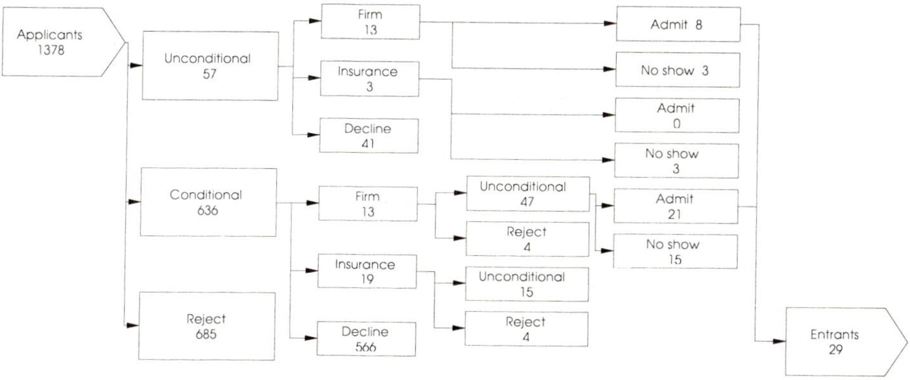

Figure 22.6 Flow of applicants into admitted students.

conditional offers. This form of analysis can provide the basis for understanding the competitive position of any university in the higher education market. It could also be used to screen applications where the target university was clearly being used as 'padding' in the application form. It would be possible to build a forecasting model to identify those likely to accept an offer.

6.4 Implications

This analysis has the potential to provide a number of marketing initiatives, which could be targeted at particular schools, universities and/or individuals. Schools could be identified individually, in the same way that entrants can be cloned, schools providing large numbers of applicants and/or entrants could also be cloned. This could be done by school type, by region, by characteristics of a school or its catchment area. The aim of such targeting would in the first instance be to increase applications, but secondly to reduce the rejection rate by increasing the success rate of applications, i.e. ensuring that applicants were applying for courses to which they were likely to be admitted and to which they wished to be admitted. Long-term relationships could be built up with individual schools on the basis of applications and/or admissions ensuring that university resources are utilised efficiently. In practical terms it might be sensible to ask each member of academic staff to act as a point of contact for a small number of schools in order to improve the sense of 'customer care', each individual could be backed up by a sophisticated information system.

Targeting competing universities could involve the rather devious ploy of tactical offers, bidding faster or lower than a rival institution in the hope of persuading applicants to come to a particular university. It would be possible to look down market and identify a rival and 'take out' their applicants, by making offers where applications would normally be rejected. This might be considered unethical.

It is at least technically possible to target individuals, either potential applicants or their parents, using commercial mailing lists, the Electoral Register and so on. However, this is unlikely to be a viable option for the present, because of the cost.

7. FUTURE DEVELOPMENTS

The potential value of this type of information for universities has been identified and shown to be able to improve their understanding of their markets. Moreover, they already have access to the data. We have undertaken detailed analysis of UCCA data for a second university which we believe has confirmed the value of our approach. By using this type of analysis, commonly used by commercial organisations, universities can improve the ways in which they plan and forecast their admissions, thereby reducing the risk and uncertainty experienced in recent years. Increasingly universities will have to be more pro-active in their relationships with institutions that provide applicants in order to maintain their market position and protect themselves from intermittent funding crises. These continuing relationships will require resources and the investment will need to be made on the basis of proven worth. The type of analysis described here has the potential to allow senior management to direct resources at the most 'productive' schools and colleges as well as providing the potential for 'cloning' schools and geographical areas to help provide growth and development. The regular monitoring and analysis of this data could be used to measure the effectiveness of activities such as visits to schools, publications sent and other marketing efforts.

It is worth commenting on the activities of some institutions in advertising on television. This kind of mass communication technique has been proven to be highly inefficient in producing measurable results compared to the direct marketing approach advocated here.

Further development of this work would involve starting again from the beginning, in order to 'scrub' the data, resolving ambiguities, omissions and other problems. For example, all addresses in the UK would have to be verified using the Royal Maile postcode database. Once the data set had been rebuilt it is possible to identify three ways in which this work could be continued, each from a quite different perspective:

- aid to marketing individual universities and courses
- behavioural studies of applicants
- geodemographic analysis of applicants.

We are now operating under UCAS and this provides slightly different information. The relevant data analysis programs are already in place and we have begun to monitor the changes in the market.

7.1 An aid to marketing

With a validated and reliable data base it would be possible to generate management reports on offers and admissions for any university, faculty, department, particular courses or for any secondary schools or colleges from which applications are received in terms of:

- historical patterns
- geographical patterns
- demographic patterns
- competitor analysis.

It would also be possible to follow the diffusion of knowledge about new courses, through the growth and spread of applications geographically and institutionally. On the basis of these analyses it would be possible to create and implement marketing plans as well as monitor their implementation in subsequent years through further data analyses. Software has been developed to link the statistical package (SPSS-X) to a data base management system (Oracle), with the transfer of data between the two packages as required, this has facilitated access to the data by non-expert users who have been provided with a simple forms-based interface. It will be possible in the future to link this to software from the Management and Administrative Computing (MAC) Initiative.

Data on existing students could also be linked to the UCCA data. Thus one might choose to keep schools and colleges informed on a regular basis of the progress of their former pupils. Where teachers or pupils from a school visit the university it would be possible to identify students from that school to meet them. In addition final degree results and subsequent careers could be linked to applicant profile, which ought to shed some additional light on selection. Given the high levels of course changes, it might be possible to use a profile of graduates to identify potential applicants, this could be especially useful for subjects not taught in schools, such as marketing.

7.2 The behaviour of applicants

Even a cursory examination of application forms and some casual discussion with students is sufficient to show that the choice of universities and courses is far from scientific and often the result of prejudice, misunderstanding and luck (bad as well as good). If universities wish to improve their marketing efforts, they need to understand the processes at work behind the completion of UCAS forms and the factors which influence applicants in their responses to offers.

Behavioural studies in a sample of schools and colleges would help determine the factors that influence the choice of universities and courses. These could be undertaken by a mixture of focus groups discussing issues and events and by an analysis of diaries kept by applicants, recording how they reached their decisions. These studies would require to cover the period up to and including completion of the UCAS form, interviews and visits and the responses of applicants to the offers received. The aim would be to complement the data analysis by identifying ways in which universities could better inform potential applicants.

7.3 Geodemographic analysis of applicants

Given funding and verification of individual student post-codes it would be possible to link the UCCA data to one of the commercially available geodemographic packages (e.g. ACORN or CACI). This would allow for the identification of productive clusters. The direct mailing of 'cold' prospective applicants would be extremely expensive and of debatable effectiveness but could aid in the siting of recruitment fairs and local seminars for schools. Locations within either productive clusters to maximise potential applications or locations in barren clusters could provide an additional level of sophistication in what has traditionally been a haphazard approach to schools liaison. Analysis of the 1991 Census would be particularly interesting, especially because it contains details of academic qualifications.

8. CONCLUSION

The market for higher education in the UK continues to change, with universities, both old and new, being forced to become much more proactive in their recruitment. Our approach to data analysis provides the basis for a complete and systematic re-assessment of individual and collective marketing activity, allowing institutions and departments to develop, implement and monitor their marketing activity. The UK government periodically exerts pressure on universities to increase student numbers in general, in particular fields of study or it may wish to increase the intake from particular socio-economic groups; our data analysis techniques, combined with the proposed behavioural analysis should make it easier to respond to such requests. However, this type of approach does not make it any easier for a university to make the structural, organisational and cultural changes necessary to respond to the changing market, these are challenges which will have to be faced by individual institutions, at best it provides a direction for such a review and at worst it would allow universities more fully to utilise the information already available to them.

Statistical analysis of applicant data could also provide a mechanism for centralised reviews of the higher education market. It would be possible to go beyond analysis of a single university data set to look at all applications through UCCA, PCAS and UCAS, for example, as part of the assessment of the viability of the proposed University of the Highlands and Islands. Analysis at the national level would be a substantial piece of work but would open up the possibility of much broader and more accurate understanding of the higher education market. Such a data set could be used to build a model of applications to universities, which could be of value determining in education policy and even economic policy.

REFERENCES

European Commission (1989) *Employment in Europe*, Commission of the European Communities, Brussels.

Green, C. (1990) Targeting New Markets. *New Directions for Higher Education*, No 71 Fall, pp. 79-89.

Kotler, P. (1982) *Marketing for Non Profit Organizations*, Prentice Hall, London.

Maclean, S. D. (1985) Marketing and the College. *Journal for Further and Higher Education in Scotland*, 9 (May), pp. 18-21.

Rapp, S. and Collins, T. (1987) *Maximarketing*, McGraw-Hill, New York.

Rickard, C. E. and Walters, J. C. (1984) Attract Academically Strong Students. *Journal of College Admissions*, No 3 Fall, pp. 35-37.

Stone, M. and Thompson, S. (1987) How far can Marketing be Applied within the Further Education Sector? *Quarterly Review of Marketing*, Autumn, pp. 16-19.

23 Saving the trees: how MCB University Press reduced its leaflet printing bills and improved its marketing response

Jonathan Barker
MCB University Press Ltd

1. INTRODUCTION

This article looks at the impact of database marketing from the perspective of a user of this technique rather from that of a system developer or maintainer. As such it will concentrate on the applications and results of the utilisation of database marketing and will not discuss the technical or logistical aspects of the database except inasmuch as they have an effect on the effectiveness or efficiency of the user's campaigns.

2. ABOUT MCB UNIVERSITY PRESS

MCB moved into publishing in 1967 with the acquisition of the journal *Management Decision*. Since then the company has grown to become one of the leading international publishers of English-language journals in the fields of management and engineering. A listing of the customer groups for whom MCB publishes journals can be found in Figure 23.1.

The company's world headquarters are situated in Bradford, West Yorkshire in the North of England and regional offices are maintained in Singapore, Brisbane, Tokyo and Washington, DC.

MCB's customers are located throughout the world with more than half outside the UK. Although all its titles are published in English, the company has a considerable subscriber base in Continental Europe. Figure 23.2 shows the breakdown of MCB customers by region.

The product range maintained by MCB covers a wide spectrum from academic titles, such as the *Journal of Economic Studies*, aimed at the university market through titles like *Target Management Development Review*, which is designed for practising managers, to secondary publishing titles such as the Anbar range of abstracting journals. Accordingly, the customer base spans libraries, companies and individual personal subscribers. Figure 23.3 illustrates the proportions of subscribers by type.

Corporate strategists
Economists
Educators
Finance Managers and Academics
General Managers
Health Care Managers
Human Resources Professionals and Academics
Information Managers
Librarians
Marketing Professionals and Academics
Quality Managers
Systems & Technology Managers
Training & Development Professionals & Academics

Figure 23.1 Customer groups of MCB University Press.

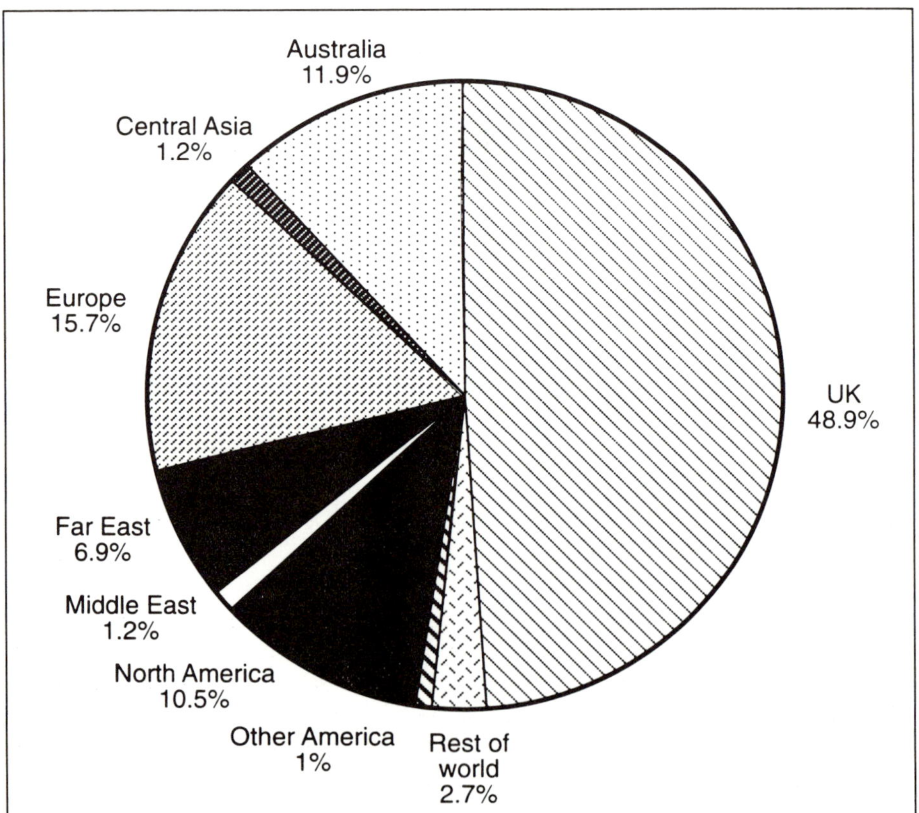

Figure 23.2 Geographical breakdown of customers.

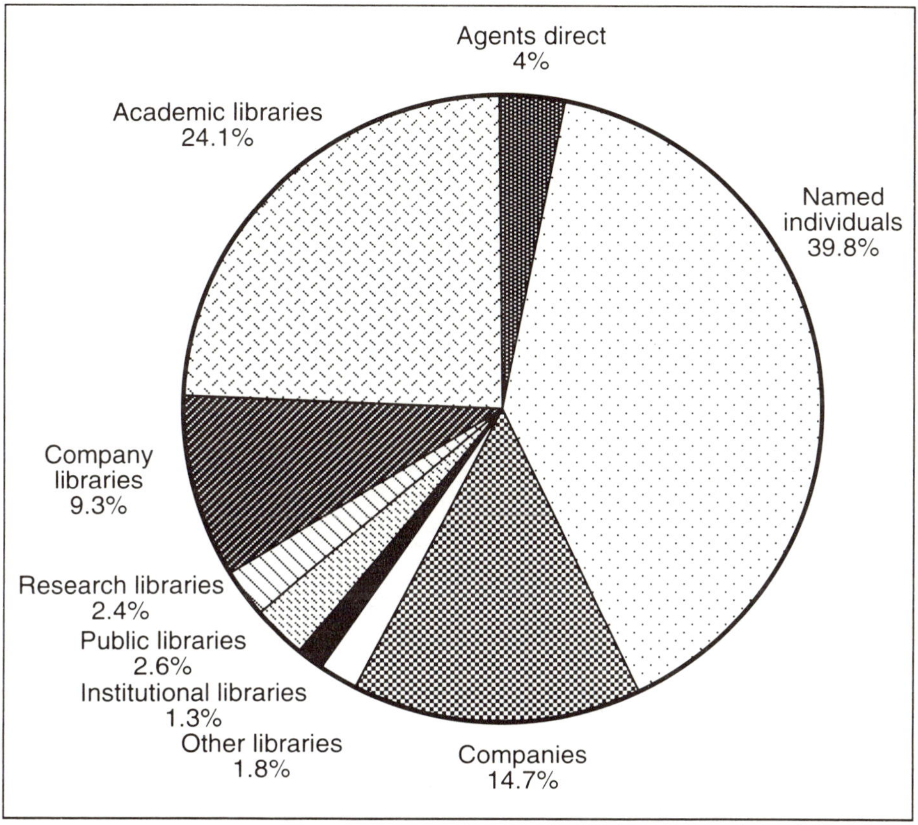

Figure 23.3 Customer breakdown by type.

Promotion of MCB journals is centred primarily on the Bradford and Brisbane offices. In 1993 MCB expects to spend some #1.5 million on promotion. The majority of promotion is undertaken via direct mail with a fraction devoted to paid advertising and loose inserts in our own and other publishers' titles. Some further promotion of MCB titles is undertaken by Subscription Agents with whom MCB has established agreements whereby the Agents will use their own databases to undertake promotion on MCB's behalf. They are paid commission on sales made via this route.

Given the very wide spread of potential subscribers to MCB journals by geographical region and customer type the promotional material and style of campaign varies considerably. Promotion must be designed to attract two basic types of potential subscriber – those who do not currently subscribe to any of

MCB's journals and those who already maintain subscriptions to one or more titles.

To attract new subscribers to the company (sales prospecting) promotional material is sent out to names and addresses maintained on external lists by list brokers. These are widely available from a range of brokers and vary in cost depending on the exclusivity and nicheing of the list. Accordingly, a list of academic libraries in the UK will be reasonably cheap but very widely targeted and very heavily used by a wide range of publishers. This is a 'cold' list and its response rate will therefore be low. A list of named individuals who have bought a particular product, say a book title, is much 'warmer' – their interest is specific and recent – and response rate will be higher. However, such a list is unique, harder to obtain and consequently more expensive.

Database marketing is used to sell further subscriptions to customers who already take one or more titles (customer development). Given that MCB knows a lot about such prospects (name, address, etc.) and has a good idea as to the subject in which such customers are interested (human resources or marketing, for example) the maintenance of a database for promotion is the most effective promotional technique.

3. THE BEGINNINGS OF DATABASE MARKETING AT MCB

MCB maintains records of in excess of 45,000 customer accounts with a typical journal list containing between 500 and 800 records. Computer files were first created to satisfy three requirements: the distribution of individual journal issues to customers; subscription recording including billing information; and management information particularly related to the capture of renewal statistics related to customer type and product.

Renewal statistics have allowed the company to derive a very accurate model of renewal behaviour and enabled the effects of product development (pagination and issue frequency) to be identified. Given the highly niched nature of MCB journals with comparatively small numbers of subscribers per title, the relationship between production costs and income as a function of price is a vital element of corporate profitability.

A further benefit deriving from accurate knowledge of likely renewal behaviour was the company's ability to estimate the amount of promotional spend allowable to gain a subscription. As early as 1978, the company was able to implement ceiling rules on promotional spend which allowed it to spend 100% of a first year subscription income to gain a new individual subscriber and 150% to gain a new library or organisational subscription based on the likelihood that renewals would cover production costs and provide the required profit.

At this stage the computer files maintained on existing customers were not used for promotional campaigns. As for current sales prospecting, external lists were purchased on which it was expected that existing MCB customers would be included. Promotional material was included in the dispatches of journal issues on a product similarity basis, i.e. a dispatch of the *Journal of Organizational Change Management* would incorporate a leaflet containing details of *Leadership and Organisation Development Journal*. (Even though many subscriptions are maintained on customers' behalf by Subscription Agents dispatch of journal issues is direct to customer.) On this basis it was not possible to exclude subscribers who already took both journals.

Initially these computer files were maintained by a bureau. This situation came about because of the high costs of computers at the time and created several difficulties:

1. It was impossible to analyse the extent to which individual journal titles were subscribed to by common customers.
2. Subscriber enquiries as to the status of their subscriptions were difficult to answer.
3. The information on subscriptions held by the bureau was up to a month out of date.

With the steadily decreasing costs of computerisation it became possible to bring the computerised subscription records in-house on to MCB's own minicomputer. A DEC VAX was purchased and a dedicated systems manager recruited. This allowed for each Customer Services Executive (CSE) to have access to the computer files via a terminal on his or her desk so that, when a customer called with a query, that customer's details could be called up instantly to provide the required information. Provision was also made for the CSE to access status reports on journal production and dispatch to answer queries on which issues a customer should have received and when future issues could be expected.

The availability of data on customers further allowed for lists of names and addresses to be generated based on journal subscriptions. The benefits of this were soon identified by the company's Marketing Services Executives (MSE) for promotional use and, before long, the system found itself 'mugged' by MSEs pulling off lists of subscribers to send out mailshots. This unexpected result of computerisation contained the seeds for serious disruption of the customer services function, but was tolerated by management because of the company's high marketing orientation.

It also prompted within the organisation an awareness of the promotional power inherent in the maintenance of a database of customer records. If unplanned, *ad hoc* use of a database designed to manage customer fulfilment was sufficiently attractive that MSEs would go to considerable lengths to access it, what more could be achieved if a specific marketing database were developed with the promotional function specifically in mind? Thus was born the third stage of database utilisation by MCB – the marketing database.

MCB University Press' dedicated marketing database went live on 30 November 1989. It was built to a specification designed by the marketing function and resides on dedicated hardware. Each MSE has a terminal linked directly to the database with which she can access the customer records and select a target audience appropriate to the promotion which is being undertaken. The data which resides on the marketing database is downloaded directly from the customer services database on a monthly basis.

The arrival at a dedicated marketing database represents the efforts and initiatives of marketing personnel themselves who, with a project sponsor amongst the company's Directors, were able to see the potential inherent in the ability to specifically target individual customers. Given that existing satisfied customers are those most likely to buy new products the impact on corporate success arising from this new ability is substantial.

4. HOW DATABASE MARKETING IS CURRENTLY USED

The arrival of MCB's marketing database was an exciting new development for the company's MSEs who realised how much more effective their work could be.

It was immediately apparent to the database's designers that the high potential arising out of the database could be endangered if its use was indiscriminate and unplanned. Worse, without rigorous planning and analysis, it would be difficult to track results from the system's usage and informed future development would be prevented.

From the outset it was decided that a series of database campaigns would be designed for use within one year's promotional activity. The target audiences used and the database selections made remained the province of the individual MSE but there would be a limited number of campaign types available. These campaigns would be subject to an annual review undertaken by the Marketing Development Unit towards the end of the year to identify which had been most effective. Suggestions for campaign improvement would be sought from the MSEs along with ideas for totally new campaigns which could be introduced. MSEs were able to design and implement their own individual campaigns to see what could be achieved but this was to be done outside work time as 'private' initiatives. Such was the interest amongst MSEs in what the database could achieve that several experiments took place.

In this way, the company ensures that only substantial programmes with considered measurement occur. Every use of the database must not only fit in with the annual agreed campaign but be logged with the Database Operations Manager, and every pre-prepared stage of the campaign fully executed and evaluated as input for the next review cycle.

During 1992 nine campaigns were available for MSEs to use. It is appropriate at this stage to describe each and indicate some of the results which have been achieved.

5. THE CAMPAIGNS

5.1 Take 2

This campaign provides the opportunity to sell one or more journals to subscribers already taking compatible MCB titles. The basic premise behind this campaign is that existing customers will have a higher propensity to buy further products than individuals who have no experience of the company's products and services. A crucial aspect in Take 2 is the identification of synergistic products. Some pairings which are the least obvious can be the most successful. For example, the journal *Executive Development* does not intrinsically have a lot in common with the journal *Executive Secretary* in terms of content. However, a mailshot addressed to the secretaries of individual subscribers to *Executive Development* has a good chance of success.

There are other factors to be taken into account – two journals can be overly compatible and, if the journal to whose subscribers a sales message is being sent is significantly more expensive than the complementary journal which is being promoted, there is the danger that the more expensive journal will be cancelled in favour of the cheaper journal.

Applied with care, this can be a very effective campaign with success rates of 1.45% recorded for individual promotions. During the first eight months of 1992 32.5% of database marketing activity made use of this campaign.

5.2 Standard Industry Classification

The SIC campaign provides the opportunity to select specific industries for the promotion of relevant journals. Companies subscribing to MCB journals are allocated a SIC, e.g. health care, manufacturing, banking, computers/electronics. At the business level of the database there may be a record relating to a subscription to *Personnel Review* such as:

Mr J Smith
Personnel Manager
ABC Bank plc
Anystreet
Anytown

If a promotion of the *Journal of Bank Marketing* is to be undertaken then this record can be retrieved using the SIC code for banking which will have been attached to it and the mailshot will be addressed to:

> The Marketing Director
> ABC Bank plc
> Anystreet
> Anytown

Of course, it is necessary to check the list of potential against existing subscribers to avoid sending mailshots to those who already subscribe.

Another usage for this type of campaign is to establish a link with the new incumbent of a position where the original subscriber has moved on. Given the estimated 35% job mobility underway in industry, there is a fair chance that a mailshot addressed to an individual may be returned as 'Gone Away'. There is a very strong chance that, although the individual name has changed, the job title will remain the same and the mailshot will get through to the appropriate person. In organisations with large mailrooms this is a particular problem as the likelihood of a mail sorter knowing that Ms X has replaced Mr Y is small.

Between January and August 1992 over 50% of database campaigns were Standard Industry Classification.

5.3 Solomon

For some journals it will be appropriate to target individuals with a specific job title, regardless of the industry in which they work. To do this the Solomon campaign selects records by the code which has been allocated to a specific job title, e.g. Marketing Manager or Chairman. The mailshot is then addressed to the named individual holding that job title.

An example of such a campaign was the selection of the codes for the Managing Director, Chief Executive and Director job titles. Fifty-five were selected and sent a mailshot for the *European Business Review* stressing the strategic importance of the Single Market. Three new subscriptions resulted from this promotion.

5.4 Bookworms

MCB publishes some books as well as journal titles. These are promoted separately and individual sales are made. Book purchasers are entered on to the database to allow for the promotion of relevant journal titles. Thus a purchaser of a book concerned with education management will be introduced to the *Journal of Educational Administration.*

There are approximately 3500 book purchasers available on the database but some of these purchases happened some time ago. With this campaign it is important to promote the relevant journal(s) within a short period of time after the initial purchase.

5.5 Fogg

This campaign, named after the hero of 'Around the World in Eighty Days', concentrates on specific geographic areas. The majority of the journals published by MCB University Press are international in nature. From time to time a journal will have a special feature or issue relating to a particular part of the world and these can be successfully linked to promotions within the region concerned. It is possible to undertake quite sophisticated selections, for example a promotion to marketing managers in wine companies in France, Italy, Germany and Bulgaria for the *International Journal of Wine Marketing*.

5.6 Resurrection

As for all publishers, there are inevitably subscriptions which lapse for MCB titles. The term 'lapsed' includes both subscriptions where an active order to cancel has been received and those where subscriptions have failed to be renewed. Lapsed subscriptions are maintained on the database because they remain potential subscribers. They may take a subscription to a cheaper journal if (as in the case of many libraries these days) budget restrictions have forced cancellation. Alternatively, the decision to cancel or not renew can be rescinded at a later date especially if lapsed customer incentives are included.

5.7 Gotcha

Much of the growth enjoyed by MCB has come in the form of acquisition of titles founded by other publishers. MCB has been very successful in this strategy because of its ability to profitably manage very niched titles with fairly small subscriptions levels. The acquisition of a journal title provides an opportunity for database marketing of compatible titles to the acquired subscribers.

An initial approach is made on the basis of welcoming the subscribers to MCB and assuring them that the level of customer care which they will receive will be the highest possible. A 'soft' promotional message is included with this, perhaps offering to send a portfolio of complementary titles.

A further letter may then be sent after dispatch of the first issue under the new publisher hoping that they have received their issue safely and suggesting that they might like a sample of another title.

5.8 Welcome Wagon

Similar to Gotcha is the Welcome Wagon campaign except that this is directed to subscribers who have taken out a new subscription to an MCB journal for the first time. Once again the emphasis is on customer care assurance with the first seed of promotion planted by the offer of a portfolio.

Welcome Wagon is also used to glean information about the customer if insufficient data was included in the original order form, e.g. job title or company business.

5.9 Samples

Requests for sample copies of journals are continually received at MCB. These can come in as a result of specific MCB promotional activity or through the potential subscriber seeing the journal in a library, for example. After the full promotion effort relating to the journal of which a sample copy was requested has been exhausted, if no subscription has resulted then the sample copy names are made available for the promotion of other compatible titles.

With the wide range of titles published by MCB it is frequently the case that another journal is closer to the potential subscriber's area of interest or falls within a predetermined price range.

One hundred and thirty one promotions to sample copy requestors were carried out in the first eight months of 1992.

6. THE 'CLUB' APPROACH

A further development of database marketing within MCB has been the development of 'clubs' for specific customer groups. Two of the three clubs which MCB has instigated are directed at enhanced customer care leading to increased propensity to purchase amongst club members. The third – the Literati club – is aimed at 'selling' MCB as a publisher to writers seeking outlets for their work and encouraging them to submit material to MCB rather than other publishers. Given that a publisher's success is directly related to the quality of the material published in its journals, this is a most important development.

The principal benefit of the club approach for the company is the extra information on customers gained. To qualify for membership individuals fill in a questionnaire on their reading and purchasing habits. In return they receive benefits including dedicated club personnel with dedicated telephone lines to answer any queries regarding current subscriptions and products of interest, newsletters and further special offers.

6.1 Library Link

As was seen in the introduction to MCB University Press, the library market is a significant sector for the company. Librarians represent a difficult challenge for MCB's marketeers. One the one hand they have large budgets (even in these more difficult times) for the purchase of journals. On the other hand they are customers rather than consumers and the arguments which can be put forward on behalf of individual journals titles to encourage a consumer to purchase are different to those which can be used for librarians.

For example, for the consumer of a journal it is an advantage if there is more information contained in the subscription through the addition of extra pages or extra issues. For the librarian (the customer) it is of no benefit (except altruistically) that there is more content to a journal and hence, in the librarian's eyes, this is no good reason to subscribe at a higher price. One might think that the benefit to the consumer (the library user) would be recognised, but librarians are aware of the relatively small percentage of material within a journal issue which is used – as opposed to might be used – and would rather purchase individual articles to specific demand.

Thus marketing to this sector is particularly difficult. It was recognised that MCB had to position itself as the 'librarian's friend' and also maximise the amount of information available about the sector to inform its marketing tactics. Thus was born Library Link with its subtitle 'Helping Us to Help You'.

The criterion against which membership of Library Link was offered was that the library concerned maintained a subscription to one or more MCB journals. The club was never intended to be a tool for prospecting for new customers but purely a means of developing existing customers.

The initial approach to a library concerning club membership is a letter explaining the benefits of the service. It was stressed in this letter that membership was by invitation only, thus engendering a feeling of 'VIP treatment' amongst recipients. Accompanying the letter was a questionnaire which sought answers in a number of areas.

The first questions sought to ensure correct name/address details for the recipient. This was followed by an enquiry into the role within the library fulfiled by the recipient. This is a crucial element for library targets because of the range of possible respondents, from clerical assistants who open the post through to the decision-makers which Library Link was seeking out. To ensure that the decision-maker information was received no matter who was filling in the questionnaire, a later question sought the names of colleagues involved in the decision-making unit.

Another variable between libraries is the subject matter in which their users are interested. For company libraries it is relatively easy to predict the subjects they will want to cover but academic libraries are more difficult. The frequent occurrence of split-site operations results in specialist libraries which need to be identified. To gather this information, the Library Link questionnaire asked respondents to rank 38 subjects as being of 'great interest', 'general interest' or 'no interest'. Sample copies of journals relevant to subjects rated of 'great interest' were then offered.

To ensure that important promotional messages were dispatched to club members at the right time, respondents were asked if there was a particular time of year when purchasing decisions were made or if this was a continuous process.

Finally, information was sought on the total number of journals for which that library maintained subscriptions and the number of new titles which were taken out each year along with the number of titles which were cancelled. The very last question asked how much money the library spent on journals per year.

Another difficulty faced in gathering data on librarian behaviour was the identification of an appropriate incentive to encourage questionnaire completion and return. As these are individuals who are, in a sense, spending other people's money (i.e. library users benefit from expended resources, not librarians), there is a risk that an incentive which benefits the librarian rather than the library could be misinterpreted as a form of bribery. The incentive which was offered sought to provide benefits for both. It took the form of a £1000 Research & Travel Bursary which the winner could use to attend a professional course or conference of their choice. Thus the individual benefited from attendance and the institution benefited from staff development which it did not have to fund. All questionnaire responses returned by a certain pre-announced date gave eligibility for inclusion in the prize draw for this bursary.

The winner of the first draw was a UK librarian who used the money to travel to an important conference in Canada. A repeat of the contest held to recruit further members resulted in a winner in Australia. As Library Link is an international venture it is open to librarians anywhere in the world and is supported by regional co-ordinators in the various MCB offices who provide a local service.

Having been in operation for some eighteen months, Library Link has identified and recruited some 1900 suitable members.

6.2 Human Resource Network

One of the professional groups for which MCB publishes a range of journal titles and which has proved itself to be particularly receptive to journal promotion is that of human resource professionals.

Accordingly, it was decided that this niche also would benefit from a 'club' approach to promotional activity and the Human Resource Network database was initiated.

Recruitment to HRN followed a similar pattern to that of Library Link utilising a questionnaire to existing subscribers. This questionnaire was somewhat shorter, again asked for correct address details, and focussed on the particular subject niches within human resources in which the respondent was interested. Given the wide range of human resource titles published by MCB, this information was required to ensure that appropriate journals were promoted.

Having been in existence for nearly a year it was decided that the Human Resource Network would offer three levels of benefit to members. This allowed HRN to reward customers who had responded to promotional activity and maintain contact with individuals who had so far proved resilient to MCB's promotional messages.

The highest level of membership is 'gold'. These members receive all the club benefits, e.g. the Contents Page Service, on a monthly basis and special offers are made to them which are not available to others. To qualify for 'gold'-level membership an individual is required to either have purchased a new subscription in the past twelve months or paid a £50 membership fee.

All members newly recruited to HRN come in as 'standard'-level members. If such members make a further purchase from the MCB portfolio they are upgraded to the 'gold' level. These members only receive the Contents Page Service on a quarterly basis and are offered just sample copies of journals without further incentives to purchase.

Some subscribers who joined HRN have not made any further purchases and have not responded to a second questionnaire which was mailed out. Such members receive a 'basic' service. Promotional material relating to journals in the subject areas in which they indicated an interest is sent to them along with information on any relevant new launches or acquisitions. If a purchase does result then such subscribers are immediately promoted up to 'standard' level.

Human Resource Network now has 1865 members throughout the world.

6.3 The Literati Club

Literati is an unusual application of database marketing techniques in that, rather than attempting to sell a product, it encourages authors who have already published with MCB to submit further material.

As with the other clubs, it includes only individuals who have prior experience with the company and does not attempt to be a database of all potential authors working the fields in which MCB publishes.

Data gathering for this database takes place at the time an author has an article accepted for publication within an MCB journal. He/she (or they) are asked to fill in a Journal Article Record Form which was originally used for production control but which has now been adapted to capture the data required for Literati.

The form also requests information on the library which the author usually uses for research and this is to be passed to the Library Link club so that promotional approaches can be made which connect the authorship of a paper by one of its users with the need for that library to maintain a subscription to the journal concerned.

At the instigation of the Literati club a retrospective exercise was carried out to capture data on authors who had published with MCB over the previous two years. Such were the perceived advantages of membership of the club that the vast majority of authors responded even though publication did not depend on compliance.

Now that a useful number of records are held on this database it can be used to target authors in particular subject areas asking them if they would like to contribute to Special Issues (journal issues which are concerned with a particular topic) or to journals which have been newly launched by MCB. Successful calls for papers have been used for titles as diverse as *Sustainable Development* which concentrates on Third World development issues, *Quality Assurance in Education* and *Pricing Strategy & Practice.*

The Literati club also sponsors MCB's 'Awards for Excellence' wherein each journal nominates a Best Author award and the company selects an Editor of the Year. Staged at London's Reform Club and preceded by an editors' workshop, this recognition of exemplary quality in journal articles has proved extremely popular.

Following its successful launch it is intended to widen the scope of Literati Club to provide a full channel of communication between MCB and its authors.

7. DATA INTEGRITY

A further major benefit of the club approach to database marketing is the recognition that the basic information held about the customer must be accurate. Even without the extra information on subject interests, etc. which the clubs have been able to gather, knowing that the name and address to which promotional material is being sent is accurate is the fundamental requirement.

To undertake the campaigns which MCB has designed certain other data about the customer need to be accurately recorded. These include the Standard Industry Classification allocated to each customer record, the job code, the format of the address and any amendments required, the geographic code, and the customer type (e.g. named individual or academic library).

It might appear easy to get such information right but, if one considers the last category – customer type – the possibilities for inaccurate coding are high. Take, for example the following address:

Mrs A Smith

The Library
ACME Marketing Consultants

This could be recorded as a named individual, a company library or a company subscription. Without a hierarchy of rules governing how individual records will be allocated, marketing database campaigns will not be able to operate at an optimal level.

Part of the problem of data integrity for MCB lies in the initial capture of the data. Because the marketing database is downloaded from the customer services database the data is first entered by Customer Services Executives from the information contained in the order form which has been sent in. Whilst the CSEs are very diligent, their prime focus is the dispatch of journal issues and the accurate billing of customers. Data which they capture for marketing purposes is not intrinsic to their work and they can have no sense of 'ownership' of that data. Accordingly a substantial amount of work has to be done on the data after it has been downloaded into the marketing database to ensure that the required information is there.

A further data integrity problem arises when MCB acquires a journal from another publisher. When this happens there is considerable pressure to get the customer records entered into MCB's customer services database and time is at a premium. Not only is this a period when mistakes are likely to occur but it is also often the case that the original publisher did not capture some of the required data such as the Standard Industry Classification.

Recognising the vital importance of data integrity the company has instigated a task force which comprises members of the Marketing Database Unit, representatives from customer services and marketing services and a member of the acquisitions team.

8. THE LEGAL ASPECTS

There are comprehensive legal requirements which need to be taken into account in direct marketing including database marketing as well as various codes of practice promulgated by a number of self-regulatory organisations (SROs) to which the industry subscribes.

The focus on legal aspects has been intensified by various draft directives issued by the European Commission in this area. These include the Directive on Data Protection, the Distance Selling Directive, the Legal Protection of Database Directive, the ISDN Directive and the Package Waste Directive.

It is part of the remit of MCB's Marketing Development Unit to maintain an awareness of developments in this area, assess their implications and implement appropriate actions. It is, of course, not only for legal reasons that MCB is rigorous in, for example, excluding the names of customers who have indicated that they do not wish to receive further product information from the database. Considerable damage can be done to the company's good name if such customers are subsequently 'pestered' with mailshots though it is necessary to warn such customers that they may still receive material from MCB where their name is included in an external list the company has rented.

9. THE FUTURE

MCB's experience with database marketing has proved that it is a worthwhile investment. After three years, however, the very success of the database has resulted in calls for ever more sophisticated capabilities. Not only do MSEs want to do more with the database but the continued growth of the organisation (when the database was introduced it was expected that the company would by now be publishing 80 titles – there are in fact over 100) both dictate that we should be looking to design the next generation.

It has been decided that, by March 1994, a fully integrated computer system will have been introduced which has the capability to satisfy both customer services and marketing services requirements with just one database. Not only will there be a new computer system but there will also be a reorganisation of the company's departments so that marketing becomes an even more integral part of the organisation.

Customers will be grouped according to their interests and a 'club' style approach will be adopted to ensure customer satisfaction and increase their propensity to buy further products and services from MCB. The level of activity will, of course, be dependent on the profile of the individual customer group but we are determined to achieve excellence in customer care at a level appropriate to the market niche.

10. CONCLUSIONS

Database marketing is a powerful tool for any organisation which either has the opportunity to cross-sell further products to existing customers or which can build up a prospecting database of suitable potential customers.

MCB has restricted itself to creating a marketing database of its existing customers and the results have been very encouraging. The company has been able to move away from the indiscriminate dispatch of thousands of leaflets to prospective and existing customers thus pleasing the customers (who are then not inundated with frequently irrelevant promotional material) and the company (which can now offer appropriate information to appropriate targets and stop wasting paper and postage).

The database was an initiative spawned by the hands-on marketers within the company. They realised the power of database marketing even before they knew to call it that. They were fortunate that MCB's Board members were equally attuned to the possibilities and supported the initiative from the beginning. This happy combination has ushered in a whole new marketing era for MCB University Press and we are convinced that future developments in this area hold out ever more possibilities for us to achieve maximum customer satisfaction and successfully market our products.

24 Using a GIS for retail analysis

John Rae
CACI Ltd

1. INTRODUCTION

Retailers think in terms of tasks which must be done, not GIS features or technology. The only reason they consider GIS systems is that they can address many of their location and marketing applications.

This article therefore discusses retail applications of a GIS. It then looks briefly at why these applications need some GIS features, and considers which features are most important. The article concludes by looking at quotes from retailers who currently have systems to suggest what is important to the retailer using a GIS.

> *"We needed a system which was adaptable and yet also sufficiently precise to contribute to all our tasks, from site evaluation, sales and competition impact forecasting, to merchandising, media and recruitment planning."*
> Jon Towson, ASDA

The comments from ASDA give a good indication of the range of tasks facing the marketing and planning departments of a large retailer and many food retailers are users of GIS systems. Of course, retailers were doing all these things before GIS came along, and many manage these tasks at present without the benefit of a GIS. Many organisations, including CACI, have developed databases, models and consultancy services to give them support.

The point is that GIS can help the retailer carry out existing analysis more effectively, or allow retailers to develop improved analysis methods.

2. THE APPLICATIONS

Location has long been the retailers holy grail, and with good reason. A retailer want to get customers buying in the store. That means there must be sufficient potential customers living within a reasonable catchment area to sustain the business, and that means he has to assess a large number of locations. Figure 24.1 shows a simple example of three alternative sites for some kind of local store, an off-licence, and a newsagent or convenience store whose trade comes from the immediate vicinity.

The figure indicates the mix of customers that is available to three different

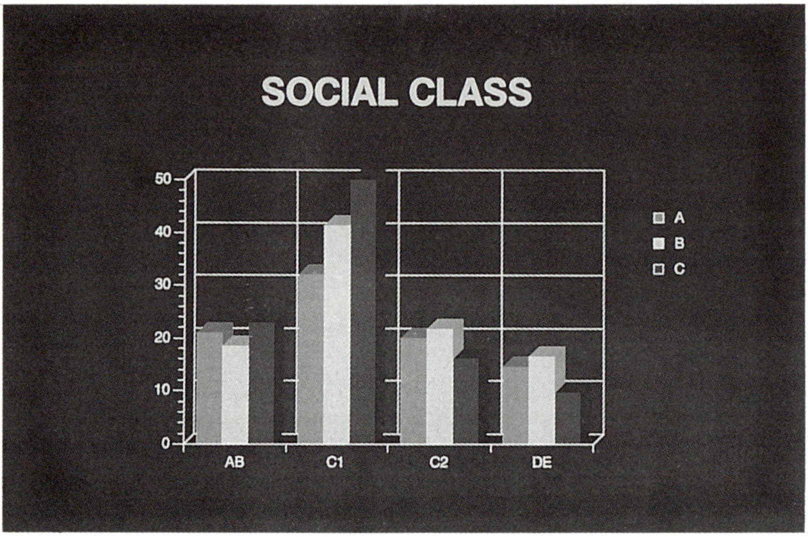

Figure 24.1

convenience stores, all situated on the north-west of Guildford within a few miles of each other. So close and yet such a different customer base. Will the retailer open stores in all three sites? Will he expect to sell the same mix of merchandise?

Another example considers three retail chains. Each sells fashion clothing, primarily targeting the 15–35 age groups, and they are all worried about the dramatic demographic changes occurring in the country. Because of the reduced rates of childbirth in the past two decades, these target ages are going to be less common in the next ten years. You might think there is nothing a retailer can do about this because the people have already been born, or in this case haven't been born (Figure 24.2).

However, like all demographic effects there are distinct local differences. Because of where they have chosen to put their branches, these three retailers are experiencing slightly different impacts. Chain C is not losing the younger end of its market but is going to lose more at the older end (Figure 24.3).

By relocating only 10 branches, all three chains can reduce their loss of business due to demographic change, but because of its unique locations, chain B can do the most to protect its business.

Of course there are other detailed issues relating to location, but these brief examples clearly illustrate why retailers need to assess sites carefully.

The data for Figures 24.1–24.3 was generated in a matter of a few minutes using a GIS. Retailers were doing similar things ten or twenty years ago – it just

DEMOGRAPHIC CHANGE OVER THE NEXT 10 YEARS

	CHAIN		
AGE	A	B	C
10 – 14	+13%	+15%	+20%
15 – 19	– 9 %	– 6 %	+ 4 %
20 – 24	–26%	–26%	–28%
25 – 34	– 3 %	– 8 %	–18%

BASED ON EXISTING PROPERTIES

CACI LIMITED

Figure 24.2

took a lot longer to generate the answers, usually days rather than minutes.

However GIS offer retailers more than simply doing the old tasks quicker. The process of assessing the impact of one store on another, or one shopping centre on another, is being treated in ever more sophisticated ways.

3. LOOKING AT CATCHMENT AREAS

Ten years ago I was often asked to assess sites such as that shown in Figure 24.4. Simply looking at the overlap of circular catchments around two site – Chichester and Bognor on the map. The retailer looked at all the people in each circle and then took a view on how much of the overlap went to each site.

Good enough in its way, but the split between the two towns is self-evidently not going to be the same throughout the overlap. After all, opposite ends of the overlap are practically adjacent to the two sites.

Nowadays improved computers make it practical to look at catchment areas and their overlap in more detail, and to more accurately model the behaviour of the shopper. After all, how many of you always go to the same shopping centre every single shopping trip?

Does your neighbour always go to the same place that you do? Does the rest of your street?

Over a period of time, retail spend in small areas will be split between the

DEMOGRAPHIC CHANGE OVER THE NEXT 10 YEARS

	CHAIN		
AGE	A	B	C
10 – 14	+14%	+ 9 %	+13%
15 – 19	– 3 %	– 10%	– 4 %
20 – 24	– 20%	– 12%	–24%
25 – 34	– 8 %	– 1 %	–12%

EXISTING PROPERTIES WITH 10 BRANCHES RELOCATED

CACI LIMITED

Figure 24.3

Figure 24.4

centres competing for that spend (Figure 24.5). In a given postal sector, the retail expenditure will split between competing local shopping centres depending upon their relative size, attractiveness and proximity.

Geographically, this means that a catchment population is no longer assessed by adding up all the people inside an area but by adding up shares of the retail market. Typically, a large share will be obtained from nearby areas and less from those further away or from areas which are near to a competing centre.

The resulting catchments no longer look like overlapping circles; indeed, they are not easy to represent simply on a map. In this example the darker the shading, the greater the share of retail spend going to the centre.

A GIS allows us to interrogate this form of catchment in more detail and, most importantly, to consider the effect of changes caused by developments within the shopping centre.

4. IMPACT STUDIES

If a new competitor is to have an impact on an existing store it must take business away by taking a share of some, or all, of the catchment area. Of course, the competitor impact is not going to be the same everywhere. There may be little effect very close to the store and a large effect to the side of the catchment nearer to the

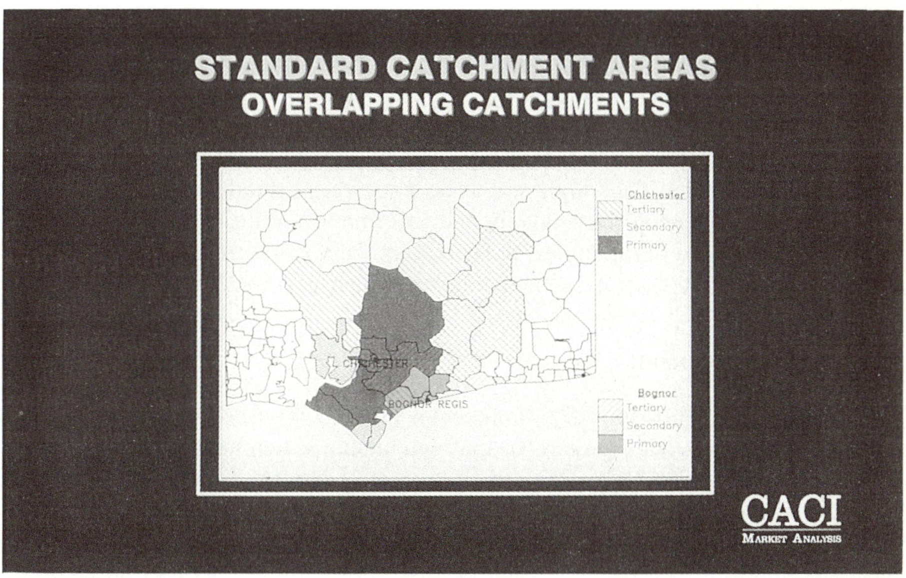

Figure 24.5

competitor. The side opposite the competitor may experience no impact at all.

Analytically, this means that the way the retail spend is shared out is altered in a different way for every small component area of the catchment!

5. MARKETING APPLICATIONS

Let us look at one more application before considering what features a retailer needs from a GIS.

Local marketing is again not something which has been brought about by the advent of GIS. People were doing leaflet drops, using local press and radio and analysing responses long before GISs were invented.

The task is conceptually very simple. The retailer knows his offer appeals to a particular subset of the population and he wishes to take advantage of the targeting of local marketing, for example a leaflet drop, to ensure his advertising reaches the right people. He needs to know who lives where.

Because every street is to some extent different, each local area will offer the retailer more or fewer of his target audience.

Leaflet drops are often distributed by postal sectors. A retailer might rank order all sectors within the catchments of all of his chain based on a targeting index related to his target customers. The report is a summary version of such a listing. Based on this the retailer can evaluate the targeting benefit of local marketing, decide how many leaflets to deliver, and give a list of them to his leafleting contractor.

6. WHICH GIS FEATURES DO RETAIL APPLICATIONS REQUIRE?

You will notice that I have so far only used two maps in my examples of retail applications of a GIS. This ought not to be a surprise – retailers are a great example of people who need the analysis and information abilities of a GIS perhaps more than they need the mapping presentation. This is not to say that retailers do not like maps, but that it is the analysis which is most important to them.

6.1 Site assessment

Basic catchment work requires some very simple GIS functionality – define a catchment and then add up data for that catchment. Catchments might be circles or polygons drawn on maps. It is really a case of having the correct data in the GIS so that useful information can be aggregated.

Some retailers, particularly those with out of town or edge of town sites, will have the majority of customers visiting their stores by car, and so will initially look at drive time catchments.

Drive times should be sensitive to small changes in store location. Moving a few hundred metres can significantly change drive time polygons, and thus the catchment population. Remember that both circles and polygons are very sensitive. A small increase in size can give a large increase in population because of the area covered. I once had a site where the 20 minute drive time included 250,000 people. Reducing to 19 minutes gave only 200,000 people and increasing to 23 minutes gave 500,000 – thus doubling the number of people for only three minutes additional drive time!

Bear in mind that there are drive time systems with poorly defined road networks or which are not sensitive to small changes in site location. As my example shows, this can lead to serious errors in subsequent analysis.

6.2 Impact analysis

Again, basic impact work requires simple GIS functionality – the ability to intersect polygons or circles.

However you will also need to be able to assign fractions of the overlap to one or other of the intersecting sites.

More detailed impact work will be based on complex interactions of catchments where different shares of each component of the catchment are assigned to each site. The GIS will need to be able to individually edit these proportions in order to add up the overall impact of a competing site.

If a GIS cannot operate in terms of proportions of data for component geographic areas, it cannot do sophisticated impact studies.

6.3 Local marketing

Local marketing can require a range of GIS functions, depending upon the local media being used. Leafleting is usually defined in terms of postal sectors. Local radio listenership areas and local press delivery or readership are also available in terms of sectors, so the GIS will probably also need to work in terms of postal sectors.

The first requirement is to be able to list every postal sector within a catchment area. This defines the universe you wish to market to. You then need to be able to add additional analysis processes.

For leafleting you can scan across all the postal sectors to identify which meet a given set of criteria and get a subset which is then leafleted. Alternatively, you can rank order the sectors and pull off the top *x*% and leaflet them. You may need the top *x*% if your main objective is efficient targeting. You may want the best *n*,000 households if you wish to optimise the marketing effect for a fixed print and delivery budget.

Essentially, the GIS needs sufficiently flexible reporting to present the information in a way most suitable for the retailer's decision process. There is no one single way of targeting leaflet drops.

Using local media is very similar to the question of overlapping catchments. The GIS needs to be able to hold media distribution areas which overlap extensively, and then work out which of the distribution areas overlap with the catchment areas.

There are four main questions which the retailer, or his agency, wish to answer

- How much of my catchment does this title reach?
- How much of my target market within this catchment does it reach?
- How much does this title deliver outside my catchment which is thus wasted spend on my part?
- Which part of the media's profile am I wanting to benefit from – am I paying premium rates but not actually reaching the groups which justify the premium rate?

The last part of local marketing is very important – analysing where the response came from in order to improve the campaign next time around. This involves loading the response data into the GIS, usually a repetitive process since response does not all arrive at the same time. A key question here is whether the GIS allows users to do this themselves or whether some 'system team' has to do it for the users. Ideally, the marketing department will need to be able to do it themselves.

6.4 Competitors

This same point of loading and updating information is a key feature when considering competitors. Competitors are always opening or closing sites, refurbishing, expanding or changing the mix of merchandise in their stores.

As a result, every competitor database is out of date the minute it is created. The only way to keep reasonably up to date is to regularly update the information. Frequently, the information comes in for individual competitors that have been visited and so the process of updating is a continuous one – another reason for it to be simple and easy to do.

Competitors can take business away if they reduce a store's catchment area. If they are sited next door the combined pulling power of the two stores can be beneficial, creating a larger catchment which the stores share between them.

To assess this the GIS must be able to aggregate data from the competition database for any location, another fairly standard GIS function.

6.5. Market share and turnover forecasting

Ultimately the retailer uses the GIS to build a forecast of his expected performance at any site. This can take many forms. The forecasting model may aim to optimise the space and merchandise mix of a store, or alternatively it may aim to predict turnover or market size.

All such models are different because each retailer is different. Every retailer will have their own preferred approach to forecasting turnover. As a result it is difficult for a GIS to provide any standard approach. Usually, however, the GIS can provide a framework of analysis tools which the retailer can use to build his customised model. An important point is that the models are usually built by a research or planning department rather than an IT department. The GIS has therefore to be sufficiently easy to use for analysts to be able to take advantage of it.

Each retailer will have different analysis needs so the reporting facilities must be easy to customise. While he was the GIS Professor at Reading University, Richard Dunn told me that most GISs he knew of were sophisticated software tools but incredibly difficult to use. In other words, it was not possible to easily customise them without specialist expertise. This is one point that is well worth remembering.

Finally, forecasting models frequently use specialist statistical techniques. Either these are built into the GIS or the GIS has to be good at transferring data to such packages, and back again. Since there are a number of good statistics packages around, there seems little point in reinventing them as part of a GIS, so the transfer of data is likely to be the important feature.

7. WHAT IS IMPORTANT TO THE RETAILER USING A GIS?

I have made a number of suggestions as to the desired properties of a GIS for a retailer. This has not come purely from me – it is based upon comments from retailing organisations who currently have a GIS. Here is a selection of quotes which is representative of the comments I receive.

> *"We needed a system that was adaptable."*
> *"We were particularly impressed by its flexibility."*
> *"CACI quickly adapted the system to our particular needs."*
> *"It has proved very user friendly."*
> *"None of the other systems was either powerful enough or specific enough to meet our needs."*
> *"We find the customised reporting particularly helpful."*
> *"We are now looking to extend the database."*
> *"Nowadays we need much more sophisticated support."*

I think these quotes support the view that retailers are most interested in making good use of their GIS systems. They hope to carry out detailed analysis for a range of applications and fully expect that their methods might evolve with time. As a result they need flexibility in their GIS system.

Across all retail categories I think it is true to say that the majority of GIS systems are PC- rather than mainframe-based, which means that there are GIS systems on the desks of location planners and marketers in a range of retailers.

8. WHAT IS IMPORTANT TO THE RETAILER USING A GIS?

8.1 Ease of use

Being easy to use is something every GIS will claim. It is also very difficult to achieve. This is because some of the analysis being undertaken is very sophisticated and if a system is designed to be sophisticated not everyone will find it easy to use. Ease of use may come more readily if the GIS has been designed with retail applications in mind.

I would suggest that any retailer looking for a GIS spends some time with real users of a number of systems so that they can be properly evaluated in a genuine working environment. Remember that the gains from the GIS will occur from using it well. It is how well you can use the system which will ultimately be the measure of its success.

8.2 Designed to meet retail applications

I have mentioned that how well you use the GIS is more important than many other factors. I think all GISs tend to reflect the applications understanding of their authors. Thus somebody with a good understanding of the issues involved in analysing the environment will tend to make such applications central to their GIS design. Similarly, a good retail GIS is likely to come from a designer with understanding of retail applications.

8.3 Support

All GIS ought to come with suitable support and training. A retailer might look for applications support – not *which button do I press* but more – *which is the best way to address this decision process*. This is not system support but application support, and since the majority of retail GIS are stand-alone PCs, I believe this aspect to be crucial to the developing use of GIS in retailers. One of the quotes I showed you said it: "Nowadays we need much more sophisticated support."

8.4 Flexibility

The need for sophisticated backup has come because over the last couple of years retailing has been a particularly difficult business. There has been a great change from the expansion trends of the mid-1980s, and retail analysts have had to change to find the answers to new questions. The analysis done by retailers has evolved, and will continue to evolve. As a result, retailers are looking for flexible GIS systems which can evolve with them. The words *adaptability* and *flexibility* occur most frequently in the comments I get from retailers with a GIS.

I have already mentioned that retailers think in terms of tasks to be done rather than GIS functions or technology. Quotes from retailers have developed this by suggesting that the retailers' needs are changing.

Like all software tools, GISs are maturing to meet the applications of their users and the software is being driven more by the applications than the technology. I consider this is a good sign, as I believe this indicates that GIS are on the way to becoming a standard tool for retailers and retail analysts.

Bibliography

The following works are either directly cited in the text of the book, or will be of interest to readers wishing to pursue further some of the themes covered. The list is not exhaustive, but contains sources of information which have proved to be of value to some of the authors who prepared the chapters making up this book.

ALEXANDER (1985)

Alexander, M 'Creative marketing and innovative consumer product decisions – some case studies' *Design Studies*, **6**(1), January 1985

BAKER (1990)

Baker, M J (Ed) 'One more time – what is marketing', in *The Marketing Book* Gower, London pp 3-9

BAKER (1991)

Baker, Michael J *Research for Marketing* Macmillan Education, Basingstoke

BAKER (1992)

Baker, Michael J *Marketing Strategy and Management* 2nd edn, Macmillan Education, Basingstoke

BAKER & ABOU-ZEID (1982)

Baker, Michael J & Abou-Zeid, E D *Successful Exporting* Westburn Publishers, Helensburgh

BAKER & HART (1989)

Baker, Michael J & Hart, S J *Marketing and Competitive Success* Philip Allen, Hemel Hempstead

BARABBA & ZALTMAN (1991)

Barabba, Vincent P & Zaltman, Gerald

Hearing the voice of the market: competitive advantage through creative use of market information Harvard Business School Press, Boston

BEAUMONT (1991)

Beaumont, J R *An Introduction to Market Analysis* CATMOG 53, Geo Books, Norwich

BEAUMONT (1991)

Beaumont J R

'Spatial Decision support systems; some comments with regard to their use in market analysis' *Environment and Planning A*, **23**(3) pp 311-318

BEAMONT & CLARKE (1992)
Beamont, J R & Clarke, M 'Strategic information management in practice for marketing', in *Perspectives on Marketing Management,* Baker, M J (Ed) Vol 2, John Wiley, London

BEAUMONT & SUTHERLAND (1992)
Beamont, J R & Sutherland, E *Information Resources Management* Butterworth-Heinemann, Oxford

BENJAMIN, DE LONG & SCOTT MORTON (1990)
Benjamin, Robert J; De Long, David W & Scott Morton, Michael S 'Electronic Data Interchange: How Much Competitive Advantage?' *Long Range Planning*, **23**(1) pp 29-40

BLATTBERG & DEIGHTON (1991)
Blattberg, R C & Deighton, J 'Interactive marketing: exploiting the age of addressability' *Sloan Management Review*, **33**(1) pp 5-14

BLYTH (1981)
Blyth, W G 'Budgetting to determine the profit contribution' *ESOMAR Annual Conference Papers*, 1981

BLYTH (1987)
Blyth, W G 'Turning data into Information. A new generation of integrated consumer research' *ESOMAR Annual Conference Papers*, 1987

BLYTH (1989)
Blyth, Bill 'The Management and valuation of marketing information' *Market Research Society Conference Paper*, 1989

BOWLES & BLYTH (1985)
Bowles, T S & Blyth, W G 'How do you like your data? Raw, al dente or stewed' *MRS Conference Papers*, 1985

BRITISH INSTITUTE OF MANAGEMENT (BIM), (1985)
Managing the Export Function: Policies and Practices in the Small and Medium Company Survey Report 26

BURDUS (1990)
Burdus, Anne 'The impact of IT on marketing' Paper to *Hoskyns/City University IT Business School Conference*, London

BUZZELL (1985)
Buzzell, Robert D (Ed) *Marketing in an electronic age* Harvard Business School Press, Boston

CHRISTOPHER, McDONALD & WILLS (1980)
Christopher, M; Mcdonald, M & Wills, G *Introducing Marketing* Pan, London

CIT RESEARCH (1981)
Advertising, marketing and the new European media CIT Research, London

CLARKE (1990)
Clarke, M 'Regional science and industry: from consultancy to technology transfer' *Environment and Planning B*, **17**, pp 257-268

CLARK & THOMAS (1992)
Clark, A M & Thomas, F G 'The Geography of the 1991 Census' *Population Trends*, **60**, London: HMSO

COBBIN, KOZAR & MICHAELE (1989)
Cobbin, Frank; Kozar, Kenneth, & Michaele, Stephen J 'Establishing Telemarketing Leadership through Information Management: Creative Concepts at AT&T American Transtech' *MIS Quarterly*, **13**(3), September 1989

CONNELL (1979)
Connell, D *The UK's Performance in Export Markets: Some Evidence from International Trade Data* Discussion Paper, NEDO

COULTAS (1990)
Coultas, Carol A 'Marketing is sold, but not satisfied' *Computerworld*, 21 May 1990 p 103

DAVIES (1992)
Davies, John M *The Essential Guide to Database Marketing* McGraw-Hill, Maidenhead

DIBB, SIMKIN, PRIDE & FERRELL (1991)
Dibb, S; Simkin, L; Pride, W M & Ferrell, O C *Marketing: Concepts and Strategies* (European Edition), Houghton Mifflin Company, London

DOCKERY (1991)
Dockery, E *The strategic use of information systems technology in banking firms and building societies* City University Working Paper No 117, April 1991

DOUGLAS (1992)
Douglas, P 'A Quality Standard for a Postcode Address File' *Mapping Awareness 92 Conference Proceedings*, Blenheim Online

DOUGLASS (1990)
Douglass, David D 'Building marketing information systems' *I/S Analyzer*, **28**(4), April 1990 pp 1-12

DRUCKER (1988)
Drucker, P 'The coming of the new organisation' *Harvard Business Review*, January/February 1988

EARLE (1989)
Earle, M J *Management Strategies for Information Technology* Prentice Hall, Englewood

Cliffs, N.J.

ESOMAR (1990)
'How to cope with data overload' Proceedings of Seminar 6-8 February 1990, ESOMAR, Amsterdam

EUROPEAN COMMISSION (1989)
Employment in Europe Commission of the European Communities, Brussels

EVANS (1979)
Evans, Christopher *The Mighty Micro* Victor Gollancz Ltd

FLAX (1984)
Flax, Stephen 'How to snoop on your competitors' *Fortune*, May 14 1984 pp 29-33

GOLD (1990)
Gold, Laurence 'High technology data collection for testing and measurement' in 'How to cope with data overload' Proceedings of Seminar 6-8 February 1990, ESOMAR, Amsterdam

GRAF (1979)
Graf, F 'Information systems for marketing' *Marketing Trends* **2**, 1-3

GREEN (1990)
Green, C 'Targeting New Markets' *New Directions for Higher Education*, No 71, Fall 1990 pp 79-89

GUNTER & FURNHAM (1992)
Gunter, Barrie & Furnham, Adrian *Consumer Profiles* Routledge, London

HANAN & CARP (1989)
Hanan, Mack & Carp, Peter *Customer Satisfaction* American Management Association, NY

HARRISON (1986)
Harrison, I D *A basic bibliography on Postcodes and Postcode applications* Working Paper 86/07, City of London Polytechnic Faculty of Computing

HARPER (1961)
Harper, Marion Jr 'A new profession to aid management' *Journal of Marketing*, January 1961 p 1

HIGBY & FARAH (1991)
Higby, Mary A & Farah, Badie N 'The status of marketing information systems, decision support systems and expert systems in the marketing function of US firms' *Information and Management* **20**(1), 1991 pp 29-48

HOLTHAM (1988)
Holtham, C 'IT Awareness for Executives' *Business Intelligence Conference Paper*

HOLTHAM (1991)
Holtham, Clive (Ed) *Executive Information Systems and Strategic Decision Support* Chapman & Hall, London

HOOLEY & LYNCH (1985)
Hooley, G J & Lynch, J 'Marketing lessons from UK's high flying companies' *Journal of Marketing Management*, **1**(1) Summer

HUGO (1967)
Hugo, I St. J *Marketing and the computer* Pergamon Press, Oxford

ITI RESEARCH LTD. (1989)
The Barclays Bank Report on Export Developments in France, Germany and the United Kingdom Barclays Bank International

JOBBER (1977)
Jobber, D 'Marketing information systems in US and British Industry' *Management Decisions* **15**(2) pp 297-304

KOTLER (1968)
Kotler, Philip 'A Design for the Firm's marketing nerve Center' in Smith, Samuel V; Brien, Richard H & Stafford, James E *Marketing Information Systems – a new era in marketing research* Houghton Mifflin, Boston, pp14-29

KOTLER (1980)
Kotler, Philip *Marketing Management* 4th edn, Prentice-Hall, Englewood Cliffs

KOTLER (1982)
Kotler, P *Marketing for Non-Profit Organisations* Prentice Hall, London

KOTLER & ARMSTRONG (1991)
Kotler, P & Armstrong, G *Principles of Marketing* 5th Ed, Prentice-Hall, Englewood Cliffs, NJ

LARRECHE (1975)
Larreche, Jean Claude *Marketing managers and models: a Search for a Better Match* INSEAD Research Paper Series, No 157

LILLIS & MCIVOR (1985)
Lillis, Charles M & McIvor, Bonnie J 'MDSSs at General Electric: Implications for the 1990s from Experiences in the 1970s and 1980s' in Buzzell, *Marketing in an electronic age* Harvard Business School Press, Boston, pp 89-106

MACLEAN (1985)
Maclean, S D 'Marketing and the College' *Journal for Further and Higher Education in Scotland* **9**, May 1985 pp 18-21

MARTIN & BRACKEN
Martin, D & Bracken, I (Editors) 'New Ways of Representing Socio-Economic Data'

Dept. of City and Regional Planning, University of Wales

MAYROS (1990)
Mayros, Van 'Have I got a system for you!' *Computerworld*, May 21 1990 pp 97-102

MORIARTY & SWARTZ (1989)
Moriarty, Rowland & Swartz, Gordon S Automation to boost sales and marketing' *Harvard Business Review*, **67**(1), Jan-Feb 1989 pp 100-108

MORRIS (1992)
Morris, C 'Lifestyle Data and GIS: an application in retail marketing' *Mapping Awareness 92 Conference Proceedings*, Blenheim Online

OASiS (1989)
The Management of Marketing Information OASiS, Maidenhead/Institute of Marketing, London

PIERCY (1990)
Piercy, N 'Developing marketing information systems', in *The Marketing Book*, Baker, M J (Ed) Gower, London pp250-269

PIERCY & EVANS (1983)
Piercy, Nigel & Evans, Martin *Managing marketing information* Croom Helm, London

POPPEL & GOLDSTEIN (1987)
Poppel, Harvey L & Goldstein, Bernard *Information Technology – the trillion dollar opportunity* McGraw Hill, New York

PUGH (1992)
Pugh,D 'What problems does a National Land Information System create?' Cambridgeshire County Council, *Mapping Awareness 92 Conference Proceedings*, Blenheim Online.

RAPER, RHIND & SHEPHERD (1992)
Raper, Rhind & Shepherd *Postcodes: The New Geography* Longman Technical and Scientific

RAPP & COLLINS (1987)
Rapp, S & Collins, T *Maximarketing* McGraw-Hill, New York

RICKARD & WALTERS (1984)
Rickard, C E & Walters, J C 'Attract Academically Strong Students' *Journal of College Admissions*, No 3, Fall 1984 pp 35-37

RICKMAN (1992)
Rickman, D 'The use of market intelligence systems within retailing' *Mapping Awareness 92 Conference Proceedings*, Blenheim Online

ROCHESTER (1990)
Rochester, Jack D 'Listening to customers' *I/S Analyzer*, **28**(12), December1990 pp 1-12

ROLLASON (1971)
Rollason, B 'What the successful exporter knows' *Exporting*, November 1971

SCHMITZ, ARMSTRONG & LITTLE (1991)
Schmitz,John D; Armstrong, Gordon D & Little, John D C 'CoverStory – Automated News Finding in Marketing' in Holtham, Clive (Ed) *Executive Information Systems and Strategic Decision Support* Chapman & Hall, London

SHAW (1988)
Shaw, Robert 'Make the database more commonplace' *Marketing Week*, September 1988 pp 55-59

SHAW & STONE (1988)
Shaw, Robert & Stone, Merlin *Database Marketing* Gower, Aldershot

SMITH, BRIEN & STAFFORD (1968)
Smith, Samuel V; Brien, Richard H & Stafford, James E *Marketing Information Systems – a new era in marketing research* Houghton Mifflin, Boston

STONE & THOMPSON (1987)
Stone, M & Thompson, S 'How far can Marketing be Applied within the Further Education Sector?' *Quarterly Review of Marketing*, Autumn 1987 pp 16-19

SUN TZU (1981)
The Art of War Hodder and Stoughton

TAKEUCHI & QUELCH (1983)
Takeuchi, H & Quelch, J A 'Quality is more than making a good product' *Harvard Business Review*, **61**(4) July/August 1983

THOMAS (1992)
Thomas, F G 'Digital Boundaries for the 1991 Census of Population in Scotland' *Geographic Information 1992*, Taylor and Francis

WALSH & ROY (1983)
Walsh, V & Roy, R *Good Design Innovation and Business Success* The Open University Design Innovation Group, DIG-01 August 1983

WEST (1987)
West, Alan *Spreadsheet marketing* Gower, Farnborough

WILLIAMS (1987)
Williams, Ian '"Dark science" brings a boost to airline profits' *Sunday Times*, 22 November 1987 p 94

WILLS (1991)
Wills, G 'Enabling customers to drive your enterprise' *Management Decision* **25**(4)

WILLS, BRUCE & DUNCAN (1991)
Wills, G; Bruce, B & Duncan, T 'Creating a marketing intelligentsia' *Marketing Intelligence and Planning* **9**(4), pp 3-20

WILLS & WILLS (1992)
Wills,G & Wills, J 'Journey to marketing clubland' *Marketing Intelligence and Planning* **10**(2), pp 22-36

WOLF (1984)
Wolf, James A 'New concepts in improving marketing productivity' *Information Industry Insights* **5**(4), Booz, Allen & Hamilton, New York